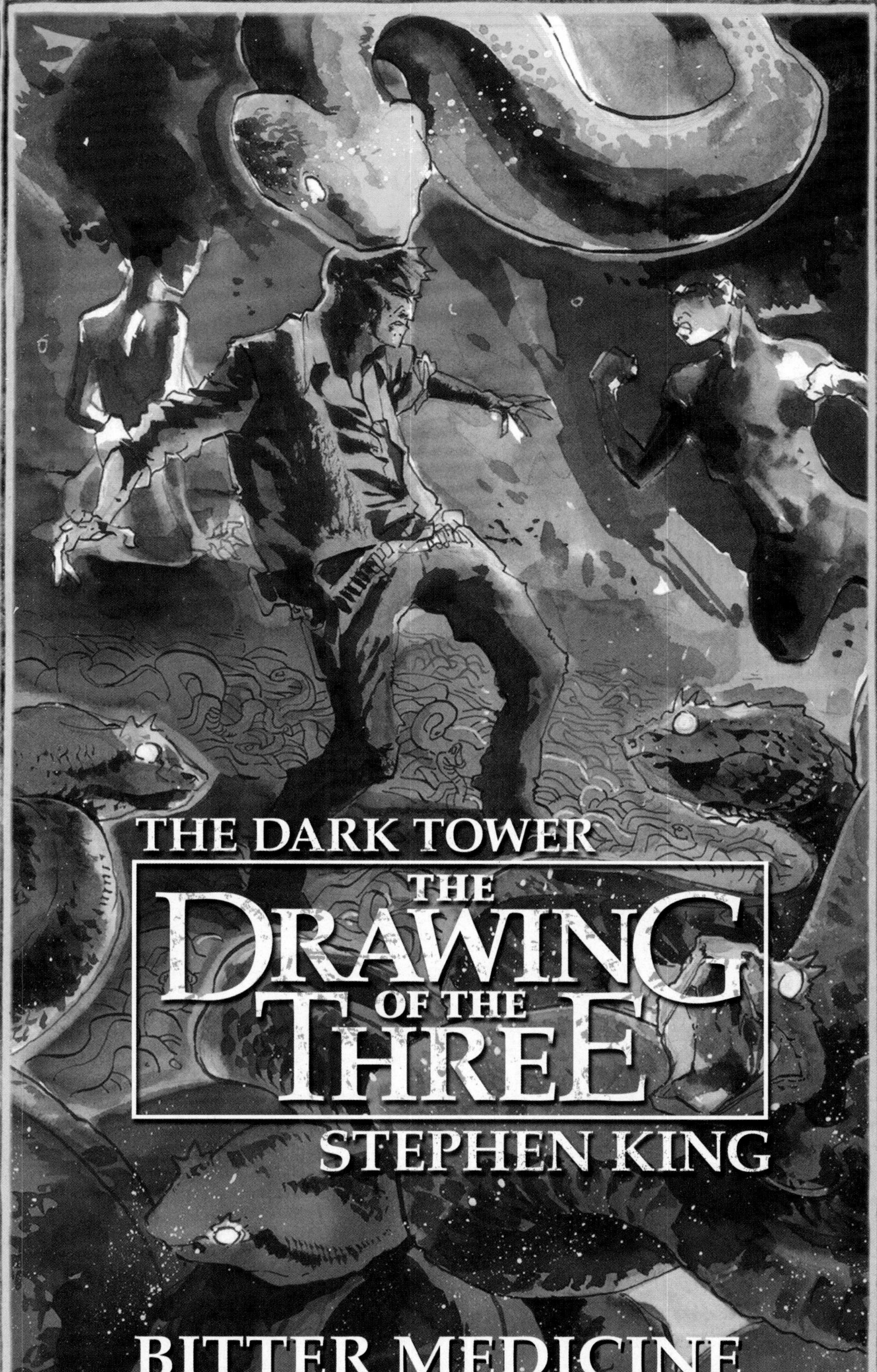
THE DARK TOWER
THE DRAWING OF THE THREE
STEPHEN KING
BITTER MEDICINE

THE DARK TOWER

THE DRAWING OF THE THREE

STEPHEN KING

CREATIVE DIRECTOR AND EXECUTIVE DIRECTOR
STEPHEN KING

PLOT AND CONSULTATION
ROBIN FURTH

SCRIPT
PETER DAVID

ARTIST
JONATHAN MARKS

COLORIST
LEE LOUGHRIDGE

LETTERING
VC'S JOE SABINO

COVER ARTIST
NIMIT MALAVIA

EDITORS
**EMILY SHAW
& MARK BASSO**

CONSULTING EDITOR
RALPH MACCHIO

BITTER MEDICINE

Collection Editor
MARK D. BEAZLEY

Associate Managing Editor
KATERI WOODY

Associate Editor
SARAH BRUNSTAD

Senior Editor, Special Projects
JENNIFER GRÜNWALD

VP Production & Special Projects
JEFF YOUNGQUIST

SVP Print, Sales & Marketing
DAVID GABRIEL

Editor in Chief
AXEL ALONSO

Chief Creative Officer
JOE QUESADA

Publisher
DAN BUCKLEY

Special Thanks to Chuck Verrill, Marsha DeFilippo & Brian Stark

DARK TOWER: THE DRAWING OF THE THREE — BITTER MEDICINE. Contains material originally published in magazine form as DARK TOWER: THE DRAWING OF THE THREE — BITTER MEDICINE #1-5. First printing 2016. ISBN# 978-0-7851-9280-0. Published by MARVEL WORLDWIDE, INC., a subsidiary of MARVEL ENTERTAINMENT, LLC. OFFICE OF PUBLICATION: 135 West 50th Street, New York, NY 10020. **Printed in Canada.** ALAN FINE, President, Marvel Entertainment; DAN BUCKLEY, President, TV, Publishing & Brand Management; JOE QUESADA, Chief Creative Officer; TOM BREVOORT, SVP of Publishing; DAVID BOGART, SVP of Business Affairs & Operations, Publishing & Partnership; C.B. CEBULSKI, VP of Brand Management & Development, Asia; DAVID GABRIEL, SVP of Sales & Marketing, Publishing; JEFF YOUNGQUIST, VP of Production & Special Projects; DAN CARR, Executive Director of Publishing Technology; ALEX MORALES, Director of Publishing Operations; SUSAN CRESPI, Production Manager; STAN LEE, Chairman Emeritus. For information regarding advertising in Marvel Comics or on Marvel.com, please contact Vit DeBellis, Integrated Sales Manager, at vdebellis@marvel.com. For Marvel subscription inquiries, please call 888-511-5480. **Manufactured between 8/19/2016 and 9/26/2016 by SOLISCO PRINTERS, SCOTT, QC, CANADA.**

10 9 8 7 6 5 4 3 2 1

THE DARK TOWER
THE DRAWING OF THE THREE
STEPHEN KING

ROLAND DESCHAIN IS A COWBOY FROM MID-WORLD ON A QUEST TO REACH THE DARK TOWER. HE IS GATHERING HIS KA-TET TO HELP HIM ON HIS JOURNEY. ONE OF THESE MEMBERS IS EDDIE DEAN, A KID FROM NEW YORK WHO HAPPENS TO BE ONE OF A SELECT FEW THAT EXIST ON MANY PLACES OF REALITY. HE IS ALSO A RECOVERING HEROIN ADDICT.

NOW EDDIE AND ROLAND ARE RECRUITING A SECOND PERSON TO JOIN THEM: THE LADY OF SHADOWS, A WOMAN CONFINED TO A WHEELCHAIR AFTER BEING HIT BY AN ONCOMING TRAIN THAT SEVERED HER LEGS.

AFTER BEING HIT ON THE HEAD WITH A BRICK AS A YOUNG GIRL, THE LADY OF SHADOWS' PERSONALITY SPLIT INTO TWO HALVES: ODETTA HOLMES AND DETTA WALKER. ODETTA HOLMES IS A POLITE, EARNEST WOMAN WHO IS ACTIVE IN THE CIVIL RIGHTS MOVEMENT. DETTA WALKER IS FULL OF RAGE AND PRONE TO ACTS OF VIOLENCE.

WHILE ODETTA WANTS TO HELP ROLAND AND EDDIE ON THEIR QUEST, DETTA IS NOT SO TRUSTFUL...

THE DARK TOWER

THE DRAWING OF THE THREE

STEPHEN KING

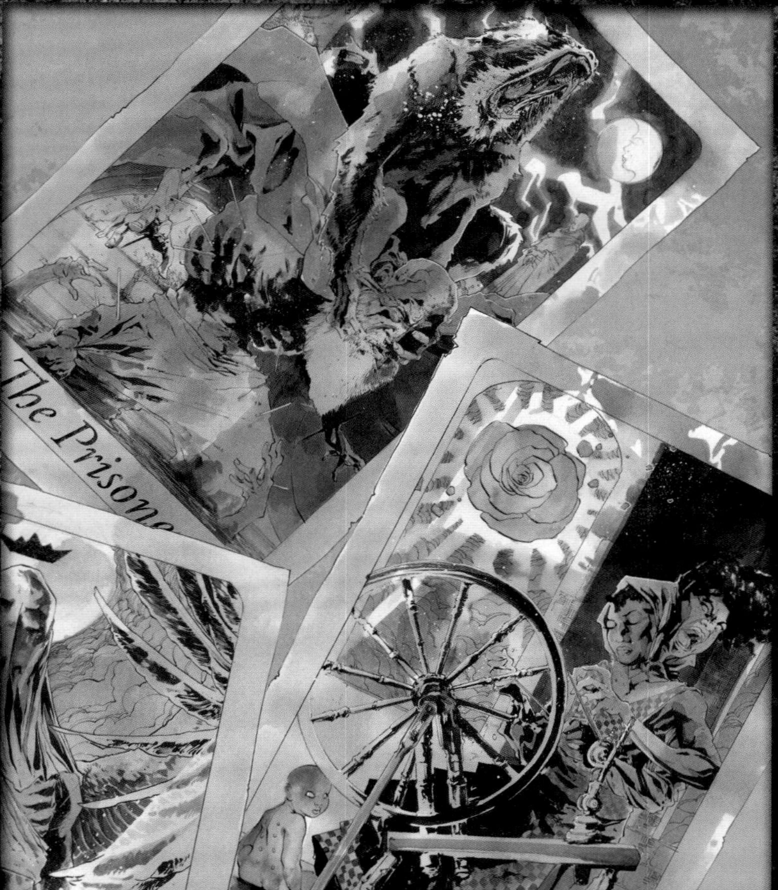

The Prisone

BITTER MEDICINE
CHAPTER ONE

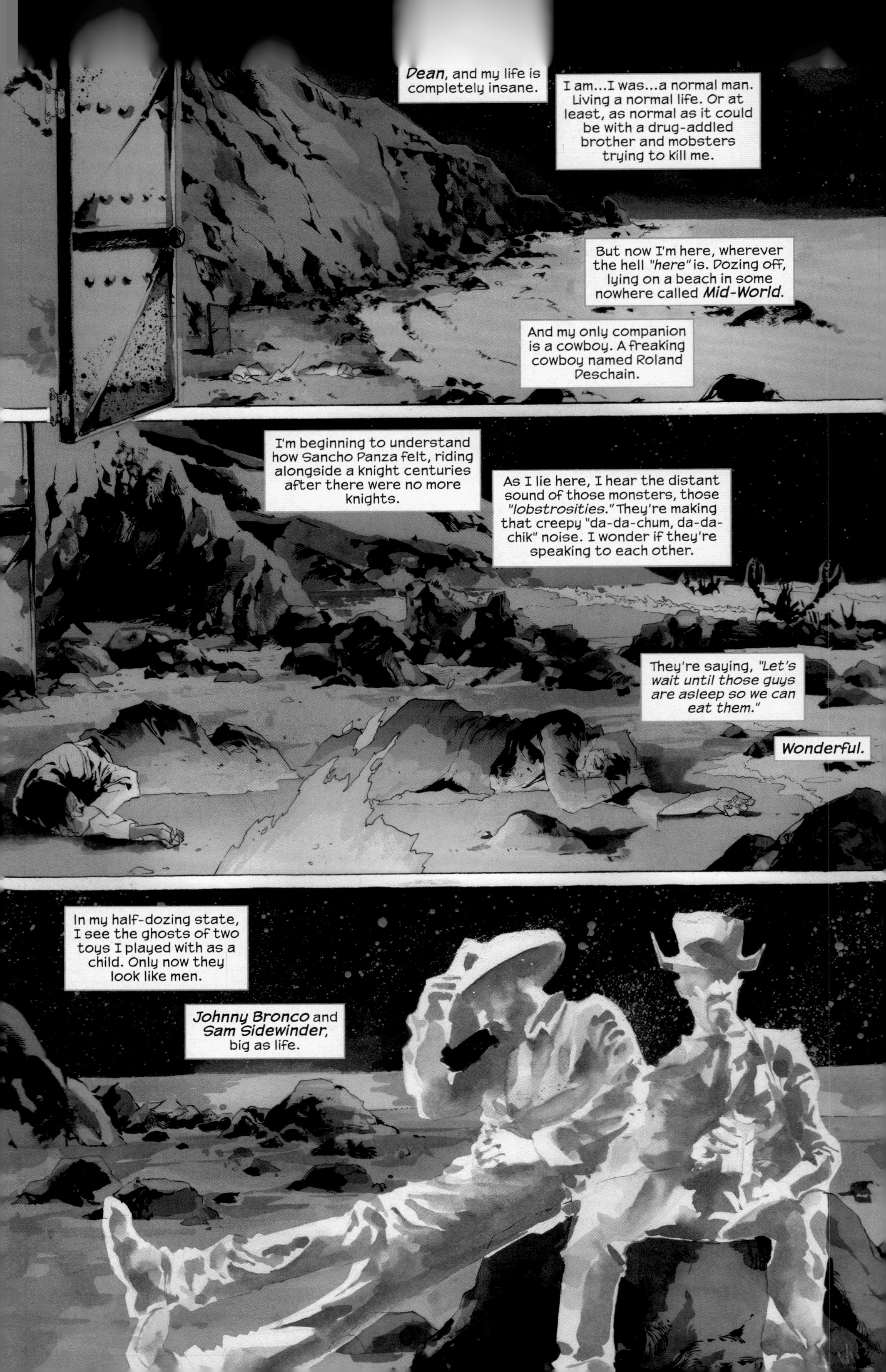
Dean, and my life is completely insane.
I am...I was...a normal man. Living a normal life. Or at least, as normal as it could be with a drug-addled brother and mobsters trying to kill me.
But now I'm here, wherever the hell "here" is. Dozing off, lying on a beach in some nowhere called Mid-World.
And my only companion is a cowboy. A freaking cowboy named Roland Deschain.
I'm beginning to understand how Sancho Panza felt, riding alongside a knight centuries after there were no more knights.
As I lie here, I hear the distant sound of those monsters, those "lobstrosities." They're making that creepy "da-da-chum, da-da-chik" noise. I wonder if they're speaking to each other.
They're saying, "Let's wait until those guys are asleep so we can eat them."
Wonderful.
In my half-dozing state, I see the ghosts of two toys I played with as a child. Only now they look like men.
Johnny Bronco and Sam Sidewinder, big as life.

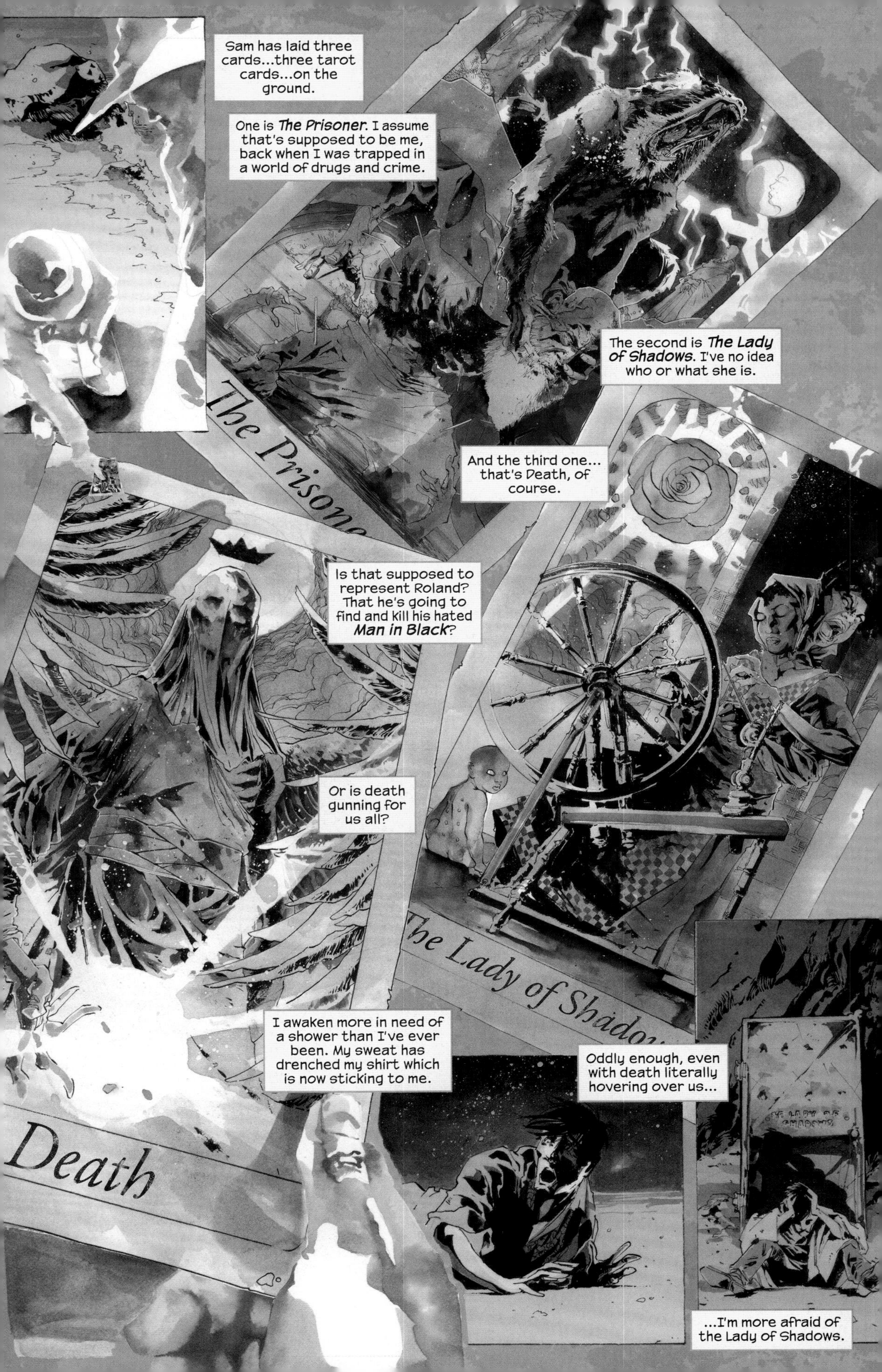

Sam has laid three cards...three tarot cards...on the ground.
One is *The Prisoner*. I assume that's supposed to be me, back when I was trapped in a world of drugs and crime.
The second is *The Lady of Shadows*. I've no idea who or what she is.
And the third one... that's Death, of course.
Is that supposed to represent Roland? That he's going to find and kill his hated *Man in Black*?
Or is death gunning for us all?
Death
I awaken more in need of a shower than I've ever been. My sweat has drenched my shirt which is now sticking to me.
Oddly enough, even with death literally hovering over us...
...I'm more afraid of the Lady of Shadows.

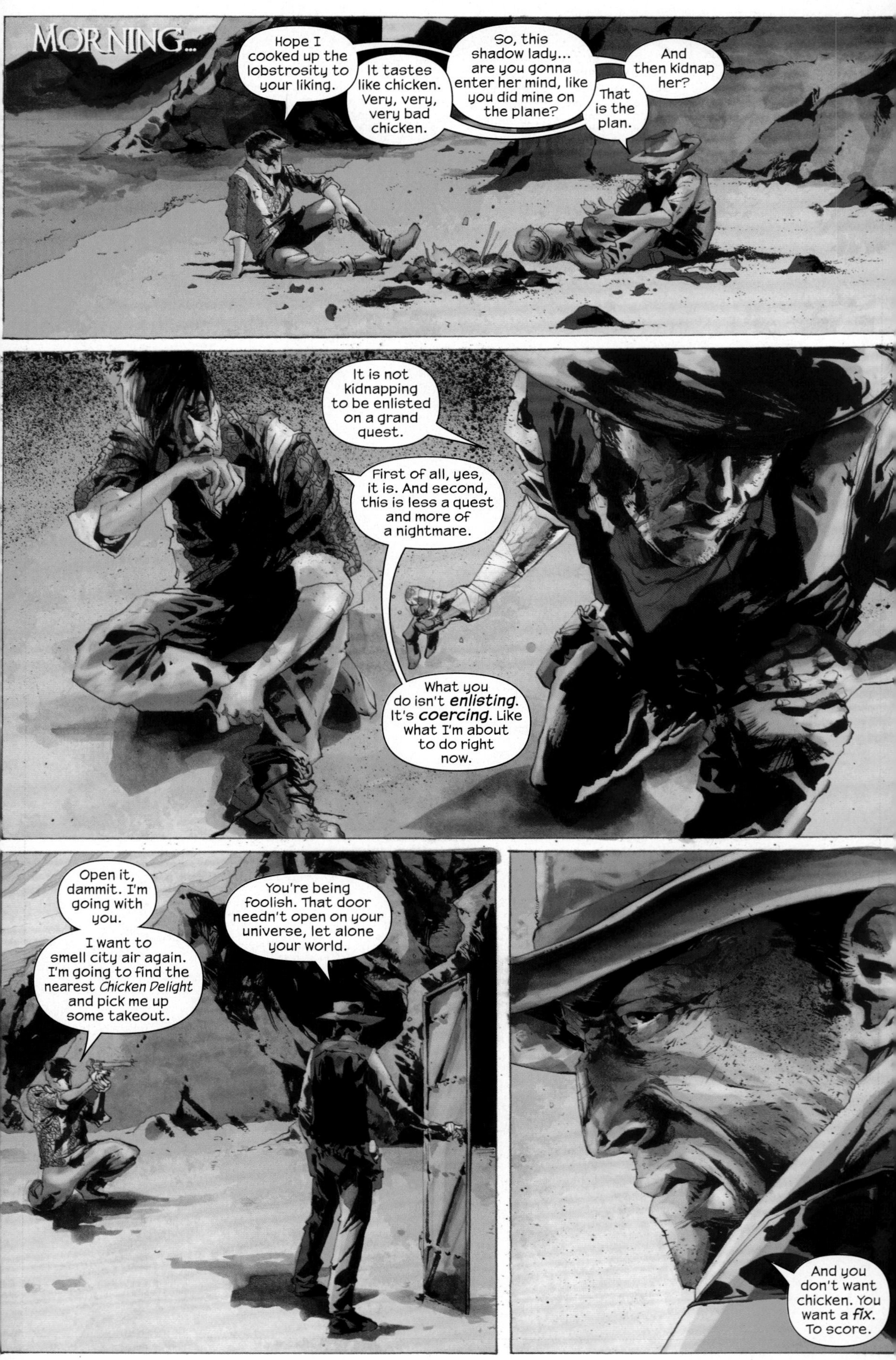
MORNING...
Hope I cooked up the lobstrosity to your liking.
It tastes like chicken. Very, very, very bad chicken.
So, this shadow lady... are you gonna enter her mind, like you did mine on the plane?
That is the plan.
And then kidnap her?
It is not kidnapping to be enlisted on a grand quest.
First of all, yes, it is. And second, this is less a quest and more of a nightmare.
What you do isn't *enlisting*. It's *coercing*. Like what I'm about to do right now.
Open it, dammit. I'm going with you.
I want to smell city air again. I'm going to find the nearest *Chicken Delight* and pick me up some takeout.
You're being foolish. That door needn't open on your universe, let alone your world.
And you don't want chicken. You want a *fix*. To score.

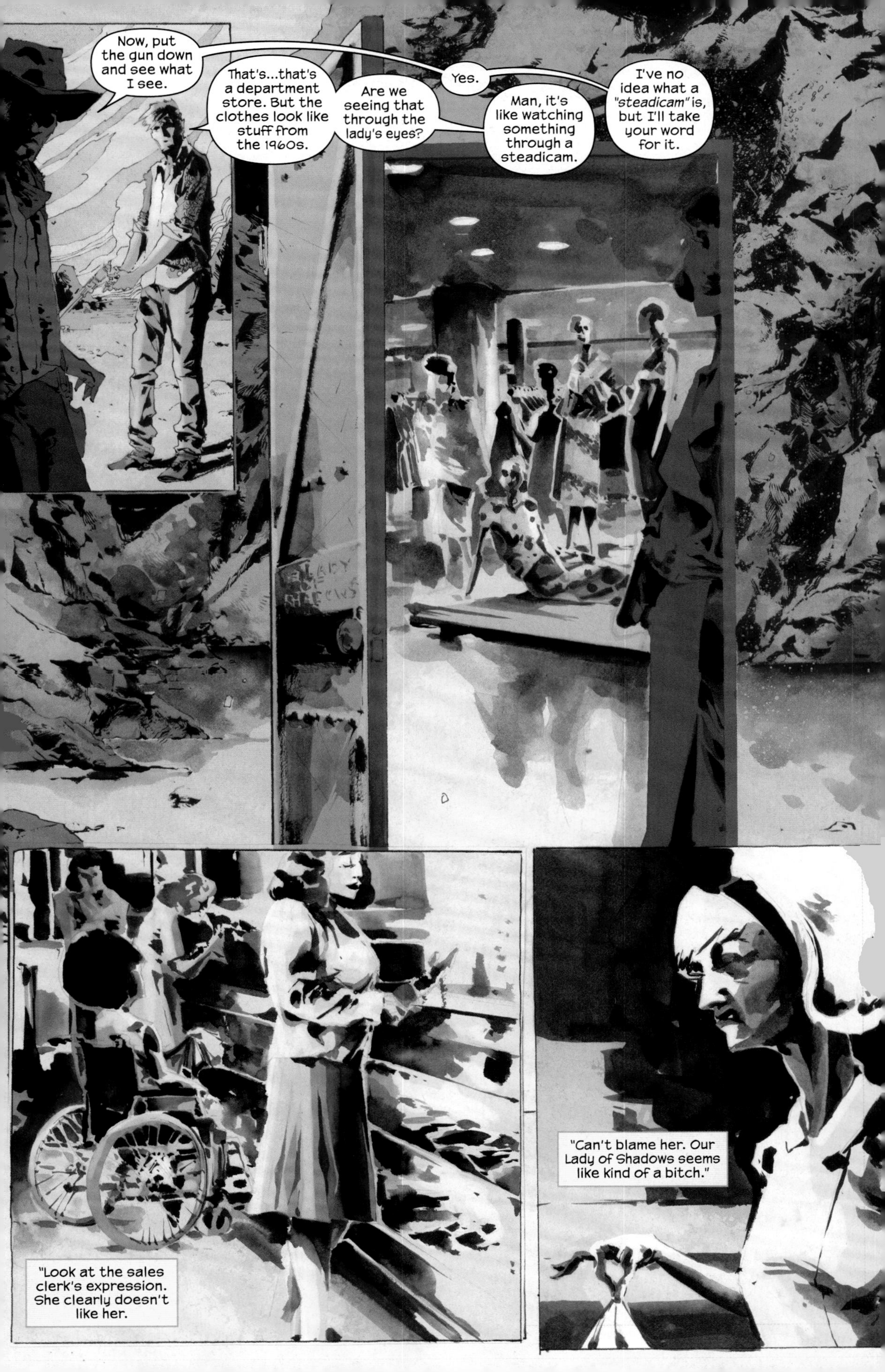
Now, put the gun down and see what I see.
That's...that's a department store. But the clothes look like stuff from the 1960s.
Are we seeing that through the lady's eyes?
Yes.
Man, it's like watching something through a steadicam.
I've no idea what a *"steadicam"* is, but I'll take your word for it.
LADY OF SHADOWS
"Look at the sales clerk's expression. She clearly doesn't like her.
"Can't blame her. Our Lady of Shadows seems like kind of a bitch."

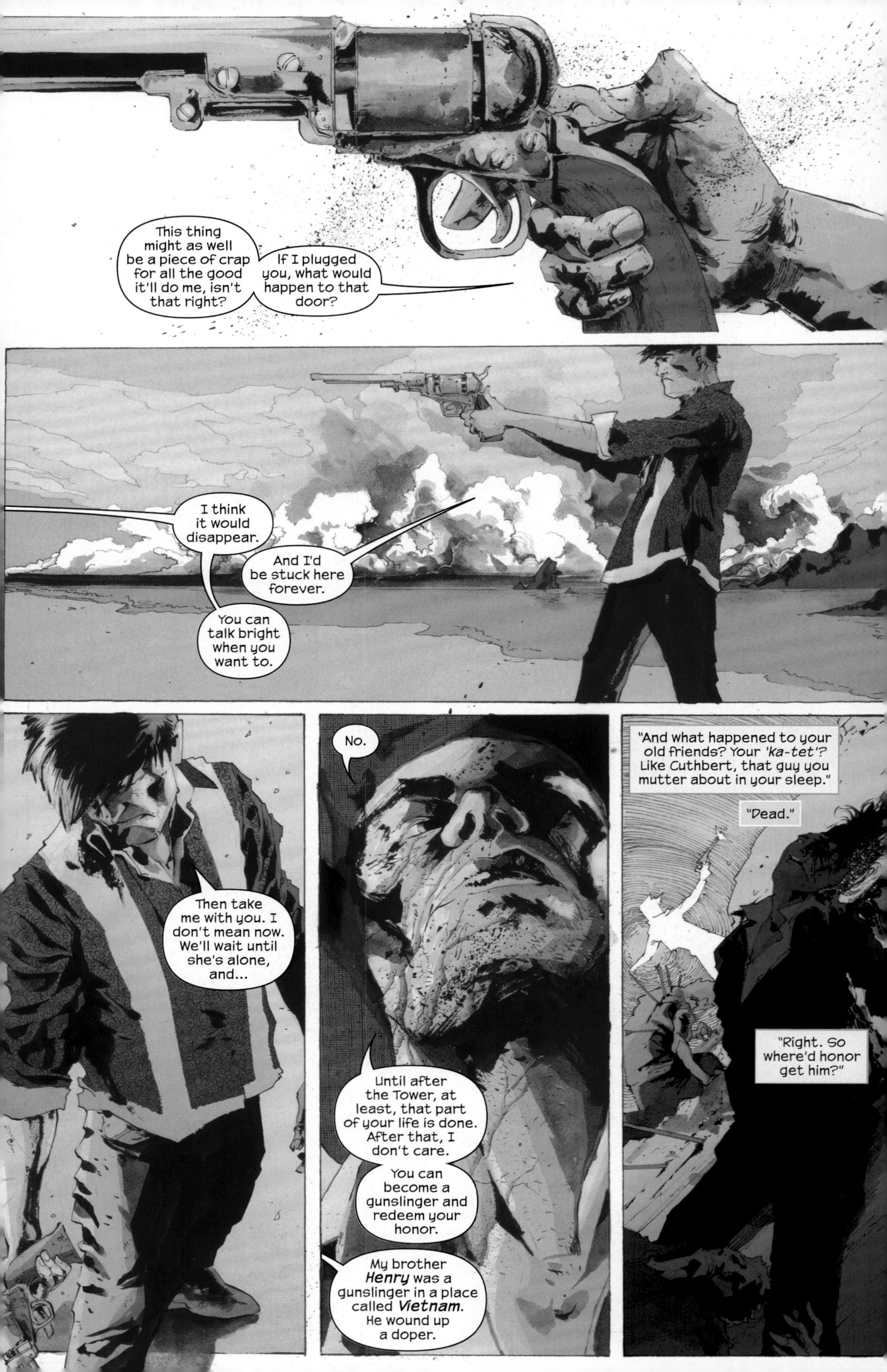
This thing might as well be a piece of crap for all the good it'll do me, isn't that right?
If I plugged you, what would happen to that door?
I think it would disappear.
And I'd be stuck here forever.
You can talk bright when you want to.
Then take me with you. I don't mean now. We'll wait until she's alone, and...
No.
Until after the Tower, at least, that part of your life is done. After that, I don't care.
You can become a gunslinger and redeem your honor.
My brother *Henry* was a gunslinger in a place called *Vietnam*. He wound up a doper.
"And what happened to your old friends? Your *'ka-tet'*? Like Cuthbert, that guy you mutter about in your sleep."
"Dead."
"Right. So where'd honor get him?"

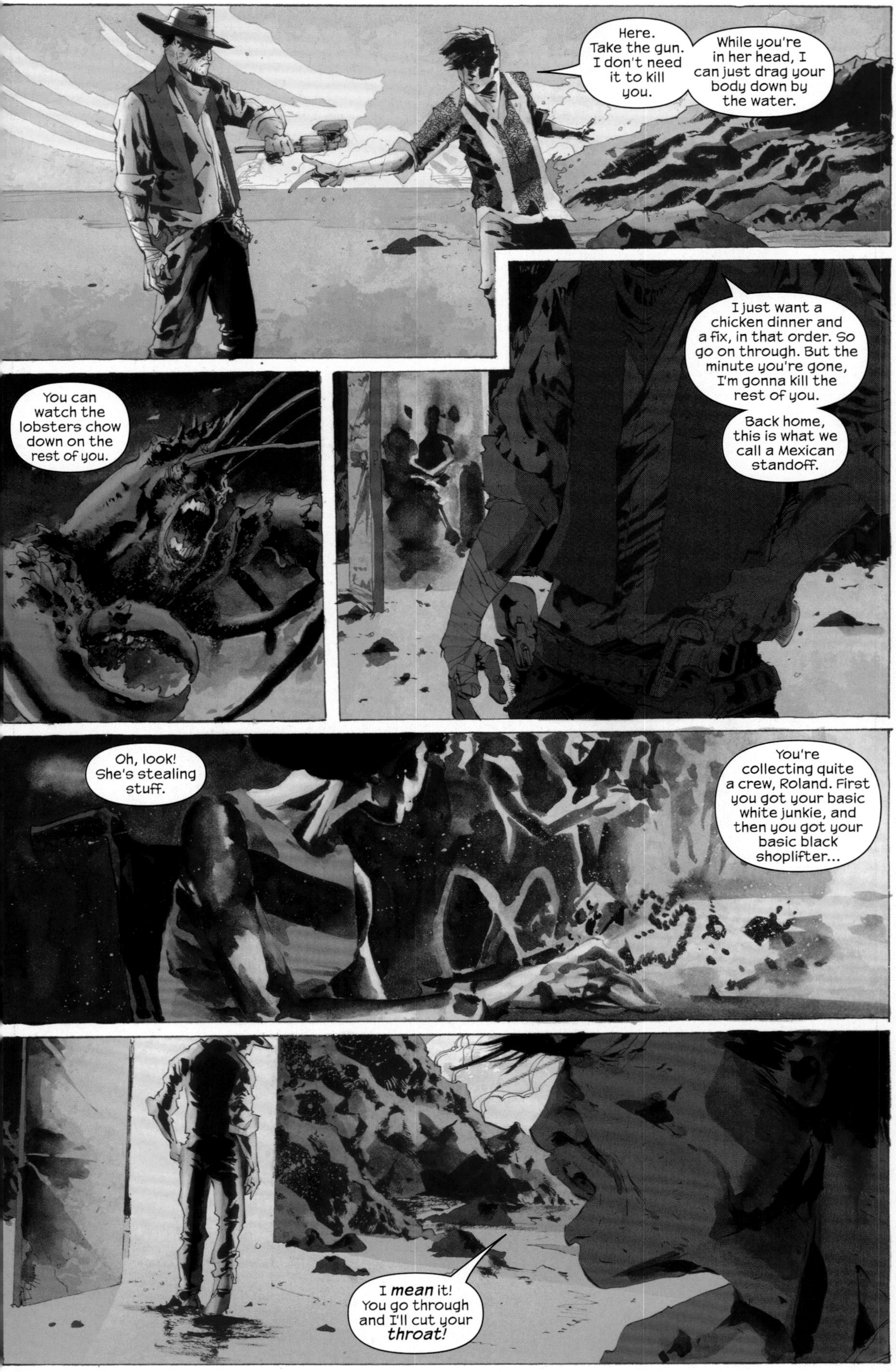
Here. Take the gun. I don't need it to kill you.
While you're in her head, I can just drag your body down by the water.
I just want a chicken dinner and a fix, in that order. So go on through. But the minute you're gone, I'm gonna kill the rest of you.
Back home, this is what we call a Mexican standoff.
You can watch the lobsters chow down on the rest of you.
Oh, look! She's stealing stuff.
You're collecting quite a crew, Roland. First you got your basic white junkie, and then you got your basic black shoplifter...
I *mean* it! You go through and I'll cut your *throat!*

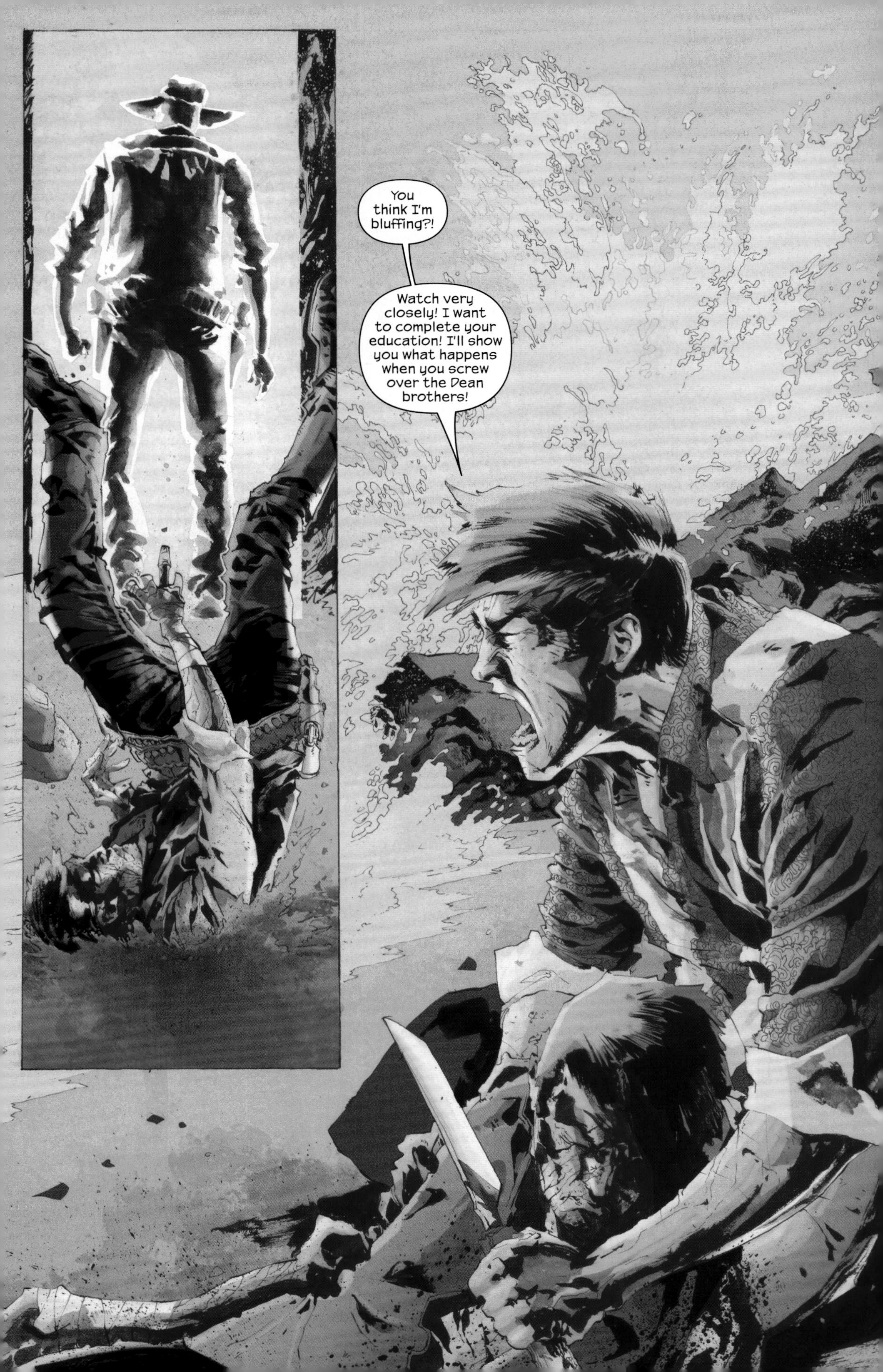
You think I'm bluffing?!
Watch very closely! I want to complete your education! I'll show you what happens when you screw over the Dean brothers!

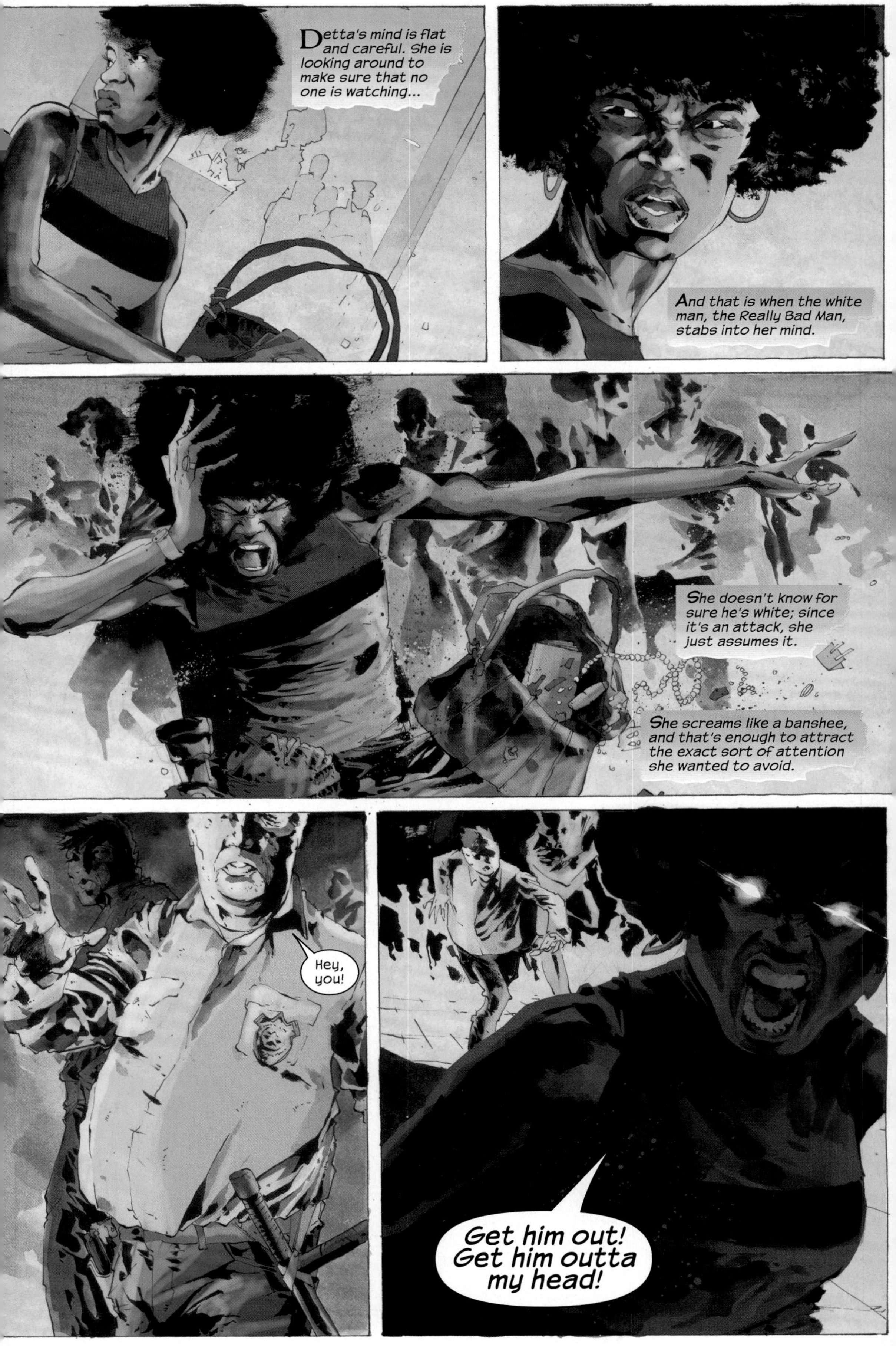
Detta's mind is flat and careful. She is looking around to make sure that no one is watching...
And that is when the white man, the Really Bad Man, stabs into her mind.
She doesn't know for sure he's white; since it's an attack, she just assumes it.
She screams like a banshee, and that's enough to attract the exact sort of attention she wanted to avoid.
Hey, you!
Get him out! Get him outta my head!

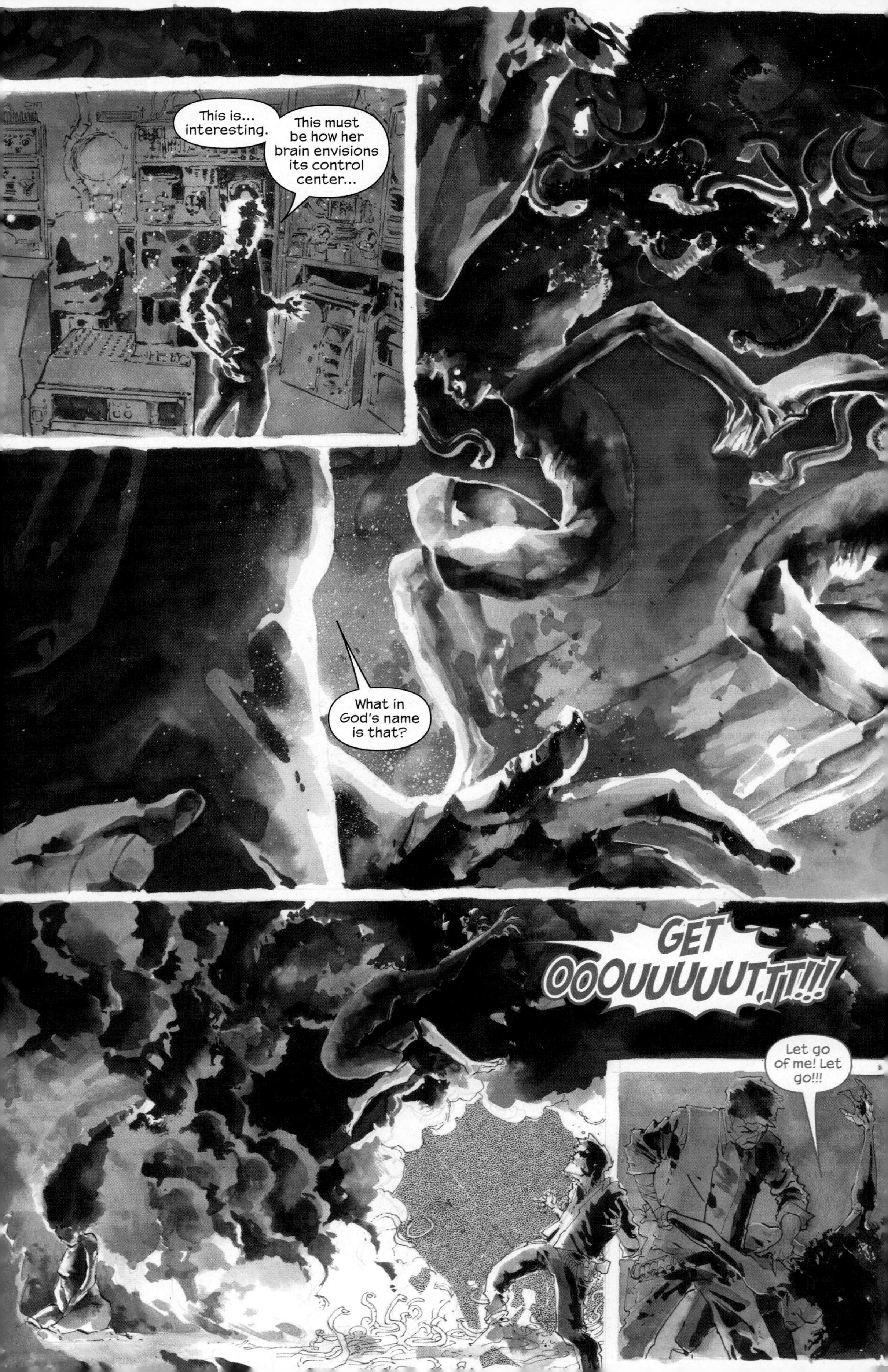
This is... interesting.
This must be how her brain envisions its control center...
What in God's name is that?
GET OOOUUUUUUTTTT!!!
Let go of me! Let go!!!

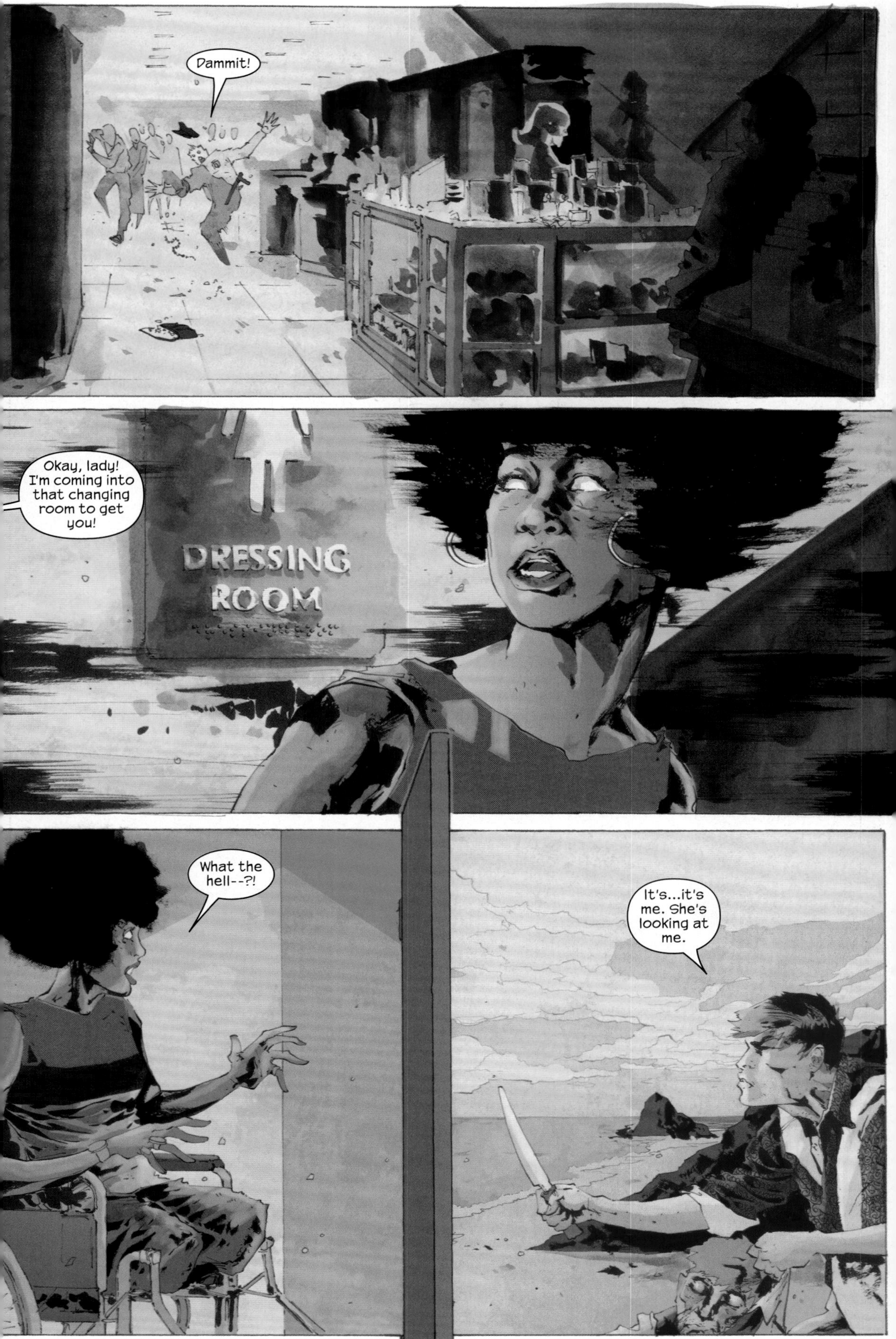
Dammit!
Okay, lady! I'm coming into that changing room to get you!
DRESSING ROOM
What the hell--?!
It's...it's me. She's looking at me.

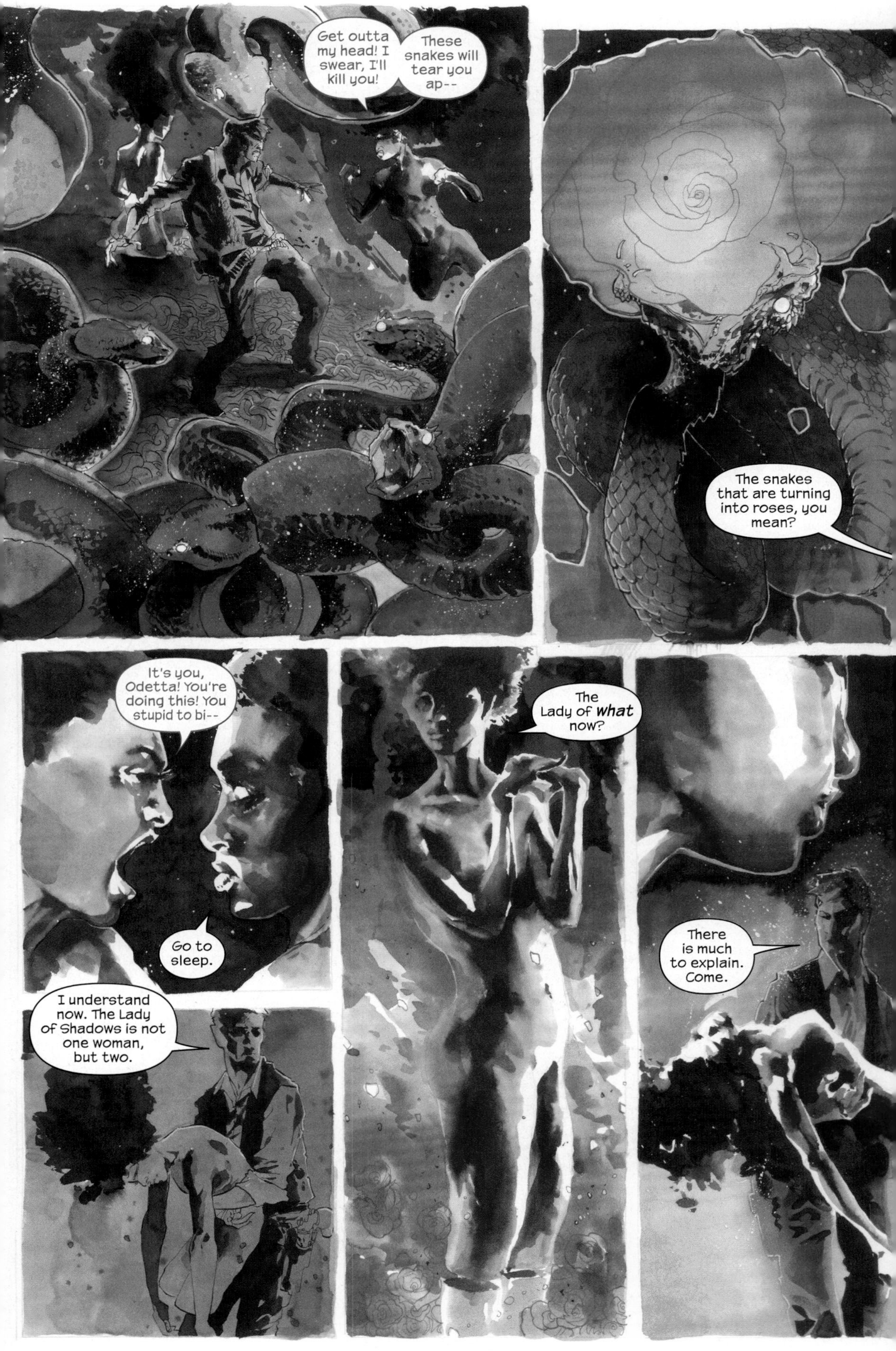
Get outta my head! I swear, I'll kill you!
These snakes will tear you ap--
The snakes that are turning into roses, you mean?
It's you, Odetta! You're doing this! You stupid to bi--
Go to sleep.
I understand now. The Lady of Shadows is not one woman, but two.
The Lady of *what* now?
There is much to explain. Come.

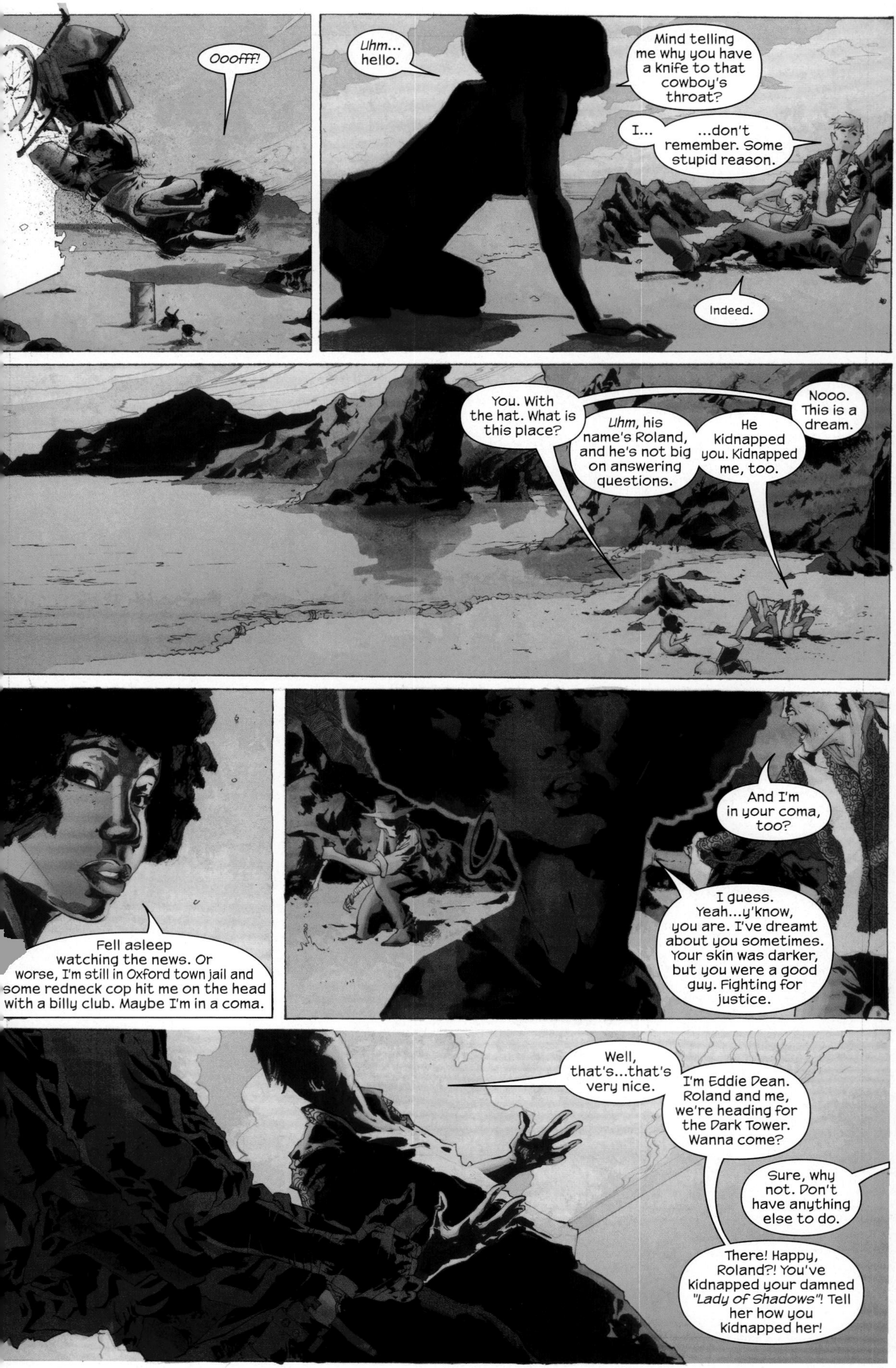
Oooffff!
Uhm... hello.
Mind telling me why you have a knife to that cowboy's throat?
I... ...don't remember. Some stupid reason.
Indeed.
You. With the hat. What is this place?
Uhm, his name's Roland, and he's not big on answering questions.
He kidnapped you. Kidnapped me, too.
Nooo. This is a dream.
Fell asleep watching the news. Or worse, I'm still in Oxford town jail and some redneck cop hit me on the head with a billy club. Maybe I'm in a coma.
And I'm in your coma, too?
I guess. Yeah...y'know, you are. I've dreamt about you sometimes. Your skin was darker, but you were a good guy. Fighting for justice.
Well, that's...that's very nice.
I'm Eddie Dean. Roland and me, we're heading for the Dark Tower. Wanna come?
Sure, why not. Don't have anything else to do.
There! Happy, Roland?! You've kidnapped your damned "Lady of Shadows"! Tell her how you kidnapped her!

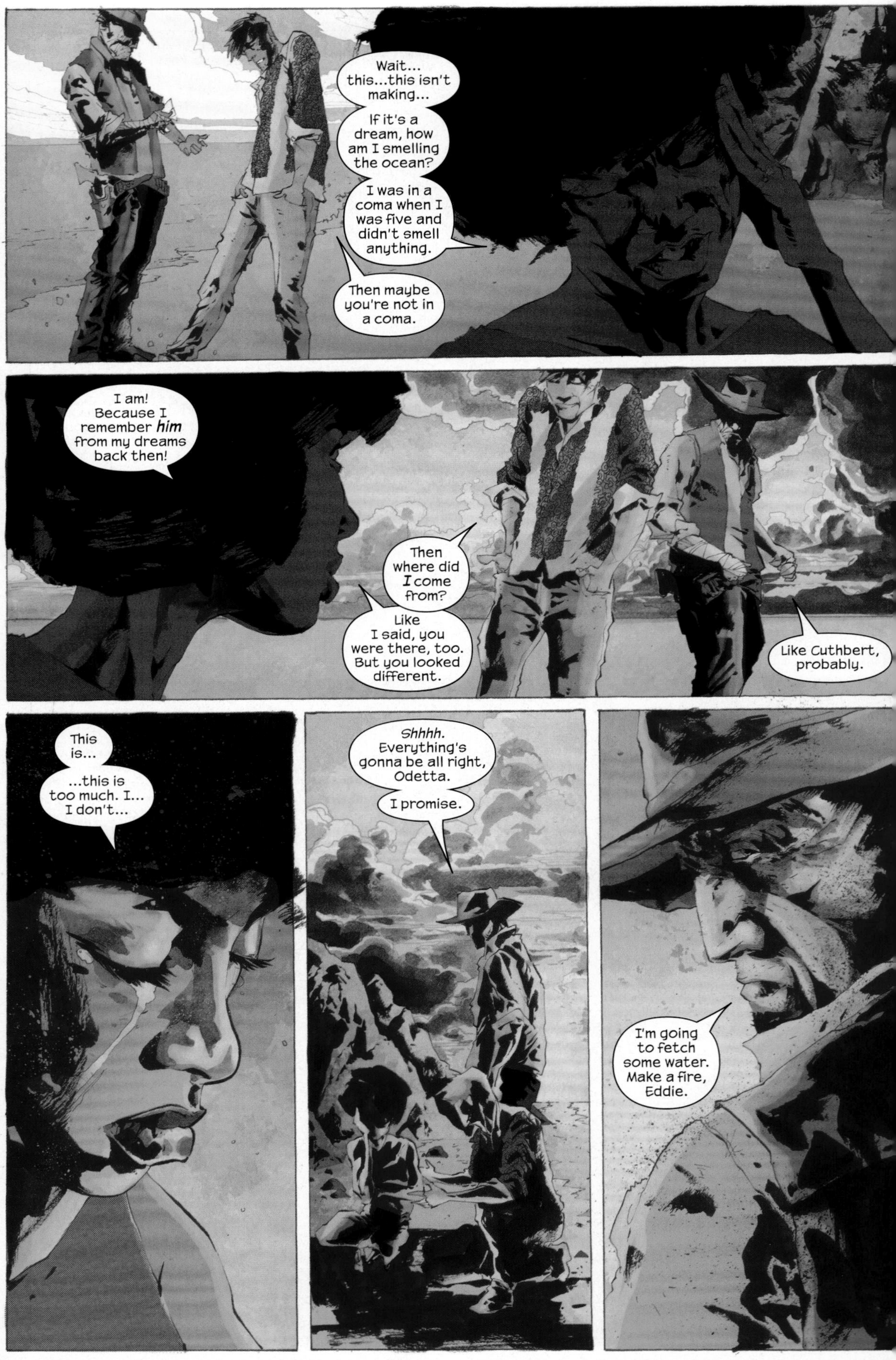
Wait... this...this isn't making...
If it's a dream, how am I smelling the ocean?
I was in a coma when I was five and didn't smell anything.
Then maybe you're not in a coma.
I am! Because I remember *him* from my dreams back then!
Then where did *I* come from?
Like I said, you were there, too. But you looked different.
Like Cuthbert, probably.
This is...
...this is too much. I... I don't...
Shhhh. Everything's gonna be all right, Odetta.
I promise.
I'm going to fetch some water. Make a fire, Eddie.

LATER...

...And that's how I wound up coming to Mid-World.

No.

I don't understand. What are you no-ing?

I believe one of two things has happened, and no matter which one it is, I am still in Oxford, Mississippi.

None of this is real.

See? Scar from an old head injury. I know what it can do to you.

I'm curious: Were you a shoplifter before your head was injured?

A *what?* I'm not a *shoplifter.*

Then why were you shoplifting jewelry?

I'm rich! And I don't wear--

--jewelry...

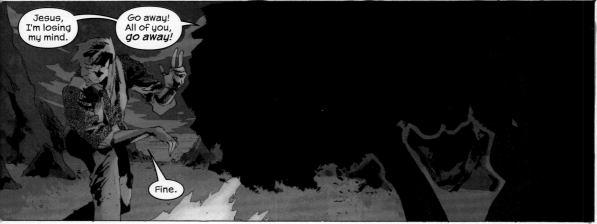

Jesus, I'm losing my mind.

Go away! All of you, *go away!*

Fine.

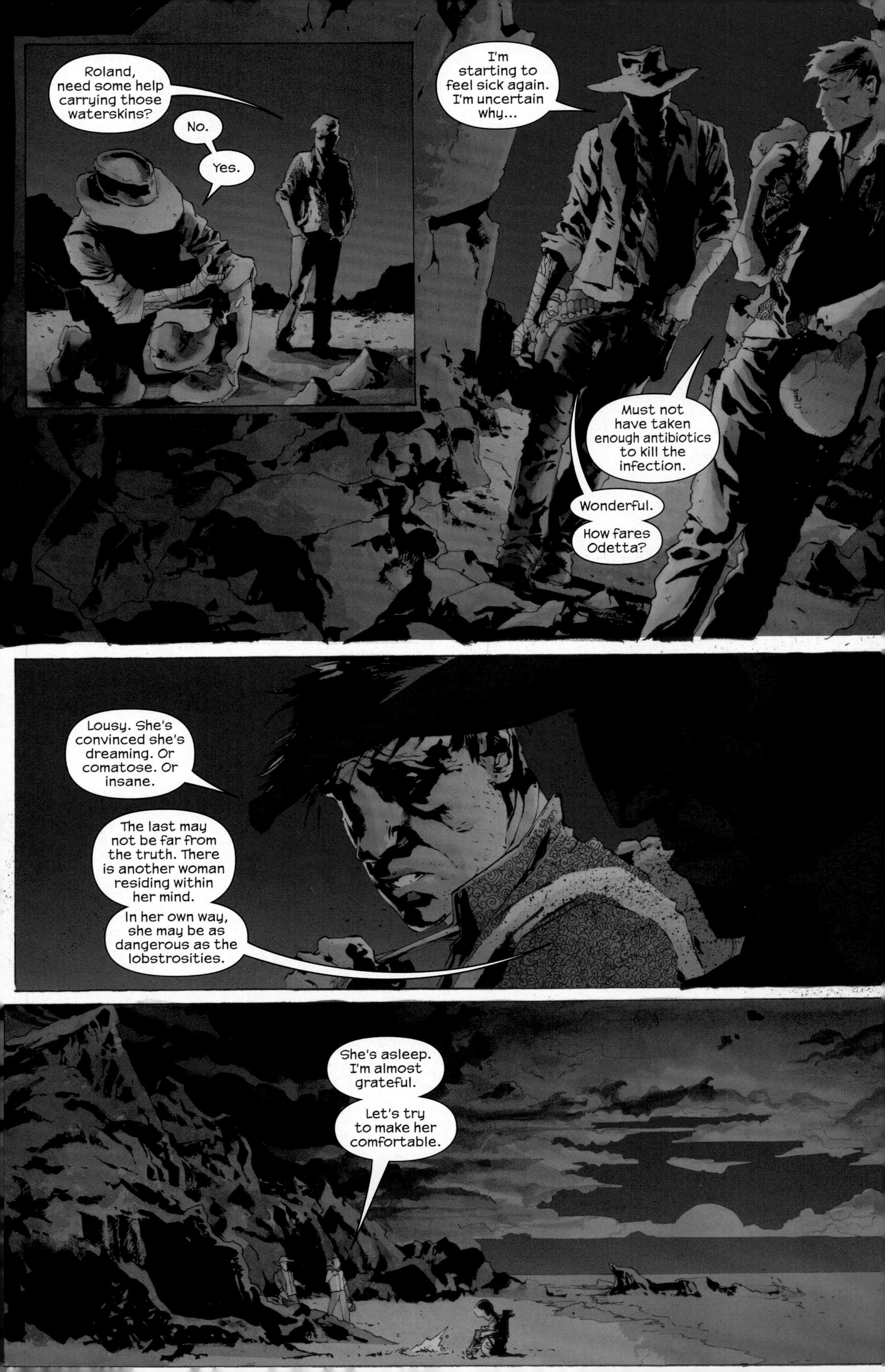
Roland, need some help carrying those waterskins?
No.
Yes.
I'm starting to feel sick again. I'm uncertain why...
Must not have taken enough antibiotics to kill the infection.
Wonderful.
How fares Odetta?
Lousy. She's convinced she's dreaming. Or comatose. Or insane.
The last may not be far from the truth. There is another woman residing within her mind.
In her own way, she may be as dangerous as the lobstrosities.
She's asleep. I'm almost grateful.
Let's try to make her comfortable.

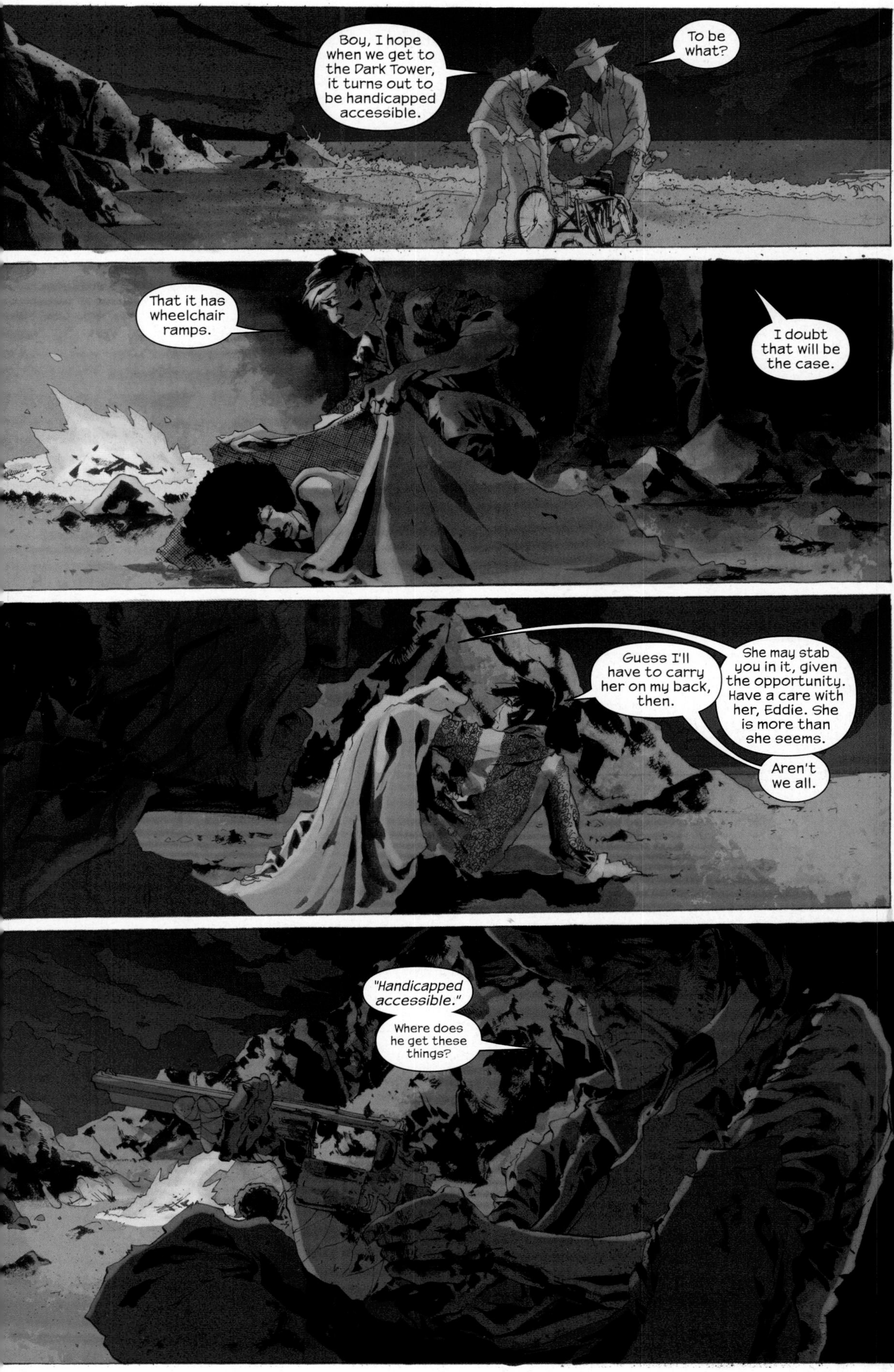
Boy, I hope when we get to the Dark Tower, it turns out to be handicapped accessible.
To be what?
That it has wheelchair ramps.
I doubt that will be the case.
Guess I'll have to carry her on my back, then.
She may stab you in it, given the opportunity. Have a care with her, Eddie. She is more than she seems.
Aren't we all.
"Handicapped accessible."
Where does he get these things?

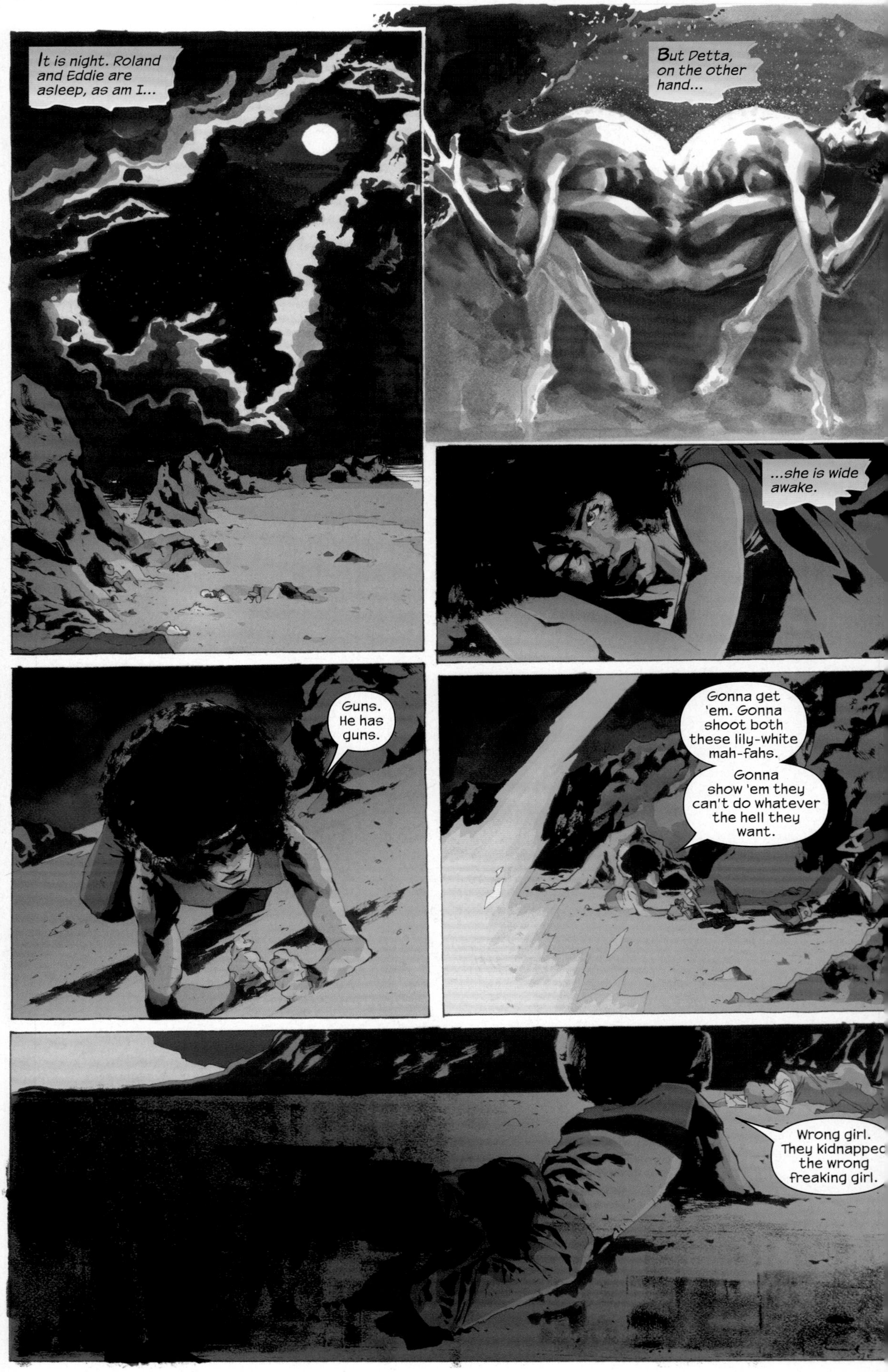
It is night. Roland and Eddie are asleep, as am I...
But Detta, on the other hand...
...she is wide awake.
Guns. He has guns.
Gonna get 'em. Gonna shoot both these lily-white mah-fahs.
Gonna show 'em they can't do whatever the hell they want.
Wrong girl. They kidnapped the wrong freaking girl.

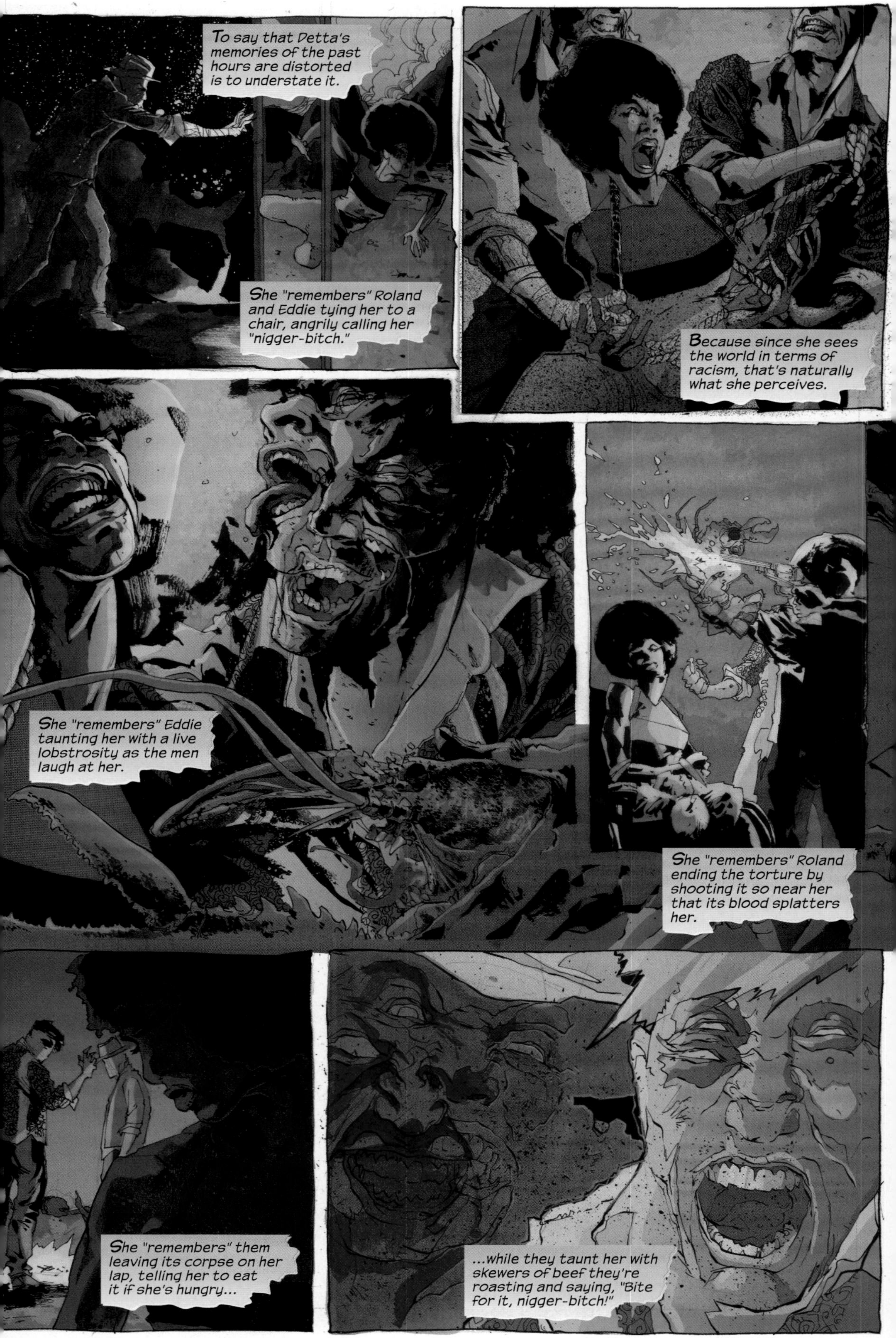
To say that Detta's memories of the past hours are distorted is to understate it.
She "remembers" Roland and Eddie tying her to a chair, angrily calling her "nigger-bitch."
Because since she sees the world in terms of racism, that's naturally what she perceives.
She "remembers" Eddie taunting her with a live lobstrosity as the men laugh at her.
She "remembers" Roland ending the torture by shooting it so near her that its blood splatters her.
She "remembers" them leaving its corpse on her lap, telling her to eat it if she's hungry...
...while they taunt her with skewers of beef they're roasting and saying, "Bite for it, nigger-bitch!"

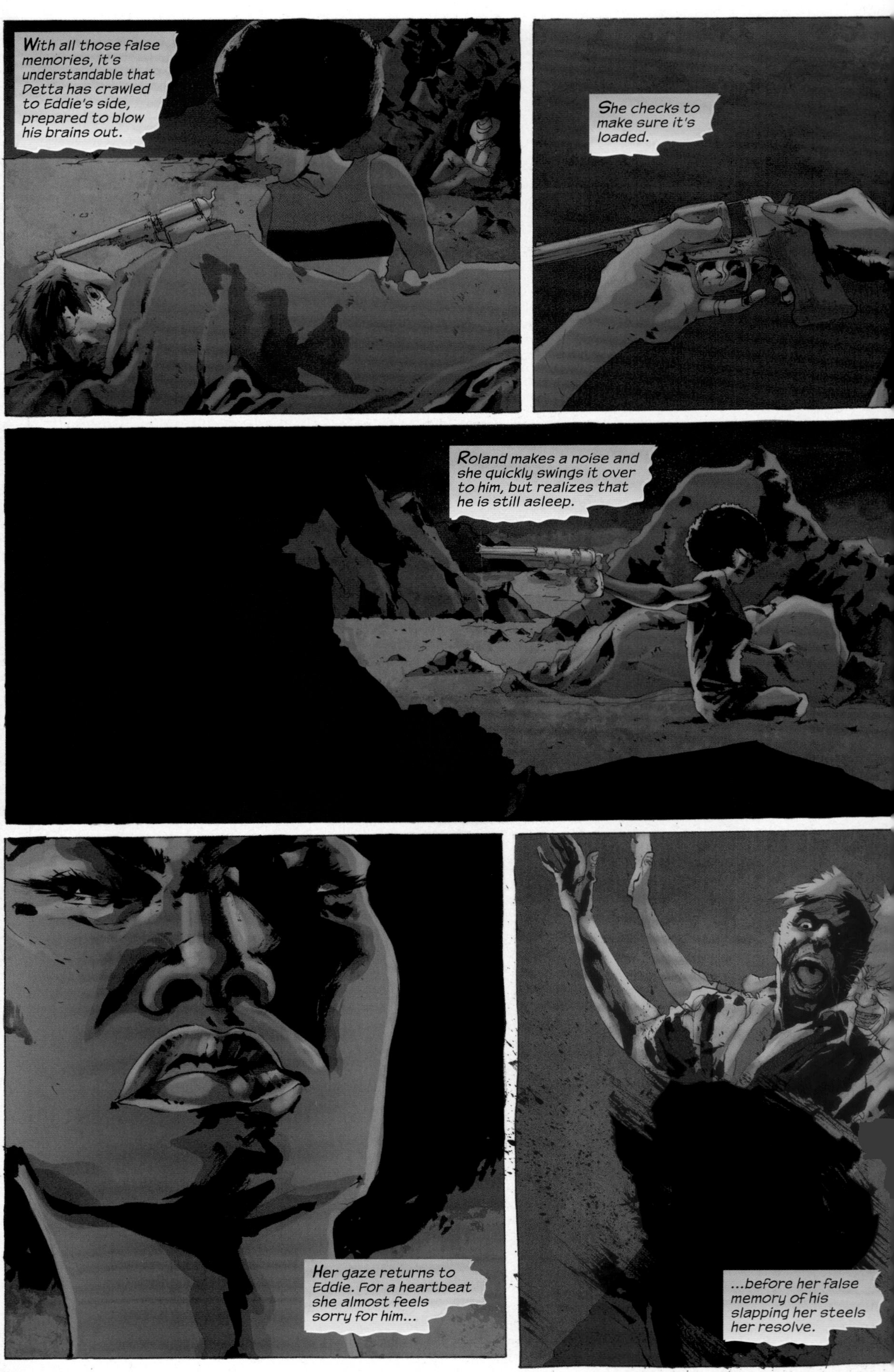
With all those false memories, it's understandable that Detta has crawled to Eddie's side, prepared to blow his brains out.
She checks to make sure it's loaded.
Roland makes a noise and she quickly swings it over to him, but realizes that he is still asleep.
Her gaze returns to Eddie. For a heartbeat she almost feels sorry for him...
...before her false memory of his slapping her steels her resolve.

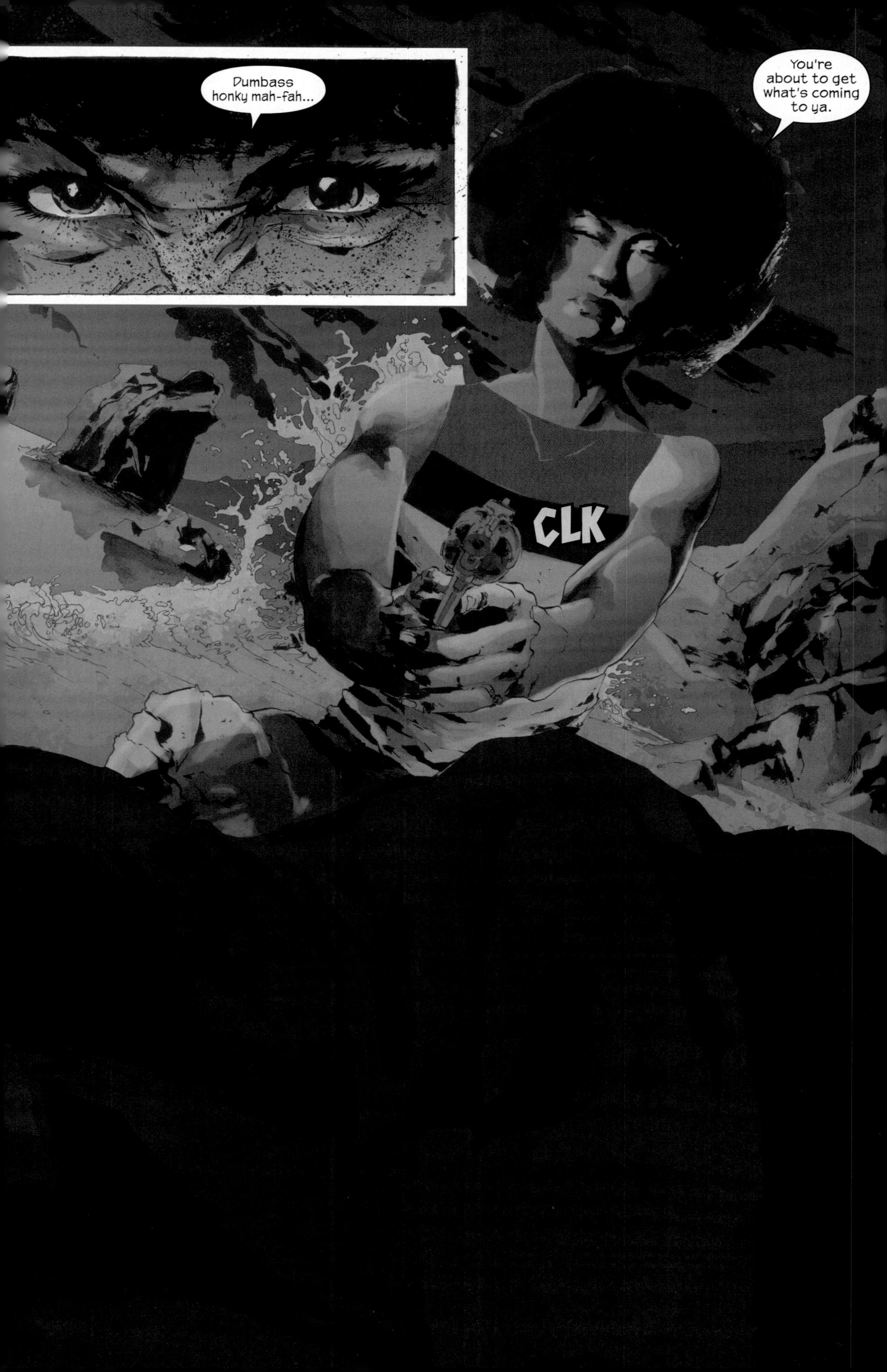
Dumbass honky mah-fah...
You're about to get what's coming to ya.
CLK

THE DARK TOWER
THE DRAWING OF THE THREE
STEPHEN KING

BITTER MEDICINE
CHAPTER TWO

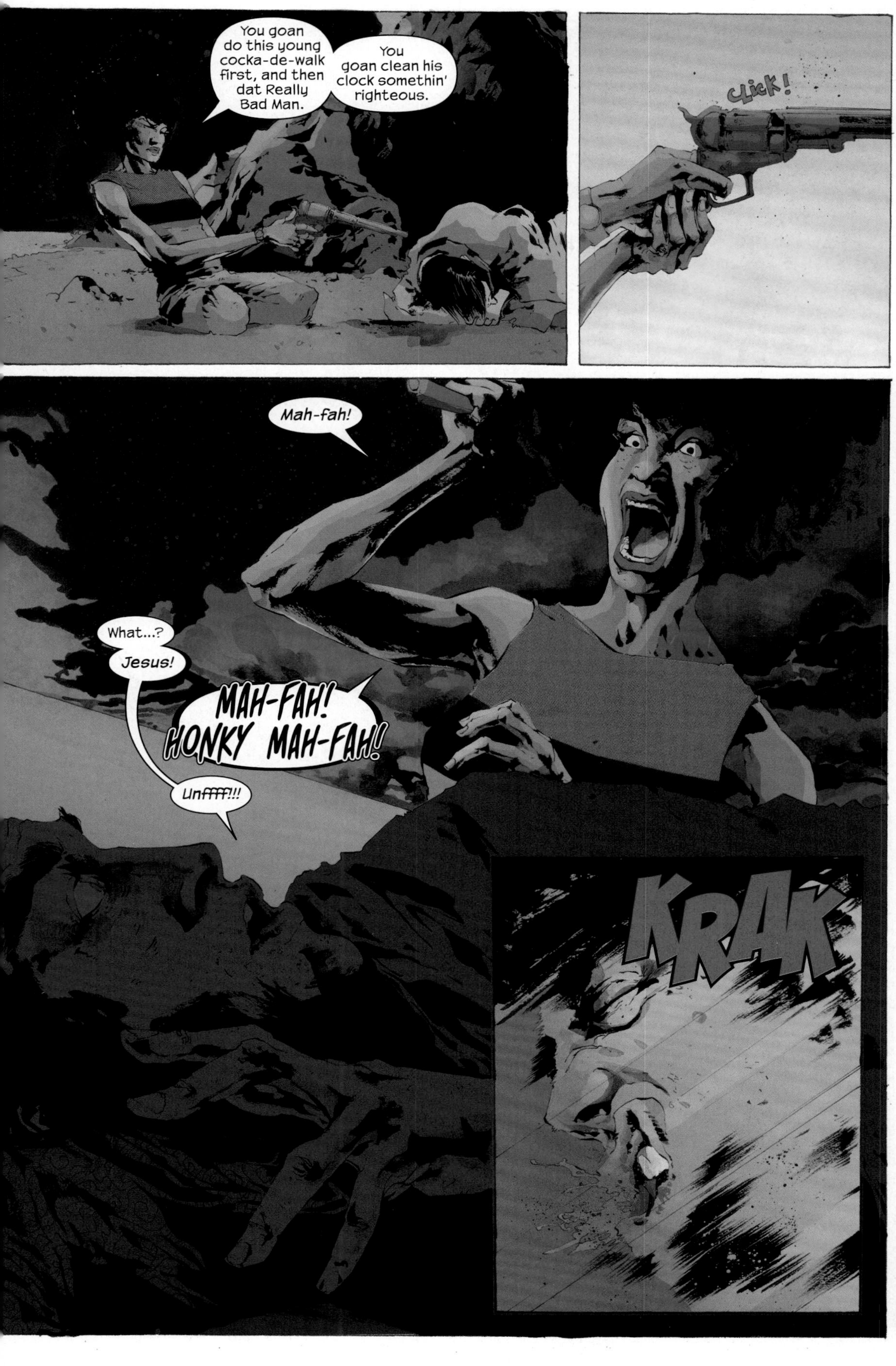
You goan do this young cocka-de-walk first, and then dat Really Bad Man.
You goan clean his clock somethin' righteous.
CLICK!
Mah-fah!
What...?
Jesus!
MAH-FAH! HONKY MAH-FAH!
Unfffff!!!
KRAK

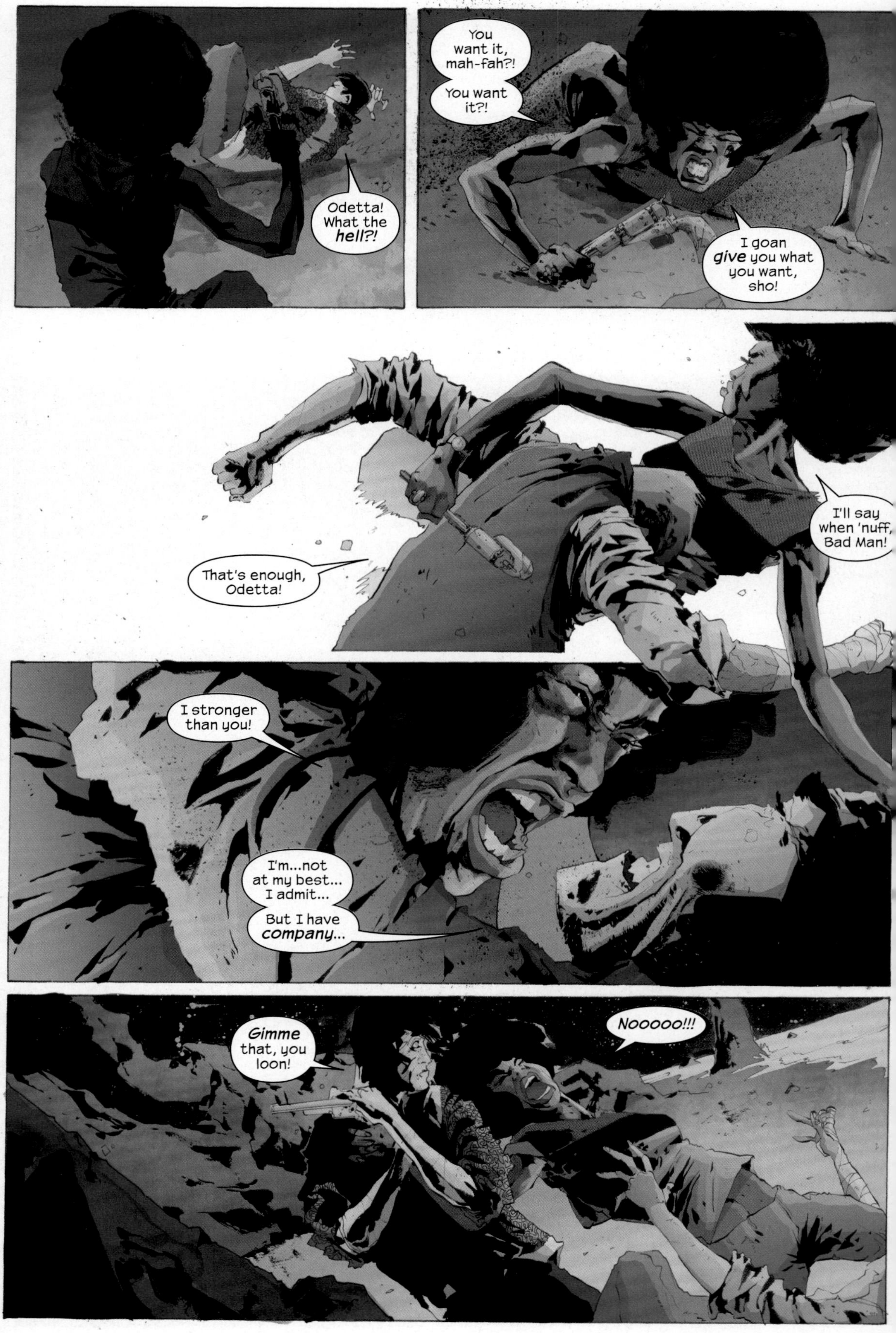
Odetta! What the *hell*?!
You want it, mah-fah?!
You want it?!
I goan *give* you what you want, sho!
I'll say when 'nuff, Bad Man!
That's enough, Odetta!
I stronger than you!
I'm...not at my best... I admit...
But I have *company*...
Gimme that, you loon!
Nooooo!!!

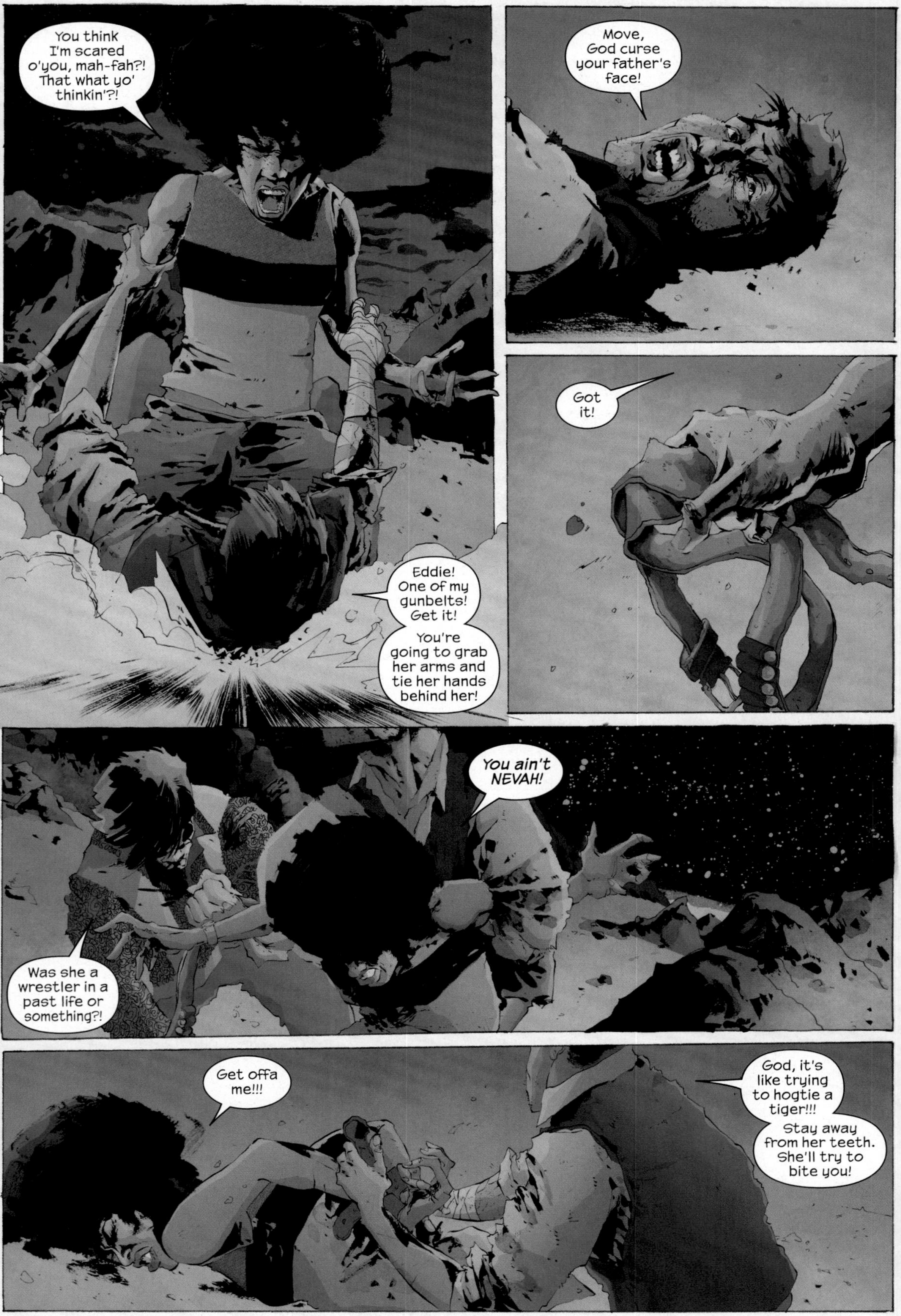
You think I'm scared o'you, mah-fah?! That what yo' thinkin'?!
Move, God curse your father's face!
Got it!
Eddie! One of my gunbelts! Get it!
You're going to grab her arms and tie her hands behind her!
You ain't NEVAH!
Was she a wrestler in a past life or something?!
Get offa me!!!
God, it's like trying to hogtie a tiger!!!
Stay away from her teeth. She'll try to bite you!

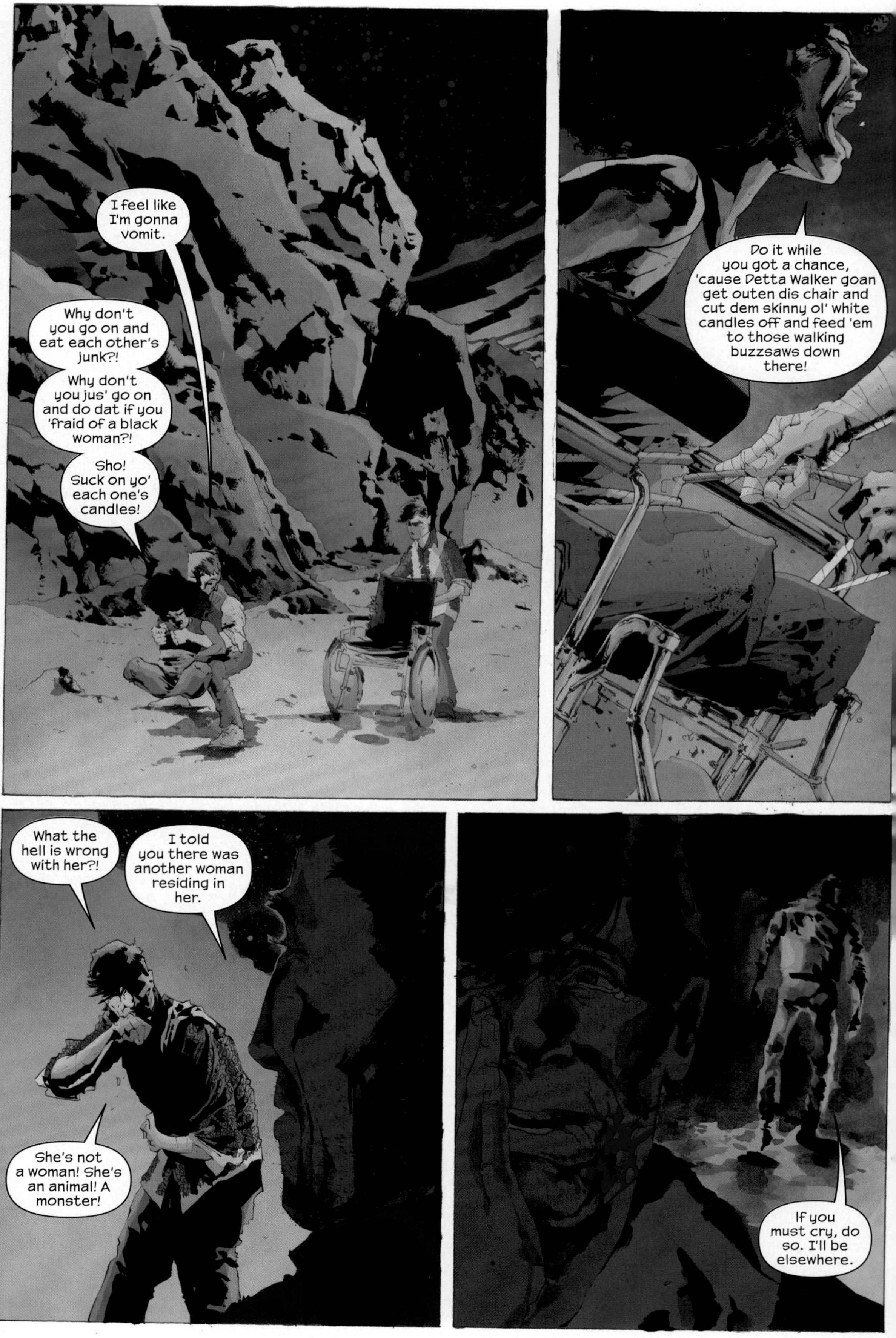
I feel like I'm gonna vomit.
Why don't you go on and eat each other's junk?!
Why don't you jus' go on and do dat if you 'fraid of a black woman?!
Sho! Suck on yo' each one's candles!
Do it while you got a chance, 'cause Detta Walker goan get outen dis chair and cut dem skinny ol' white candles off and feed 'em to those walking buzzsaws down there!
What the hell is wrong with her?!
I told you there was another woman residing in her.
She's not a woman! She's an animal! A monster!
If you must cry, do so. I'll be elsewhere.

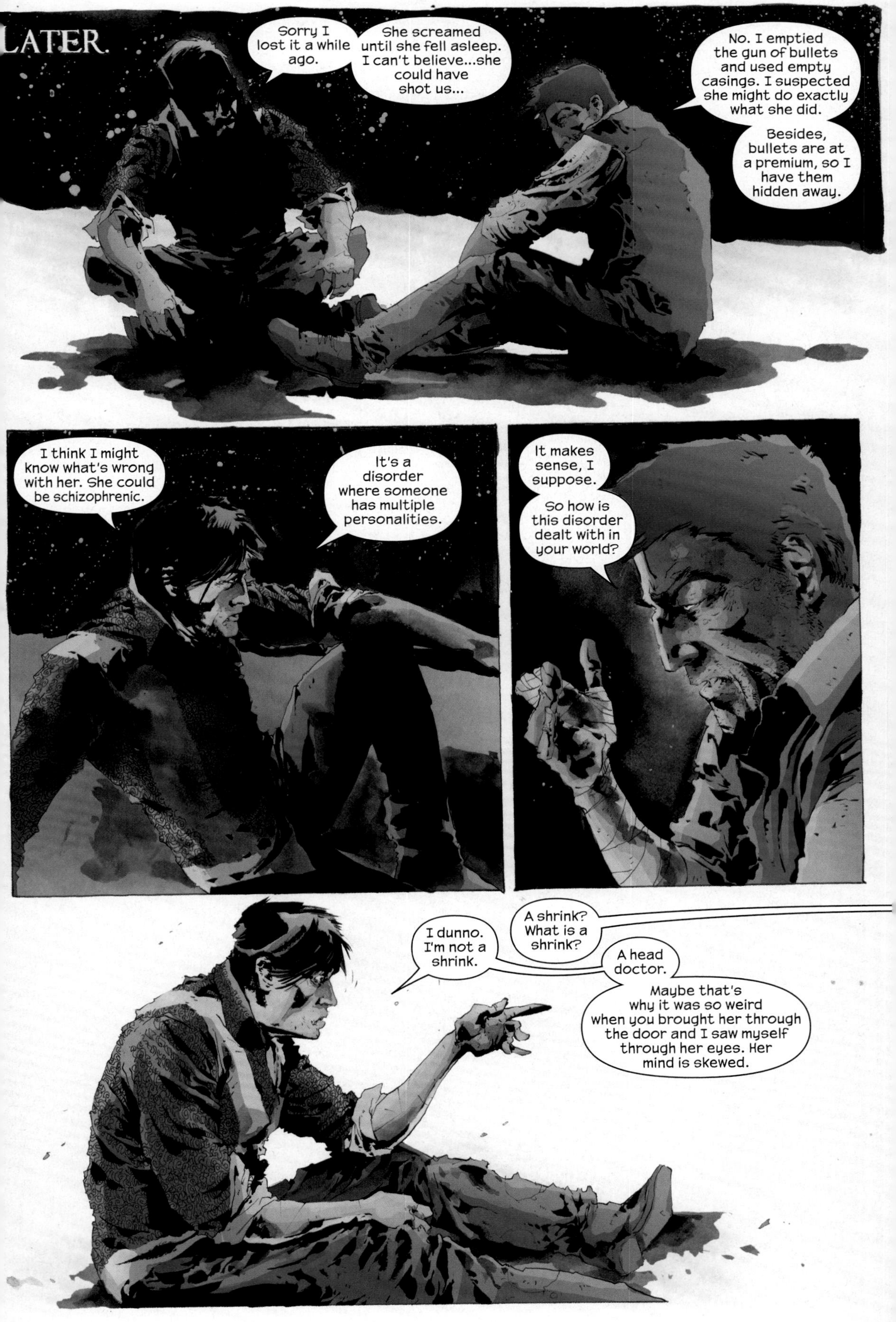
LATER.
Sorry I lost it a while ago.
She screamed until she fell asleep. I can't believe...she could have shot us...
No. I emptied the gun of bullets and used empty casings. I suspected she might do exactly what she did.
Besides, bullets are at a premium, so I have them hidden away.
I think I might know what's wrong with her. She could be schizophrenic.
It's a disorder where someone has multiple personalities.
It makes sense, I suppose.
So how is this disorder dealt with in your world?
I dunno. I'm not a shrink.
A shrink? What is a shrink?
A head doctor.
Maybe that's why it was so weird when you brought her through the door and I saw myself through her eyes. Her mind is skewed.

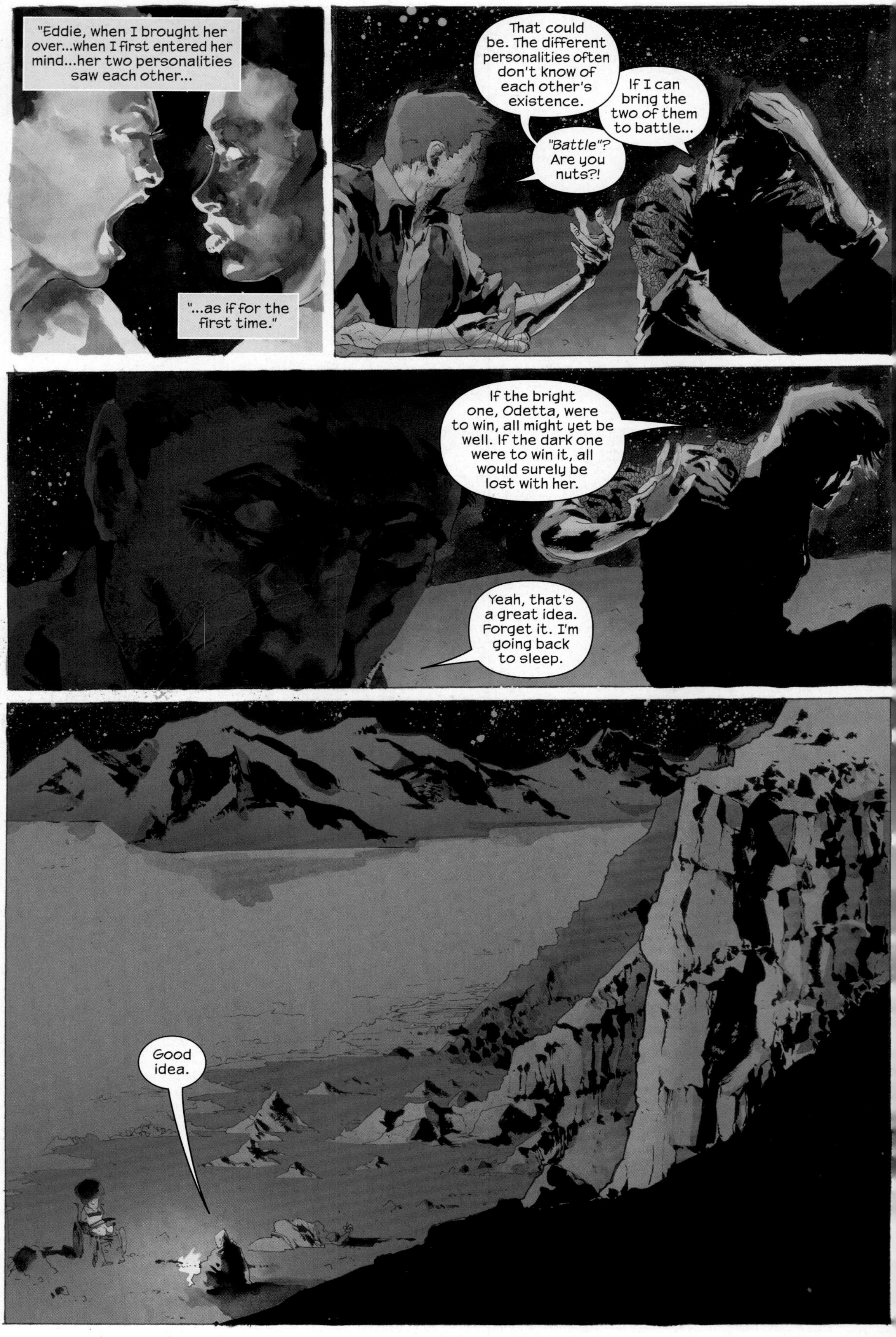
"Eddie, when I brought her over...when I first entered her mind...her two personalities saw each other...
"...as if for the first time."
That could be. The different personalities often don't know of each other's existence.
If I can bring the two of them to battle...
"Battle"? Are you nuts?!
If the bright one, Odetta, were to win, all might yet be well. If the dark one were to win it, all would surely be lost with her.
Yeah, that's a great idea. Forget it. I'm going back to sleep.
Good idea.

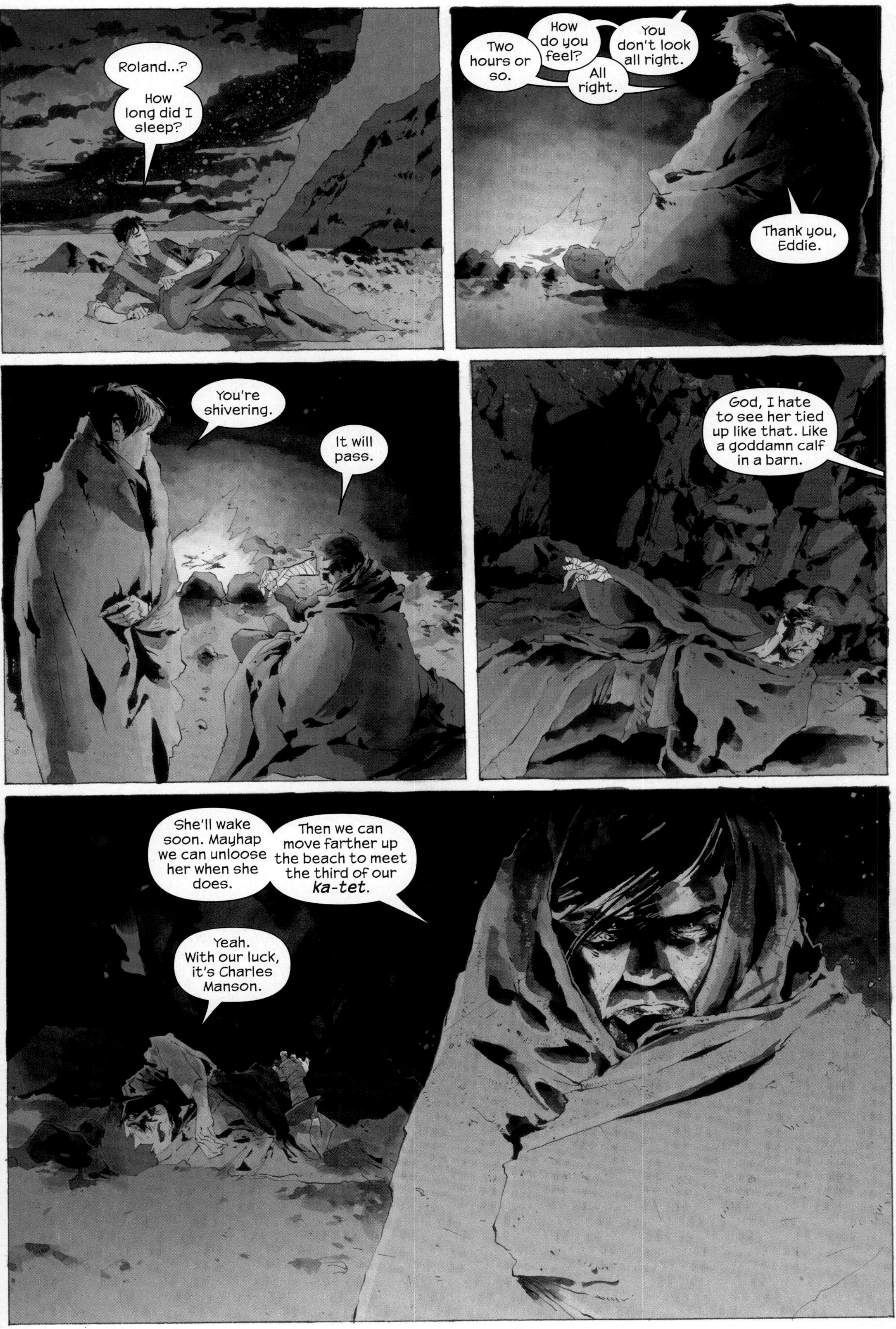
Roland...?
How long did I sleep?
How do you feel?
Two hours or so.
You don't look all right.
All right.
Thank you, Eddie.
You're shivering.
It will pass.
God, I hate to see her tied up like that. Like a goddamn calf in a barn.
She'll wake soon. Mayhap we can unloose her when she does.
Then we can move farther up the beach to meet the third of our *ka-tet*.
Yeah. With our luck, it's Charles Manson.

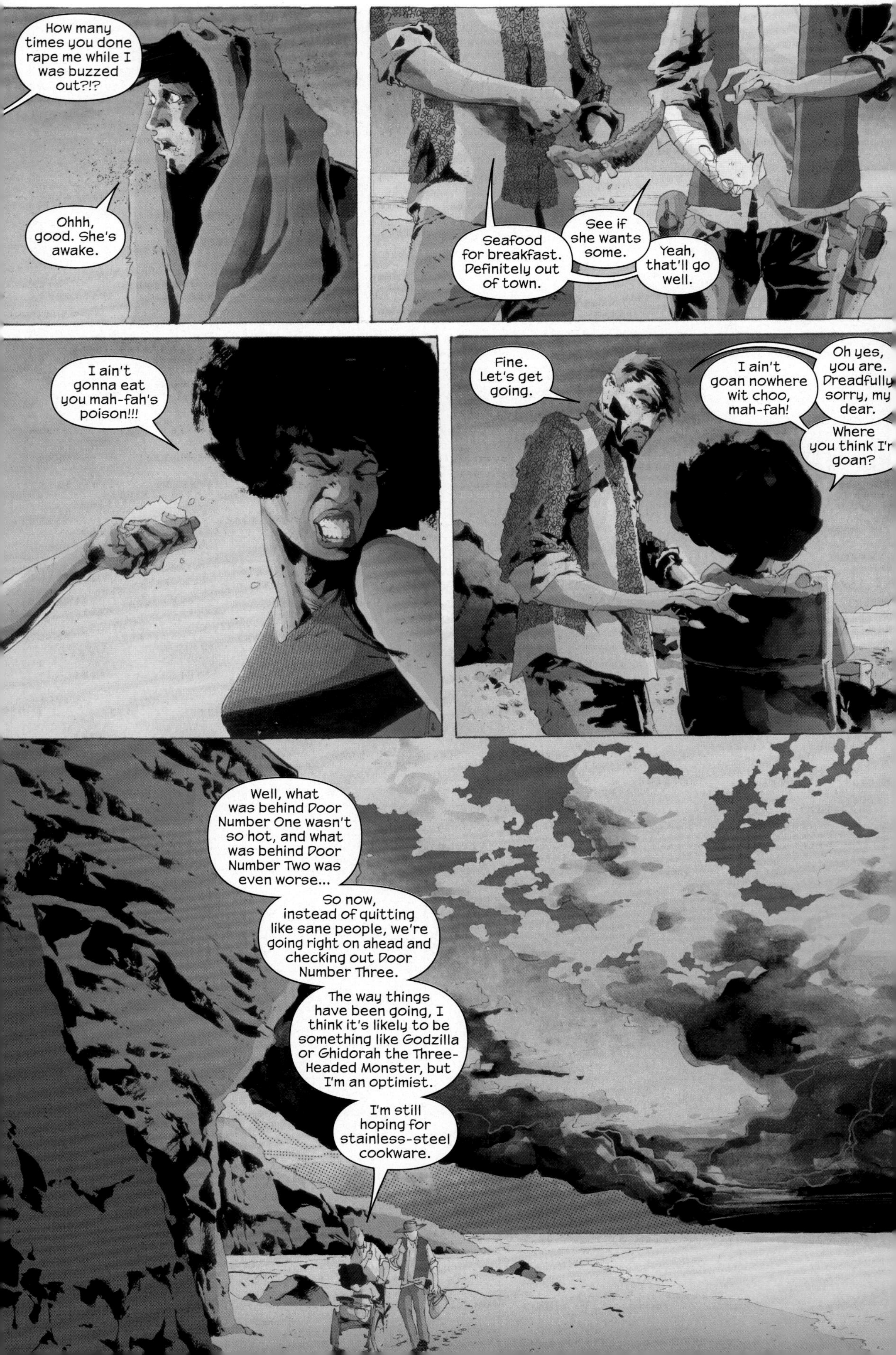
How many times you done rape me while I was buzzed out?!?
Ohhh, good. She's awake.
Seafood for breakfast. Definitely out of town.
See if she wants some.
Yeah, that'll go well.
I ain't gonna eat you mah-fah's poison!!!
Fine. Let's get going.
I ain't goan nowhere wit choo, mah-fah!
Oh yes, you are. Dreadfully sorry, my dear.
Where you think I'm goan?
Well, what was behind Door Number One wasn't so hot, and what was behind Door Number Two was even worse...
So now, instead of quitting like sane people, we're going right on ahead and checking out Door Number Three.
The way things have been going, I think it's likely to be something like Godzilla or Ghidorah the Three-Headed Monster, but I'm an optimist.
I'm still hoping for stainless-steel cookware.

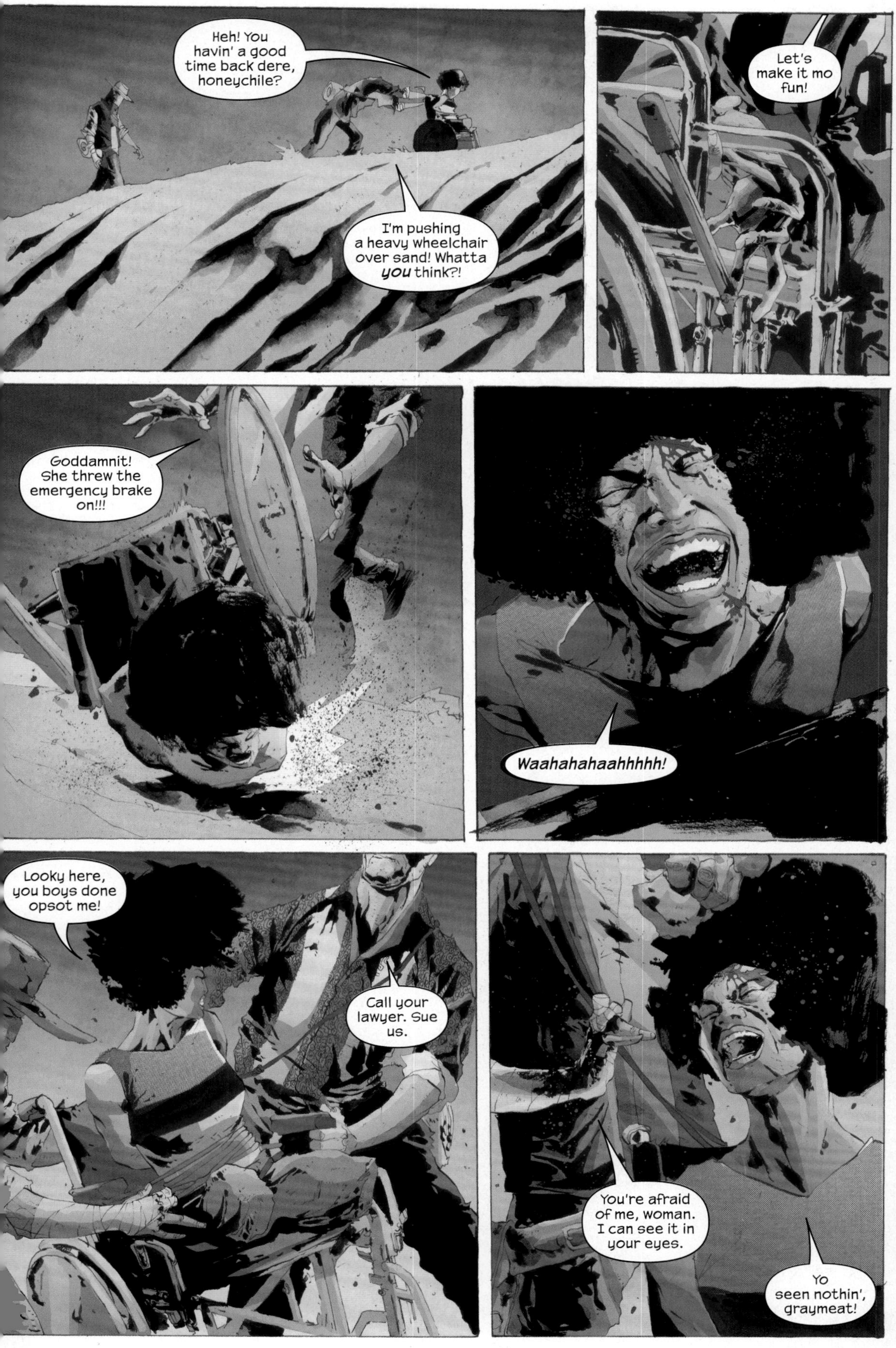
Heh! You havin' a good time back dere, honeychile?
I'm pushing a heavy wheelchair over sand! Whatta *you* think?!
Let's make it mo fun!
Goddamnit! She threw the emergency brake on!!!
Waahahahaahhhhh!
Looky here, you boys done opsot me!
Call your lawyer. Sue us.
You're afraid of me, woman. I can see it in your eyes.
Yo seen nothin', graymeat!

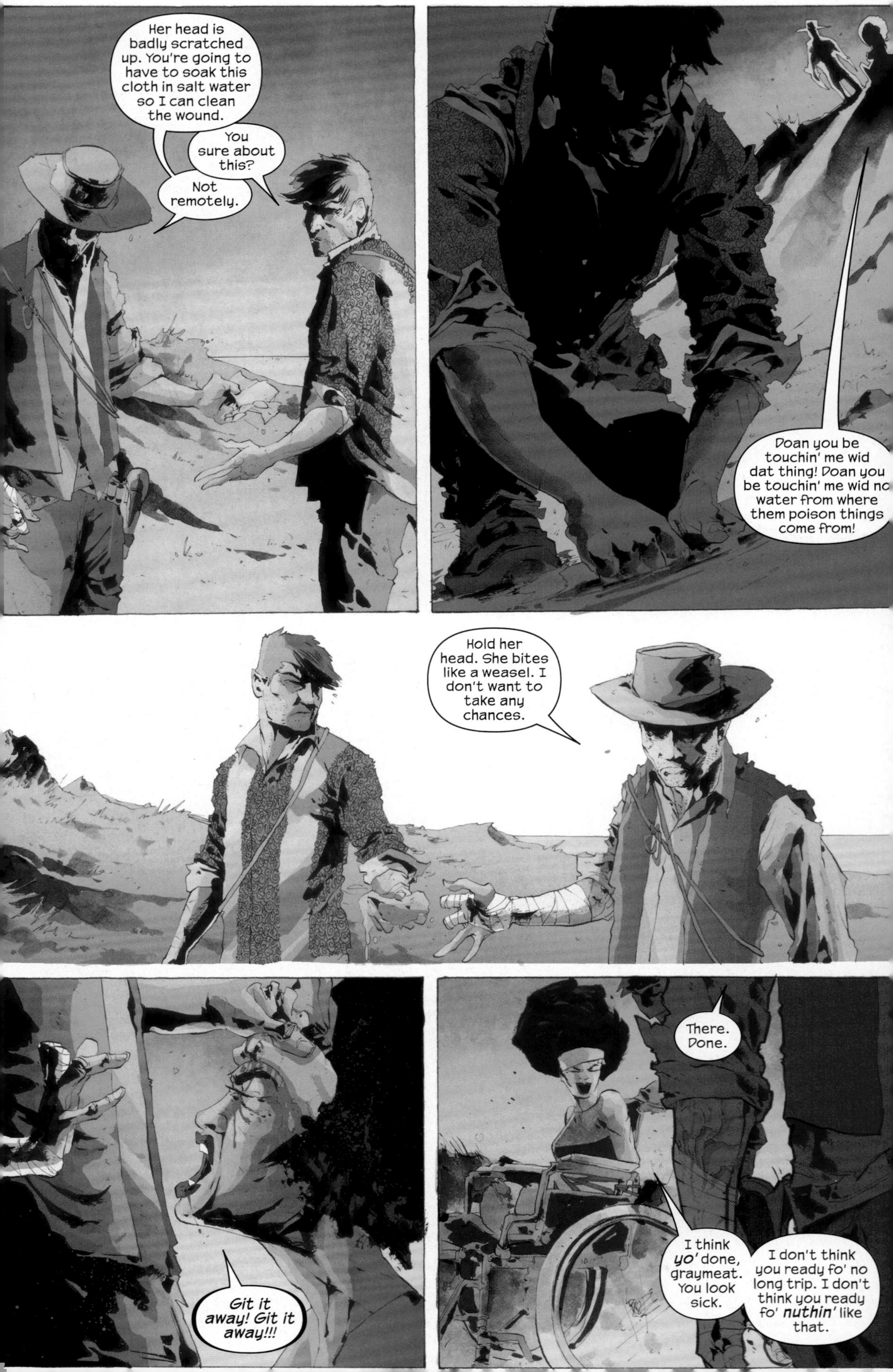

Her head is badly scratched up. You're going to have to soak this cloth in salt water so I can clean the wound.
You sure about this?
Not remotely.
Doan you be touchin' me wid dat thing! Doan you be touchin' me wid no water from where them poison things come from!
Hold her head. She bites like a weasel. I don't want to take any chances.
Git it away! Git it away!!!
There. Done.
I think *yo'* done, graymeat. You look sick.
I don't think you ready fo' no long trip. I don't think you ready fo' ***nuthin'*** like that.

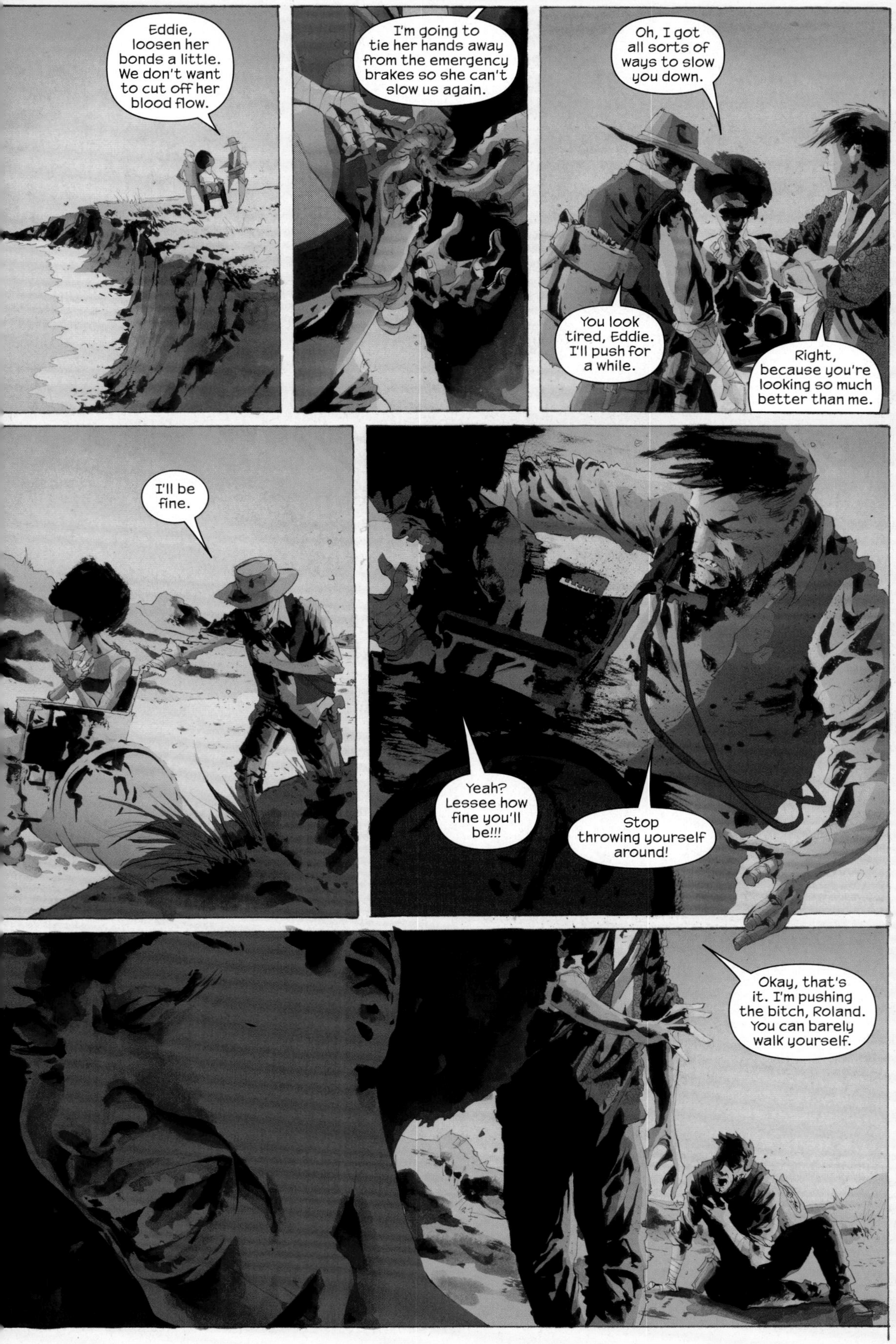
Eddie, loosen her bonds a little. We don't want to cut off her blood flow.
I'm going to tie her hands away from the emergency brakes so she can't slow us again.
Oh, I got all sorts of ways to slow you down.
You look tired, Eddie. I'll push for a while.
Right, because you're looking so much better than me.
I'll be fine.
Yeah? Lessee how fine you'll be!!!
Stop throwing yourself around!
Okay, that's it. I'm pushing the bitch, Roland. You can barely walk yourself.

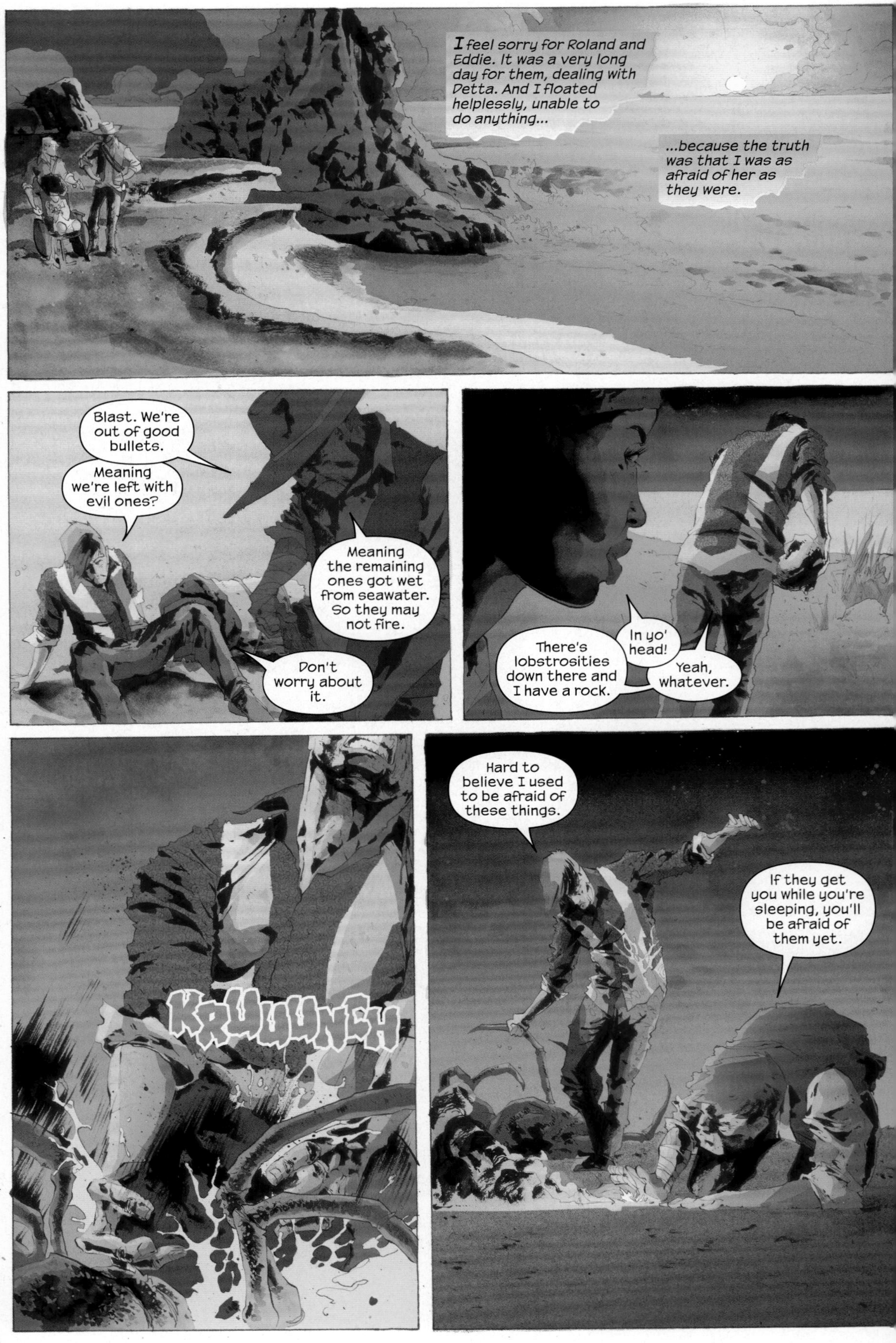
I feel sorry for Roland and Eddie. It was a very long day for them, dealing with Detta. And I floated helplessly, unable to do anything...
...because the truth was that I was as afraid of her as they were.
Blast. We're out of good bullets.
Meaning we're left with evil ones?
Meaning the remaining ones got wet from seawater. So they may not fire.
Don't worry about it.
There's lobstrosities down there and I have a rock.
In yo' head!
Yeah, whatever.
KRUUUNCH
Hard to believe I used to be afraid of these things.
If they get you while you're sleeping, you'll be afraid of them yet.

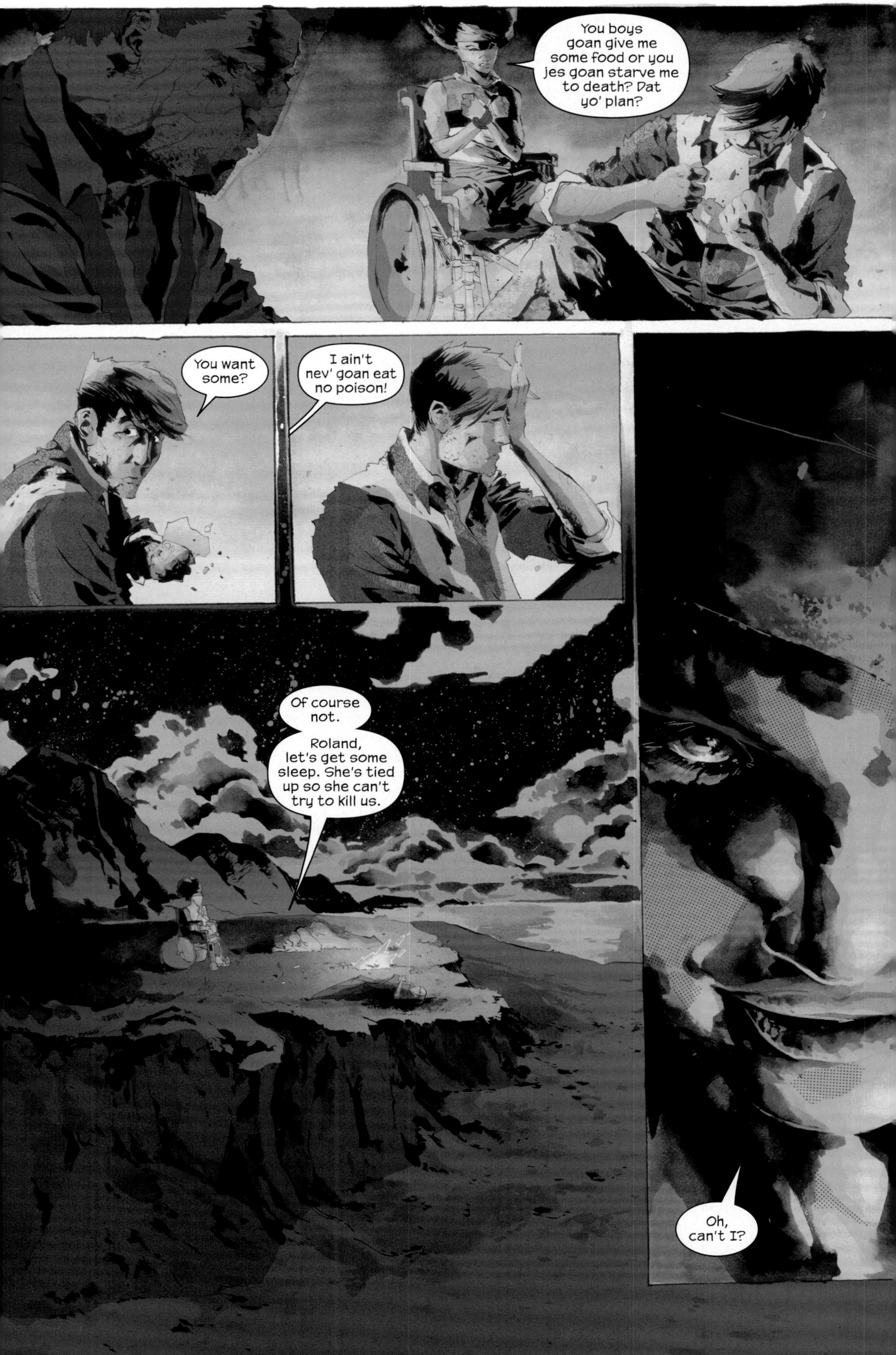

You boys goan give me some food or you jes goan starve me to death? Dat yo' plan?
You want some?
I ain't nev' goan eat no poison!
Of course not.
Roland, let's get some sleep. She's tied up so she can't try to kill us.
Oh, can't I?

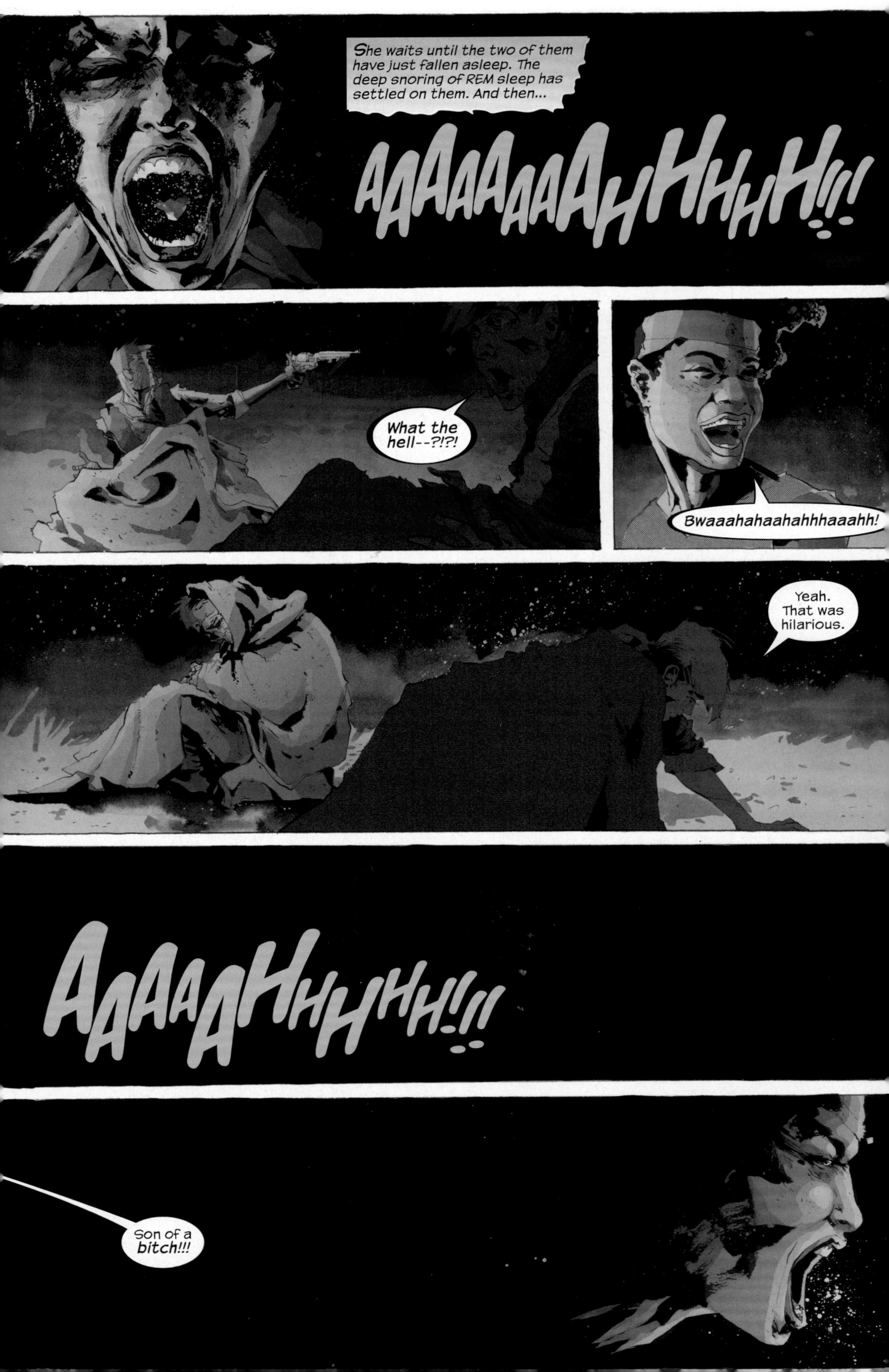
She waits until the two of them have just fallen asleep. The deep snoring of REM sleep has settled on them. And then...
AAAAAAAAAHHHHH!!!
What the hell--?!?!
Bwaaahahaahahhhaaahh!
Yeah. That was hilarious.
AAAAAHHHHH!!!
Son of a bitch!!!

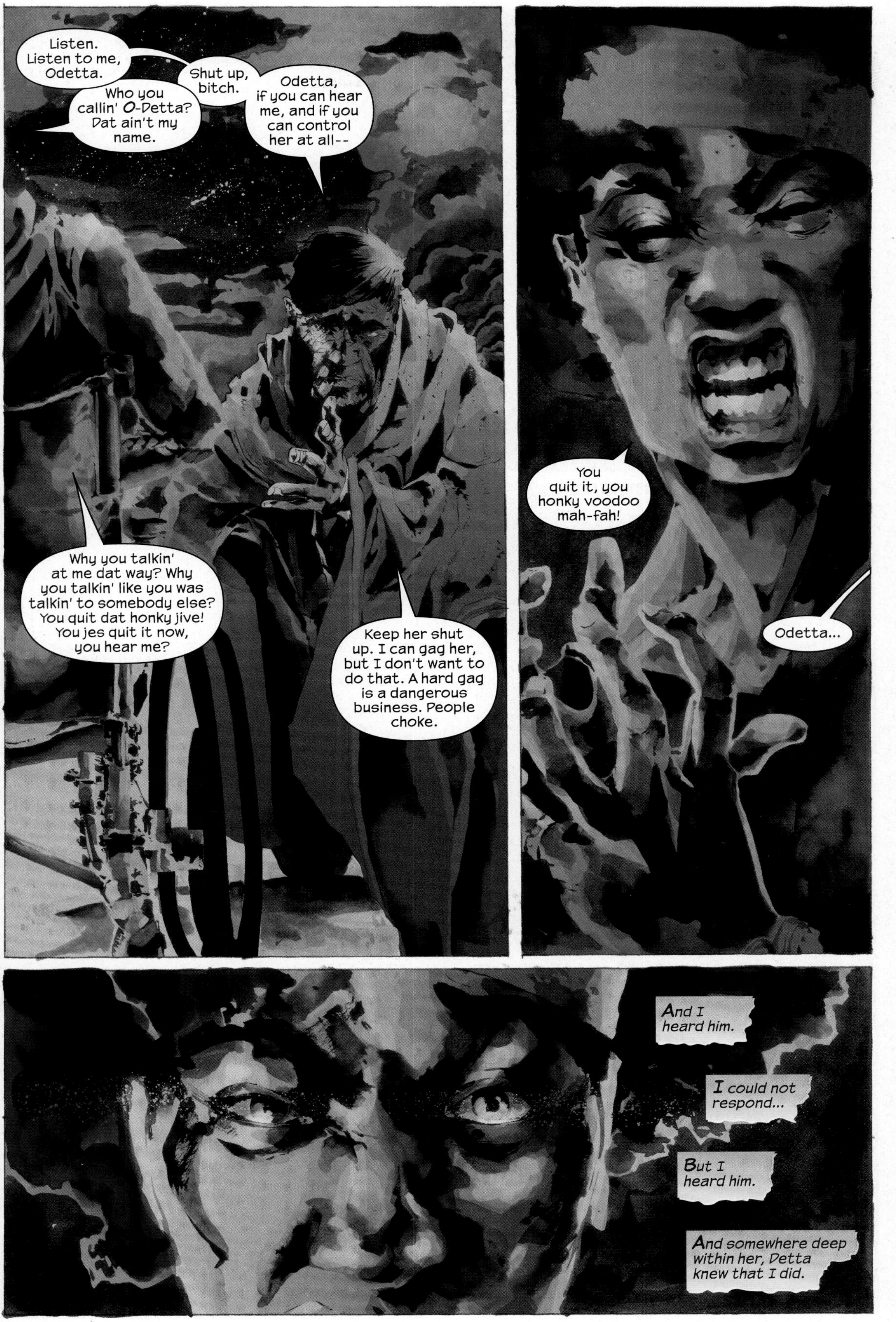
Listen. Listen to me, Odetta.
Shut up, bitch.
Who you callin' O-Detta? Dat ain't my name.
Odetta, if you can hear me, and if you can control her at all--
Why you talkin' at me dat way? Why you talkin' like you was talkin' to somebody else? You quit dat honky jive! You jes quit it now, you hear me?
Keep her shut up. I can gag her, but I don't want to do that. A hard gag is a dangerous business. People choke.
You quit it, you honky voodoo mah-fah!
Odetta...
And I heard him.
I could not respond...
But I heard him.
And somewhere deep within her, Detta knew that I did.

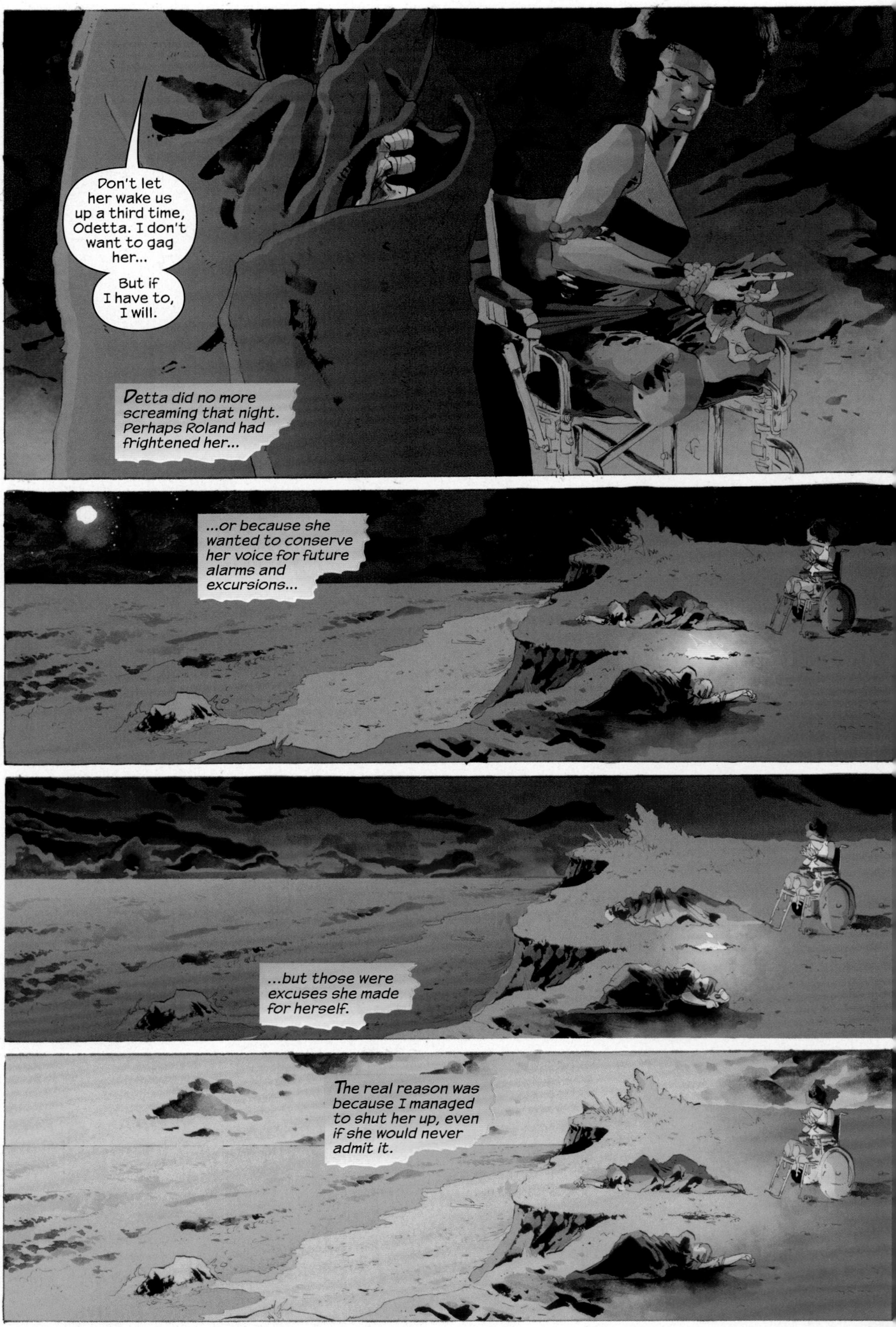
Don't let her wake us up a third time, Odetta. I don't want to gag her...
But if I have to, I will.
Detta did no more screaming that night. Perhaps Roland had frightened her...
...or because she wanted to conserve her voice for future alarms and excursions...
...but those were excuses she made for herself.
The real reason was because I managed to shut her up, even if she would never admit it.

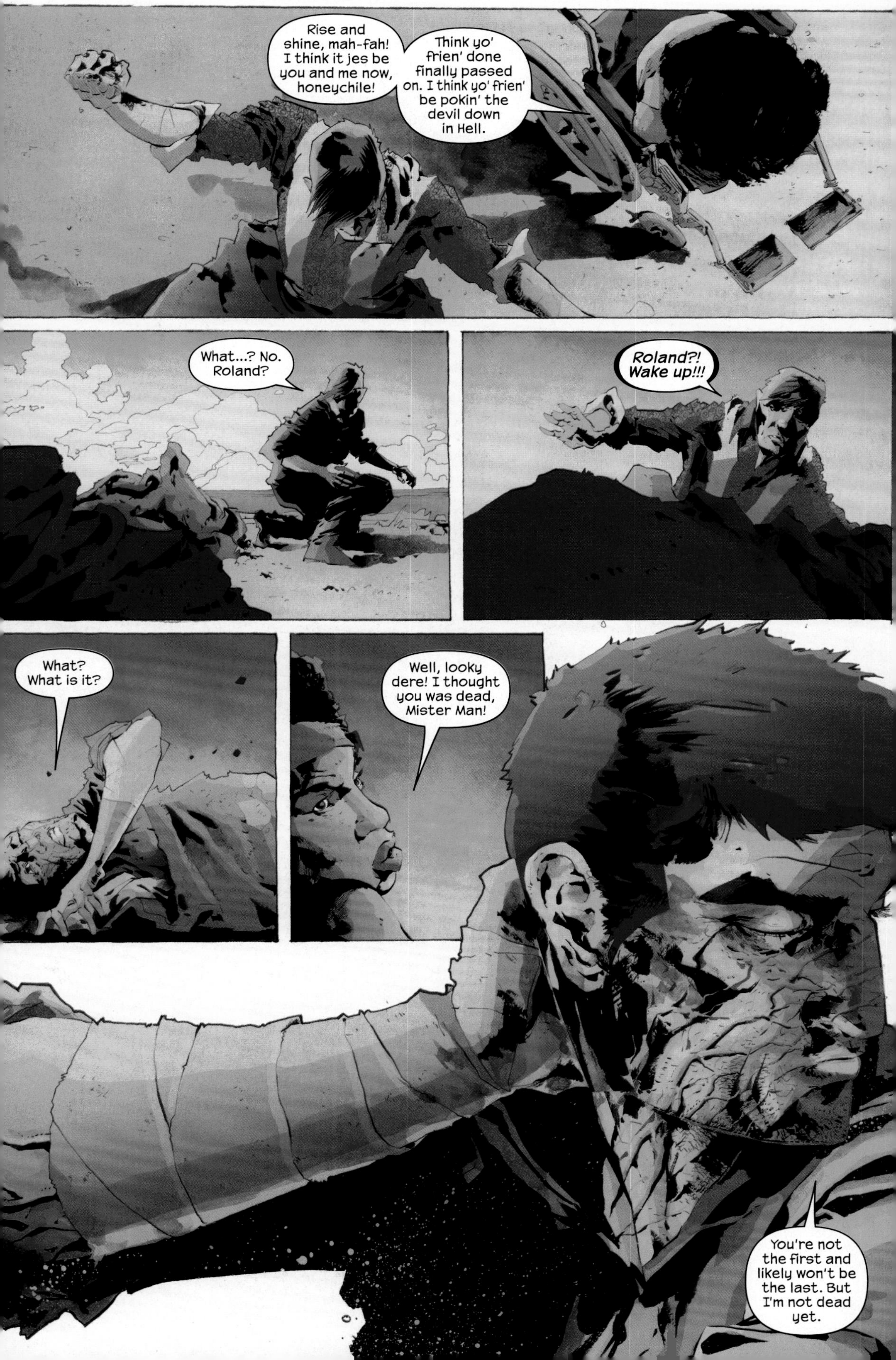
Rise and shine, mah-fah! I think it jes be you and me now, honeychile!
Think yo' frien' done finally passed on. I think yo' frien' be pokin' the devil down in Hell.
What...? No. Roland?
Roland?! Wake up!!!
What? What is it?
Well, looky dere! I thought you was dead, Mister Man!
You're not the first and likely won't be the last. But I'm not dead yet.

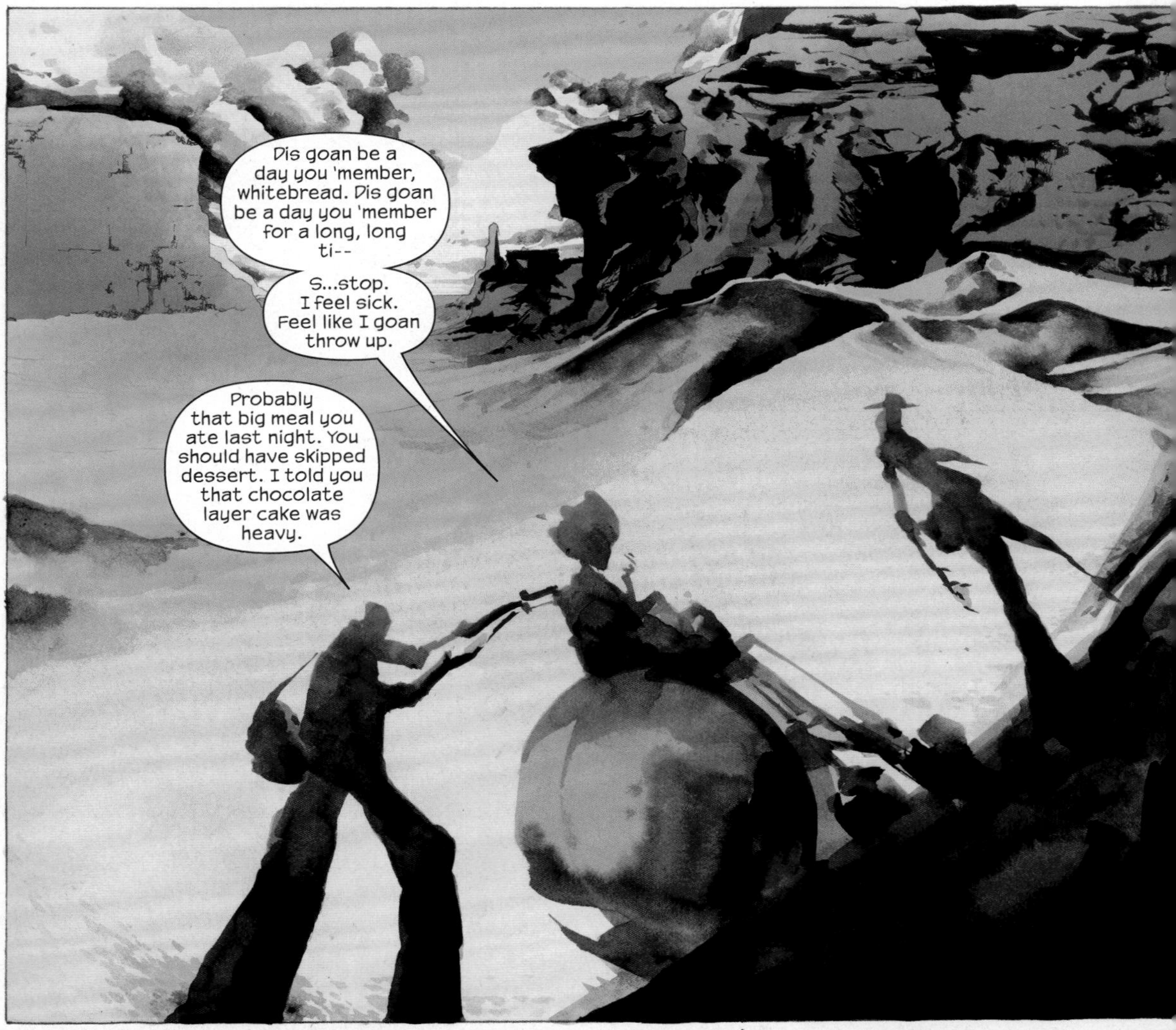
Dis goan be a day you 'member, whitebread. Dis goan be a day you 'member for a long, long ti--
S...stop. I feel sick. Feel like I goan throw up.
Probably that big meal you ate last night. You should have skipped dessert. I told you that chocolate layer cake was heavy.

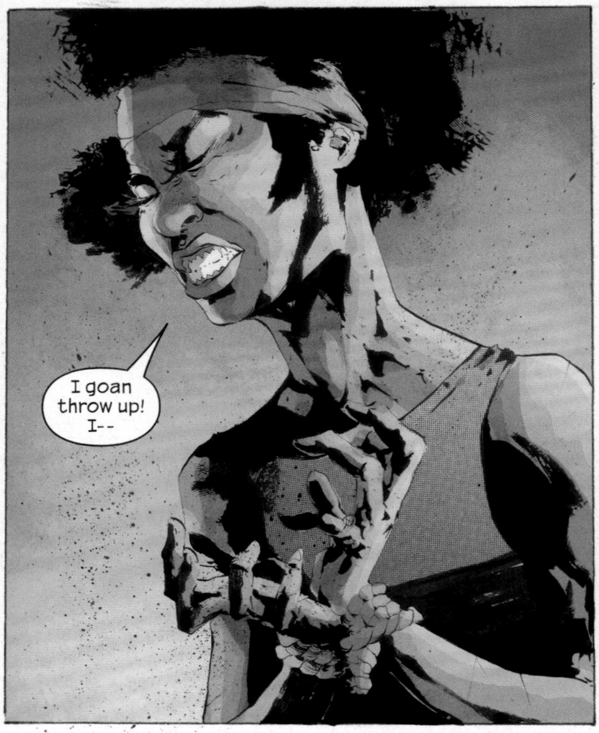
I goan throw up! I--

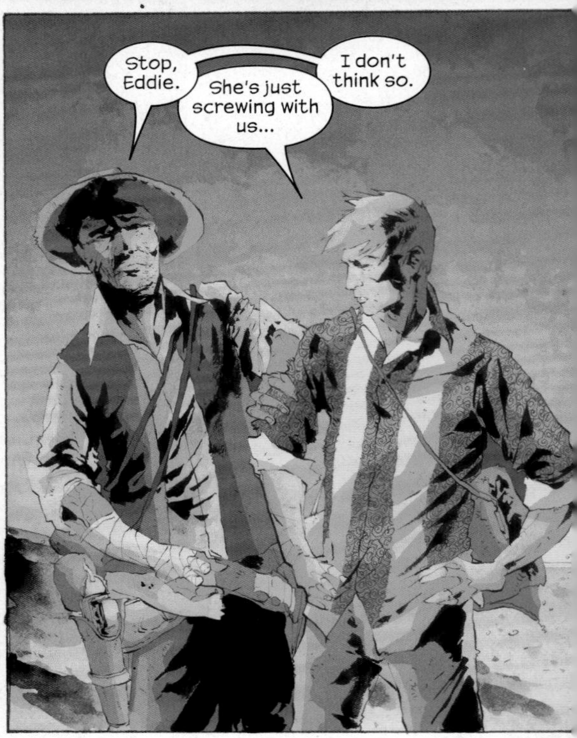
Stop, Eddie.
She's just screwing with us...
I don't think so.

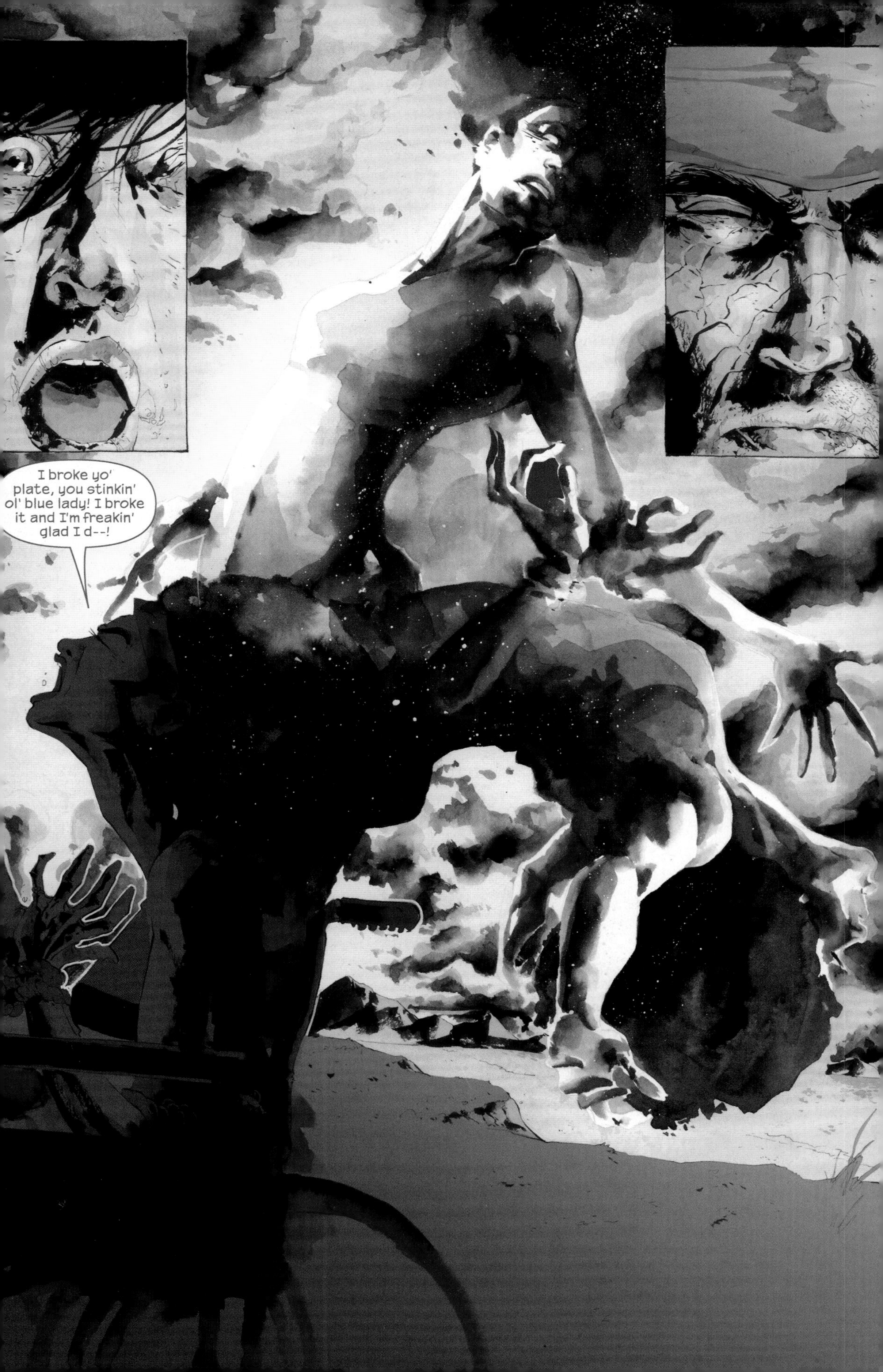
I broke yo' plate, you stinkin' ol' blue lady! I broke it and I'm freakin' glad I d--!

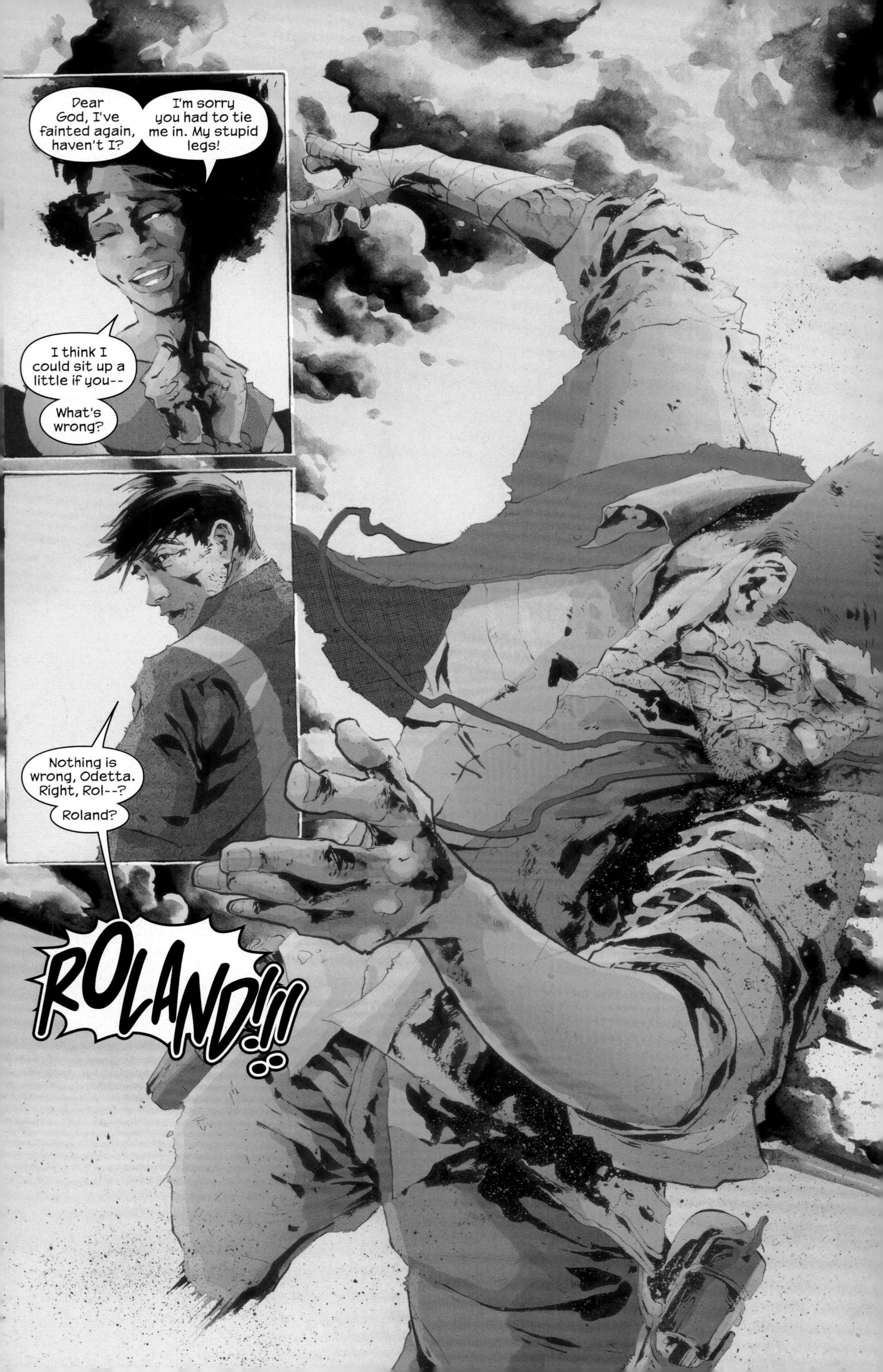
Dear God, I've fainted again, haven't I?
I'm sorry you had to tie me in. My stupid legs!
I think I could sit up a little if you--
What's wrong?
Nothing is wrong, Odetta. Right, Rol--?
Roland?
ROLAND!!!

THE DARK TOWER
THE DRAWING OF THE THREE
STEPHEN KING

BITTER MEDICINE
CHAPTER THREE

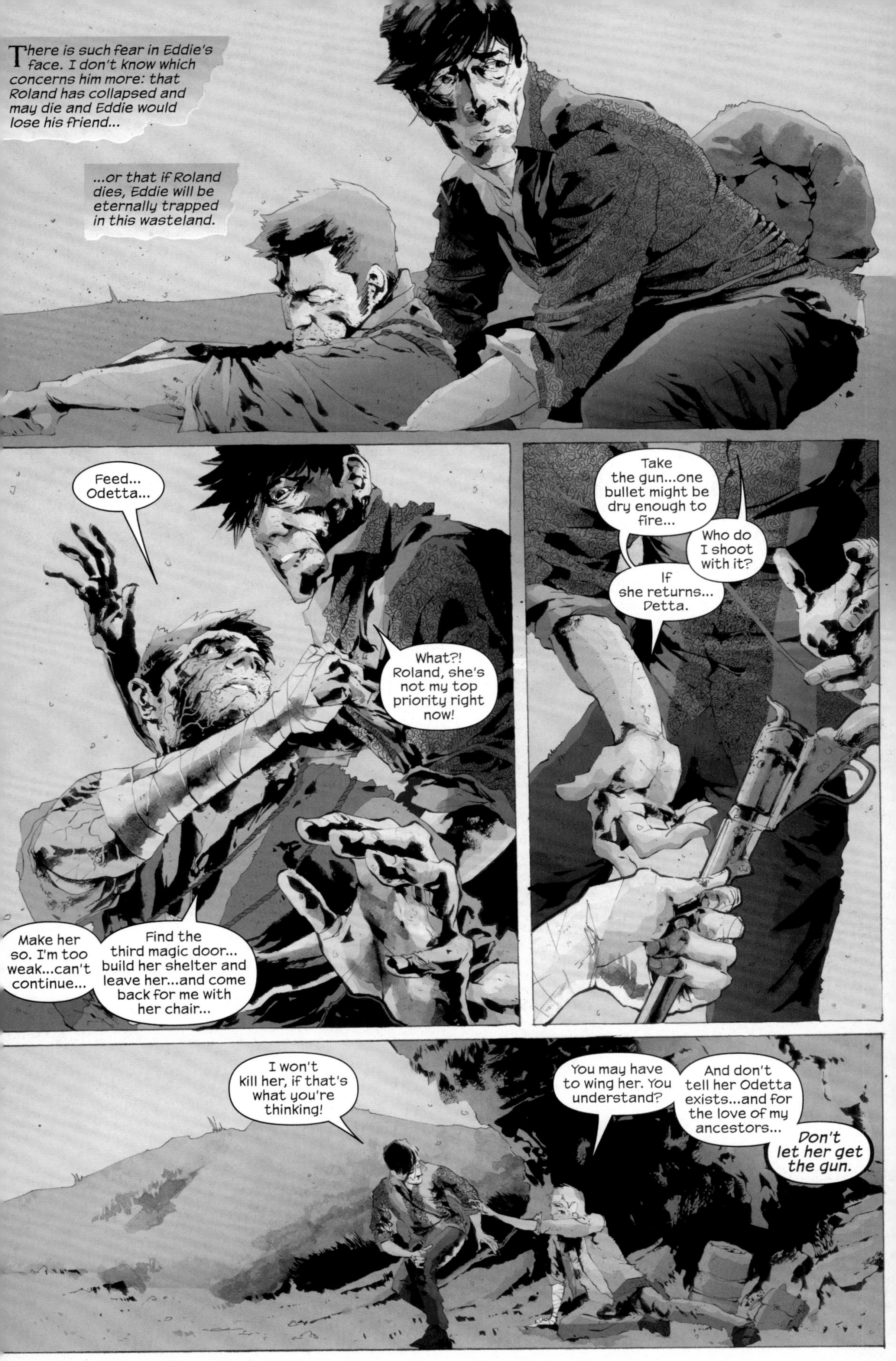
There is such fear in Eddie's face. I don't know which concerns him more: that Roland has collapsed and may die and Eddie would lose his friend...
...or that if Roland dies, Eddie will be eternally trapped in this wasteland.
Feed... Odetta...
What?! Roland, she's not my top priority right now!
Make her so. I'm too weak...can't continue...
Find the third magic door... build her shelter and leave her...and come back for me with her chair...
Take the gun...one bullet might be dry enough to fire...
Who do I shoot with it?
If she returns... Detta.
I won't kill her, if that's what you're thinking!
You may have to wing her. You understand?
And don't tell her Odetta exists...and for the love of my ancestors...
Don't let her get the gun.

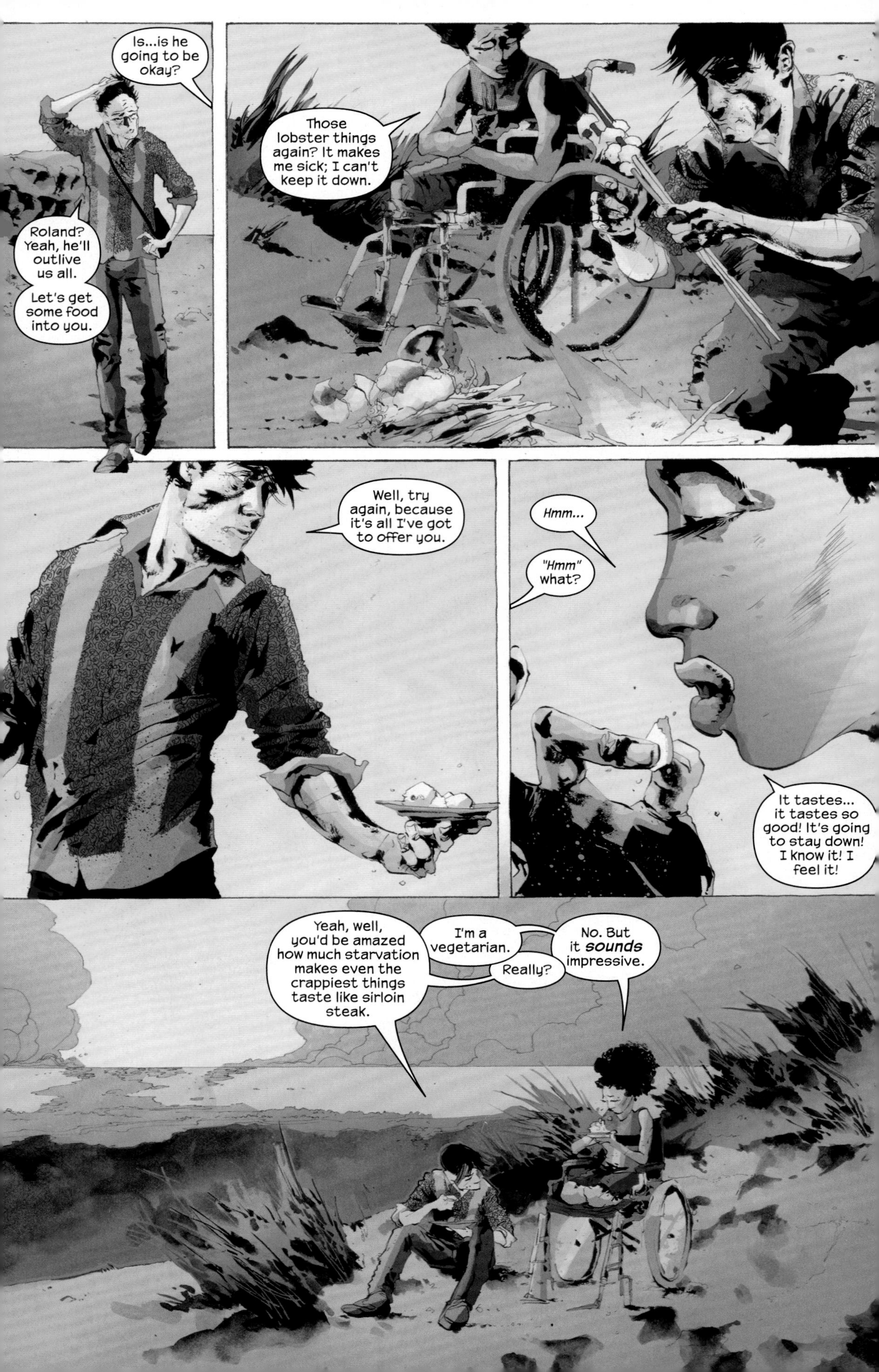

Is...is he going to be okay?
Roland? Yeah, he'll outlive us all.
Let's get some food into you.
Those lobster things again? It makes me sick; I can't keep it down.
Well, try again, because it's all I've got to offer you.
Hmm...
"*Hmm*" what?
It tastes... it tastes so good! It's going to stay down! I know it! I feel it!
Yeah, well, you'd be amazed how much starvation makes even the crappiest things taste like sirloin steak.
I'm a vegetarian.
Really?
No. But it ***sounds*** impressive.

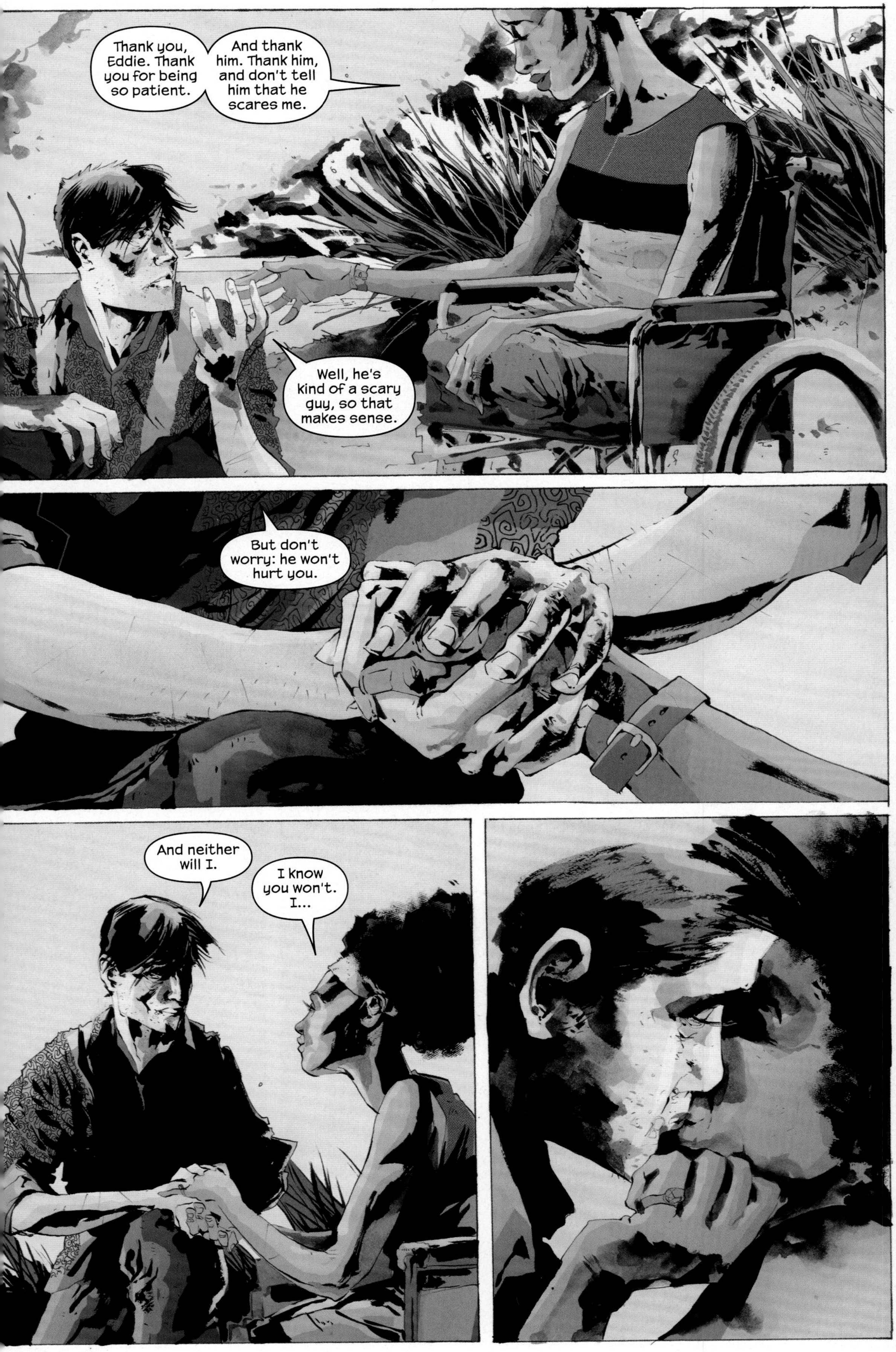
Thank you, Eddie. Thank you for being so patient.
And thank him. Thank him, and don't tell him that he scares me.
Well, he's kind of a scary guy, so that makes sense.
But don't worry: he won't hurt you.
And neither will I.
I know you won't. I...

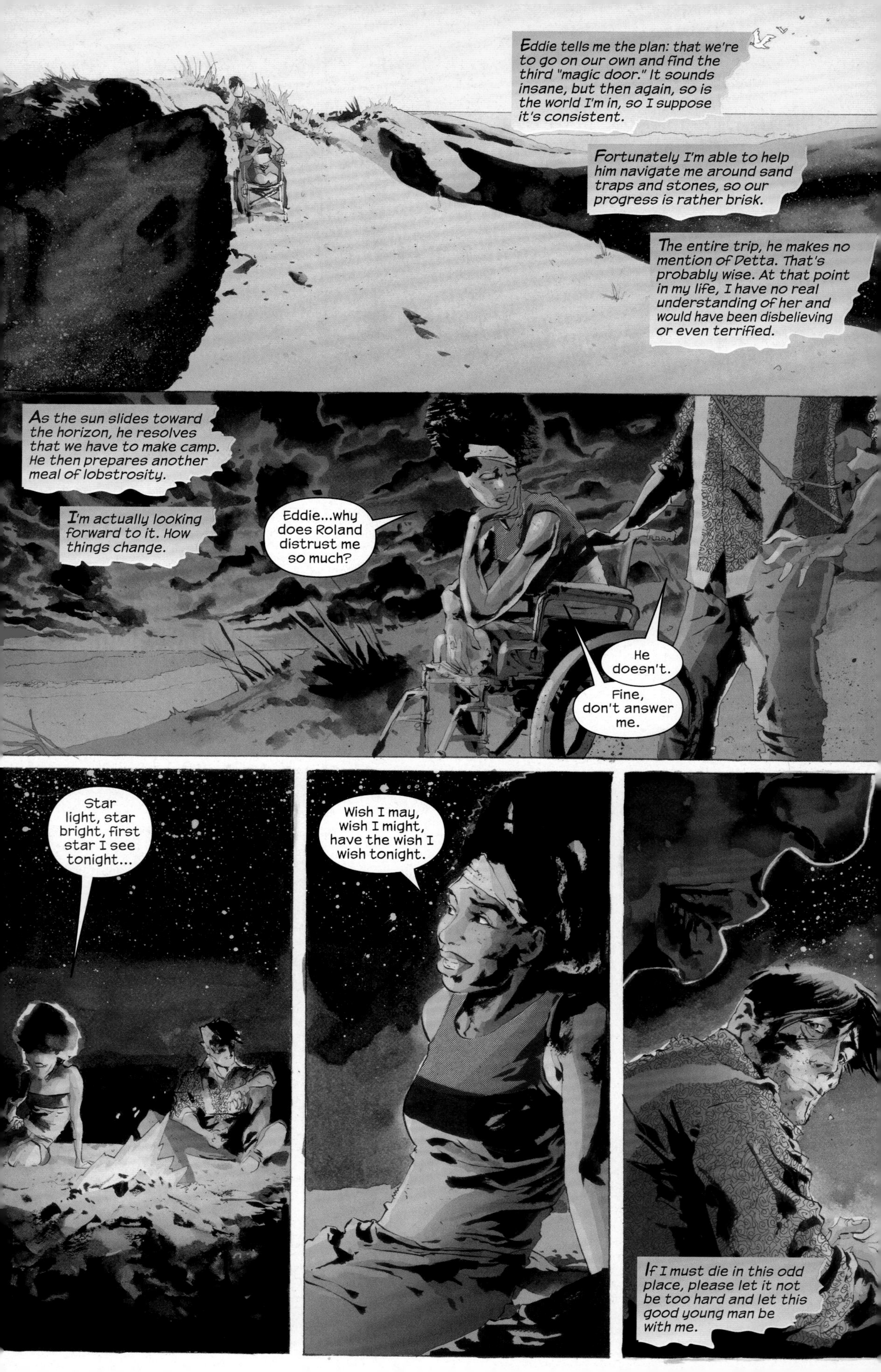
Eddie tells me the plan: that we're to go on our own and find the third "magic door." It sounds insane, but then again, so is the world I'm in, so I suppose it's consistent.
Fortunately I'm able to help him navigate me around sand traps and stones, so our progress is rather brisk.
The entire trip, he makes no mention of Detta. That's probably wise. At that point in my life, I have no real understanding of her and would have been disbelieving or even terrified.
As the sun slides toward the horizon, he resolves that we have to make camp. He then prepares another meal of lobstrosity.
I'm actually looking forward to it. How things change.
Eddie...why does Roland distrust me so much?
He doesn't.
Fine, don't answer me.
Star light, star bright, first star I see tonight...
Wish I may, wish I might, have the wish I wish tonight.
If I must die in this odd place, please let it not be too hard and let this good young man be with me.

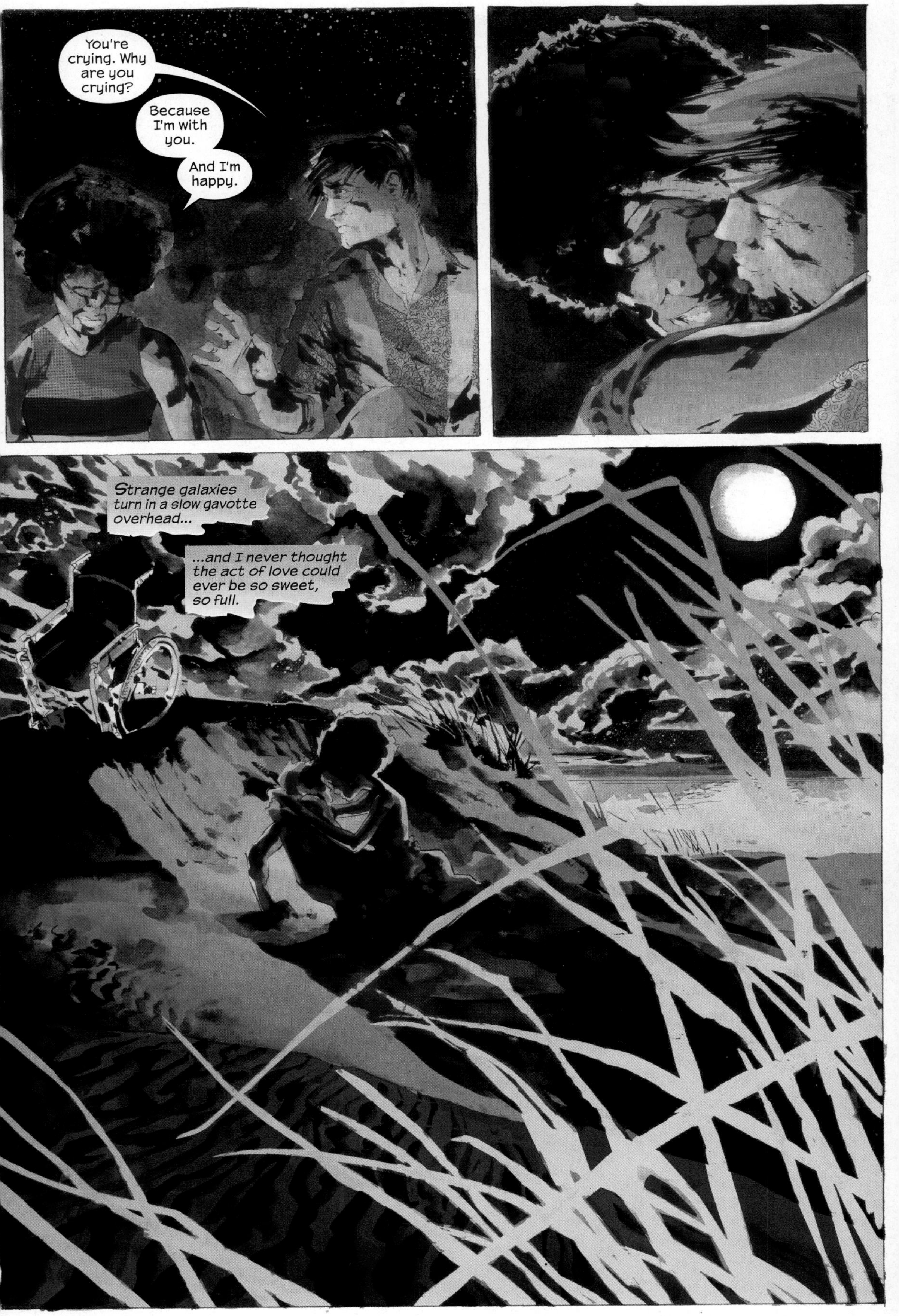
You're crying. Why are you crying?
Because I'm with you.
And I'm happy.
Strange galaxies turn in a slow gavotte overhead...
...and I never thought the act of love could ever be so sweet, so full.

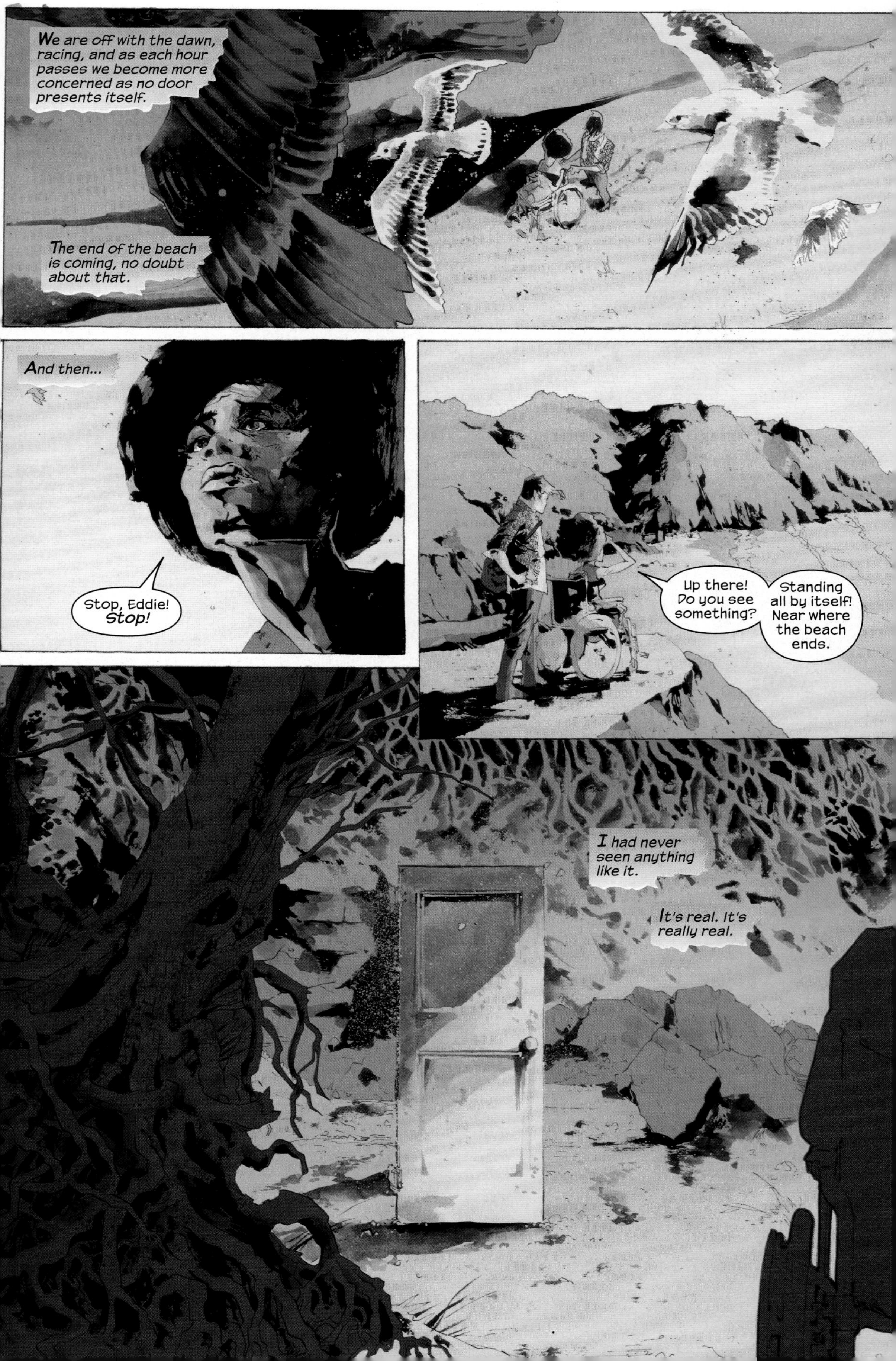
We are off with the dawn, racing, and as each hour passes we become more concerned as no door presents itself.
The end of the beach is coming, no doubt about that.
And then...
Stop, Eddie! Stop!
Up there! Do you see something?
Standing all by itself! Near where the beach ends.
I had never seen anything like it.
It's real. It's really real.

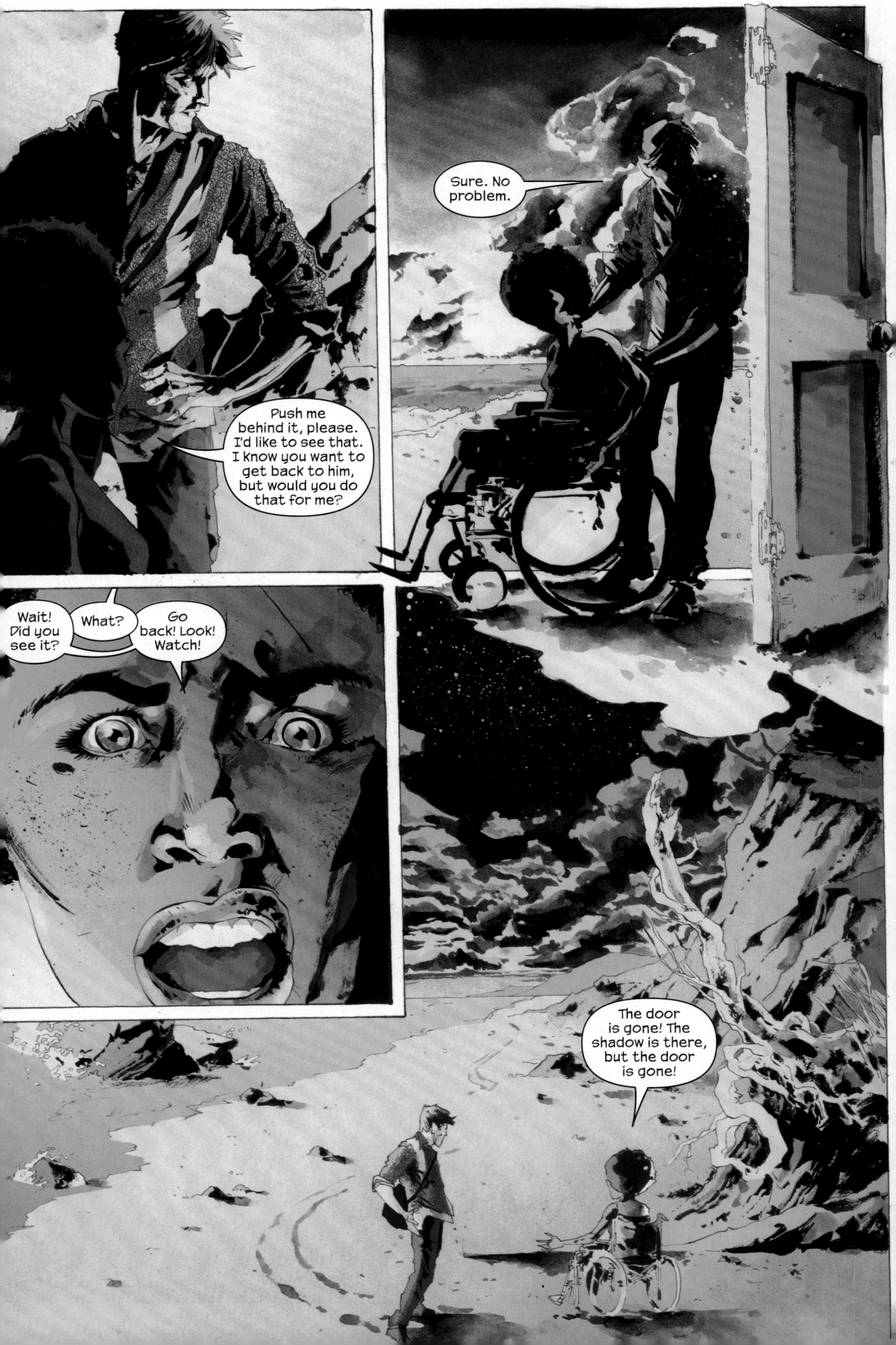
Push me behind it, please. I'd like to see that. I know you want to get back to him, but would you do that for me?
Sure. No problem.
Wait! Did you see it?
What?
Go back! Look! Watch!
The door is gone! The shadow is there, but the door is gone!

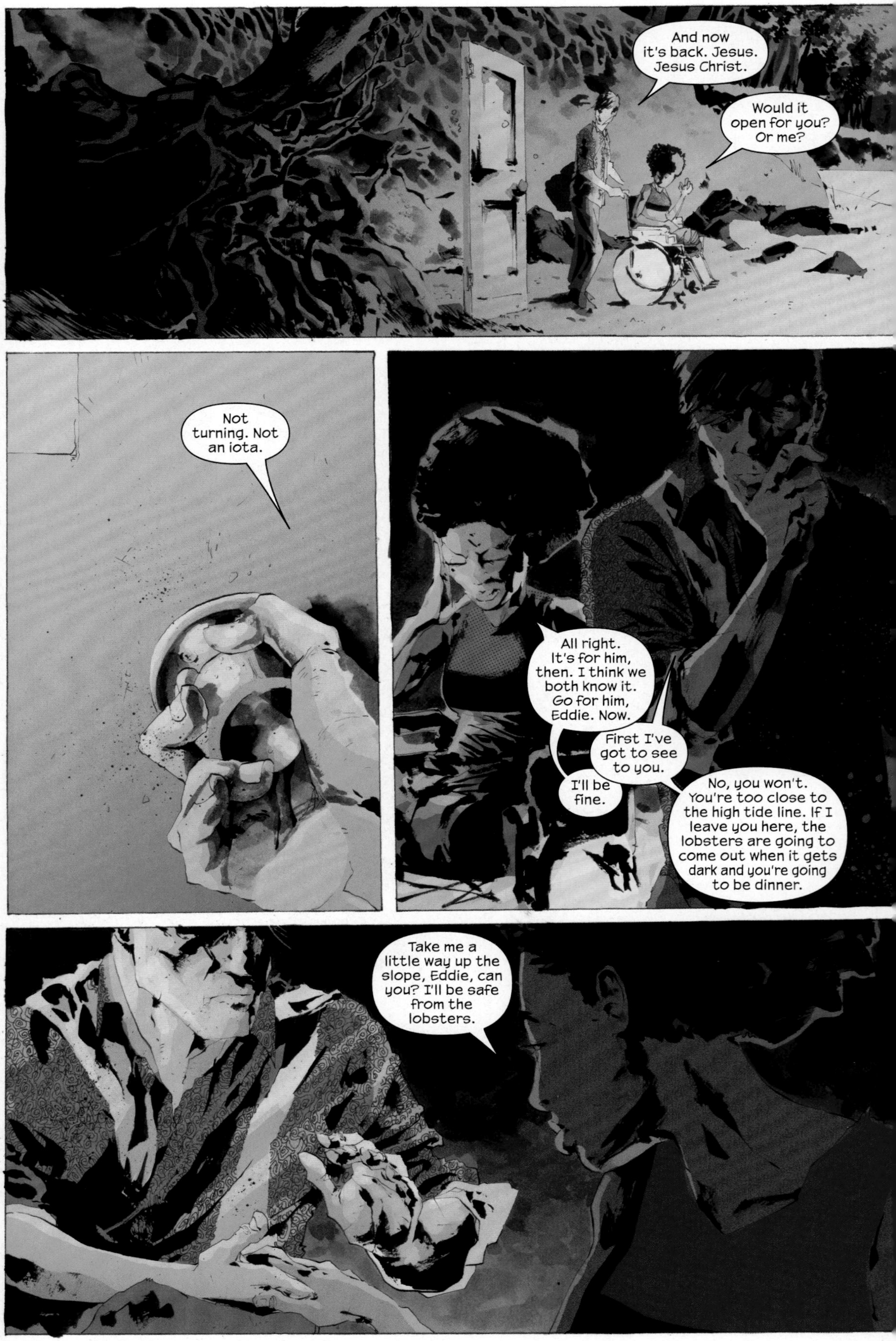
And now it's back. Jesus. Jesus Christ.
Would it open for you? Or me?
Not turning. Not an iota.
All right. It's for him, then. I think we both know it. Go for him, Eddie. Now.
First I've got to see to you.
I'll be fine.
No, you won't. You're too close to the high tide line. If I leave you here, the lobsters are going to come out when it gets dark and you're going to be dinner.
Take me a little way up the slope, Eddie, can you? I'll be safe from the lobsters.

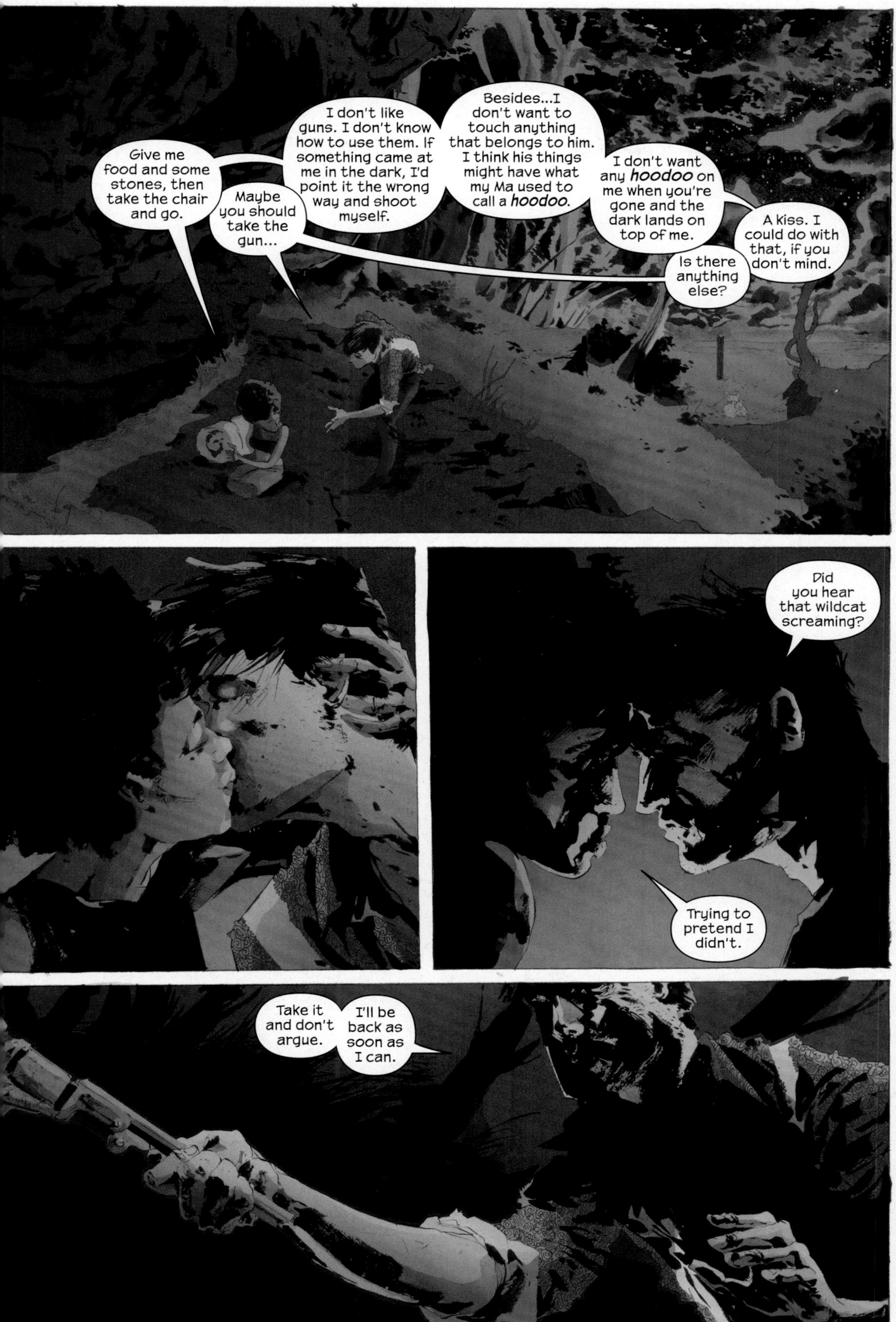
Give me food and some stones, then take the chair and go.
Maybe you should take the gun...
I don't like guns. I don't know how to use them. If something came at me in the dark, I'd point it the wrong way and shoot myself.
Besides...I don't want to touch anything that belongs to him. I think his things might have what my Ma used to call a *hoodoo*.
I don't want any ***hoodoo*** on me when you're gone and the dark lands on top of me.
Is there anything else?
A kiss. I could do with that, if you don't mind.
Did you hear that wildcat screaming?
Trying to pretend I didn't.
Take it and don't argue.
I'll be back as soon as I can.

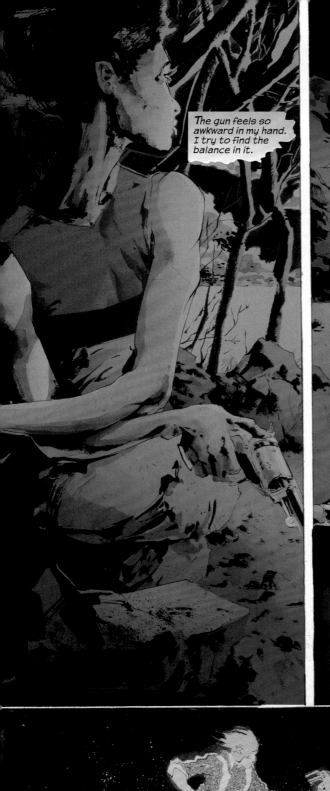

The gun feels so awkward in my hand. I try to find the balance in it.

As for Eddie...

He runs.

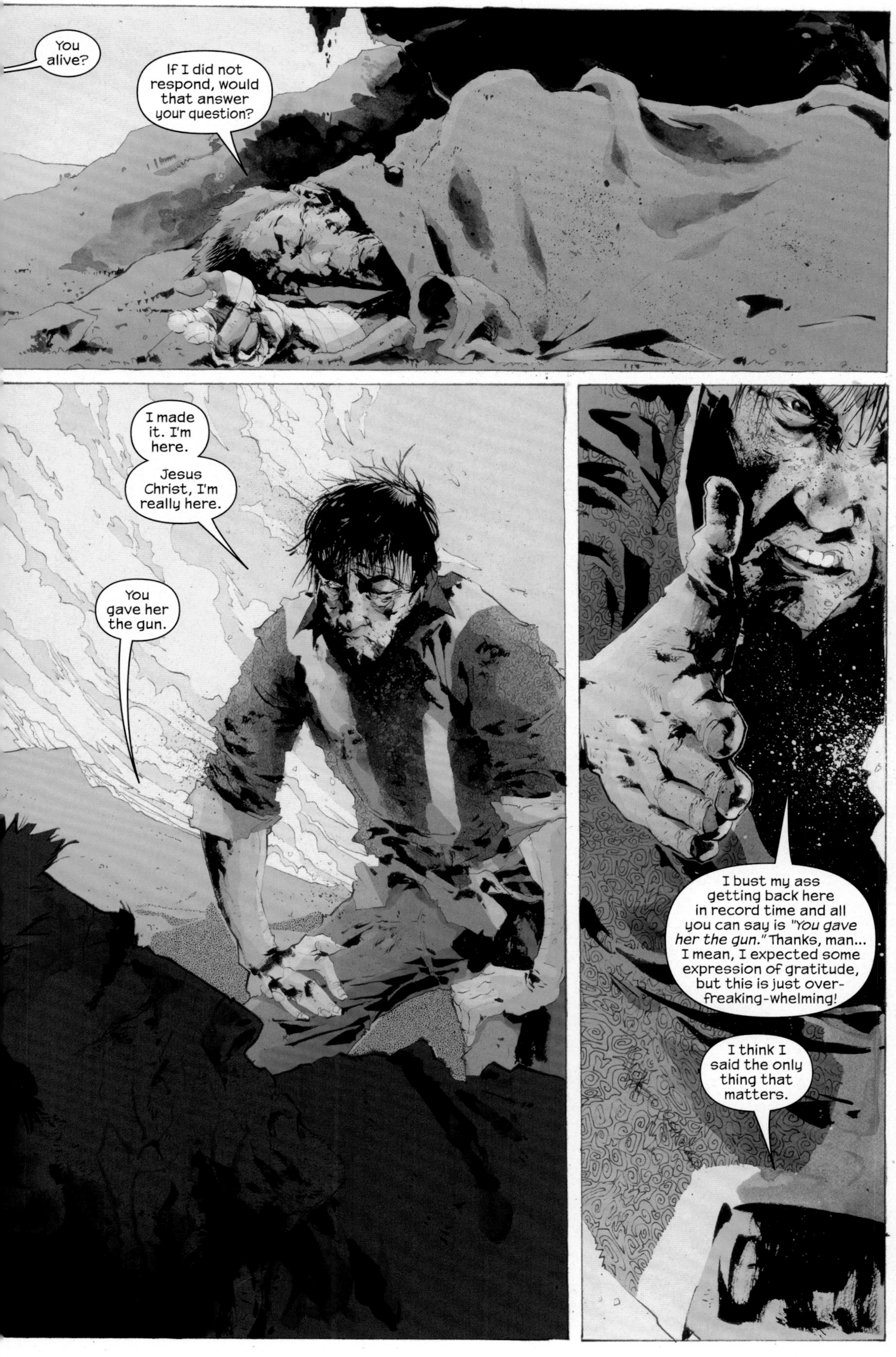
You alive?
If I did not respond, would that answer your question?
I made it. I'm here.
Jesus Christ, I'm really here.
You gave her the gun.
I bust my ass getting back here in record time and all you can say is *"You gave her the gun."* Thanks, man... I mean, I expected some expression of gratitude, but this is just over-freaking-whelming!
I think I said the only thing that matters.

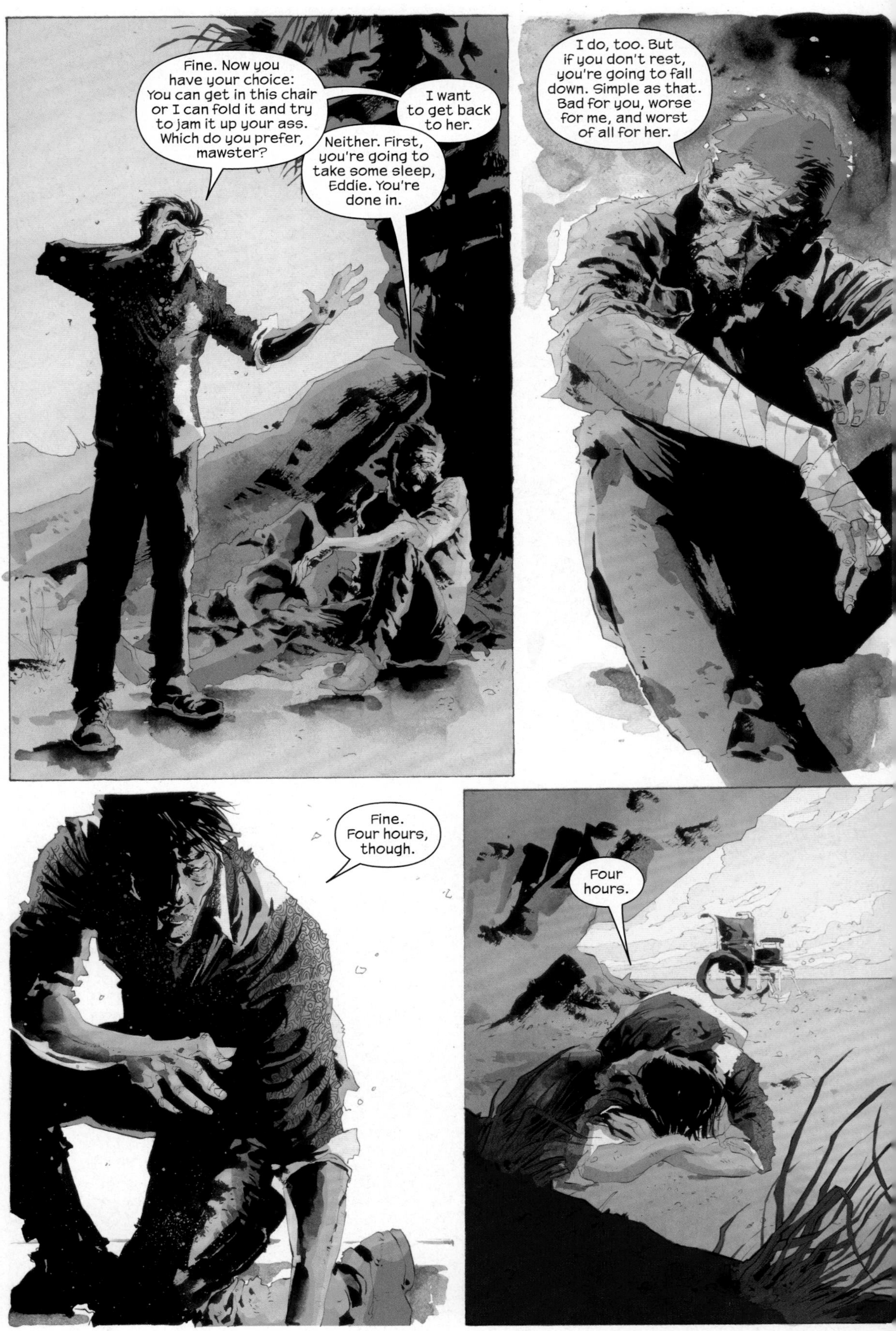
Fine. Now you have your choice: You can get in this chair or I can fold it and try to jam it up your ass. Which do you prefer, mawster?
I want to get back to her.
Neither. First, you're going to take some sleep, Eddie. You're done in.
I do, too. But if you don't rest, you're going to fall down. Simple as that. Bad for you, worse for me, and worst of all for her.
Fine. Four hours, though.
Four hours.

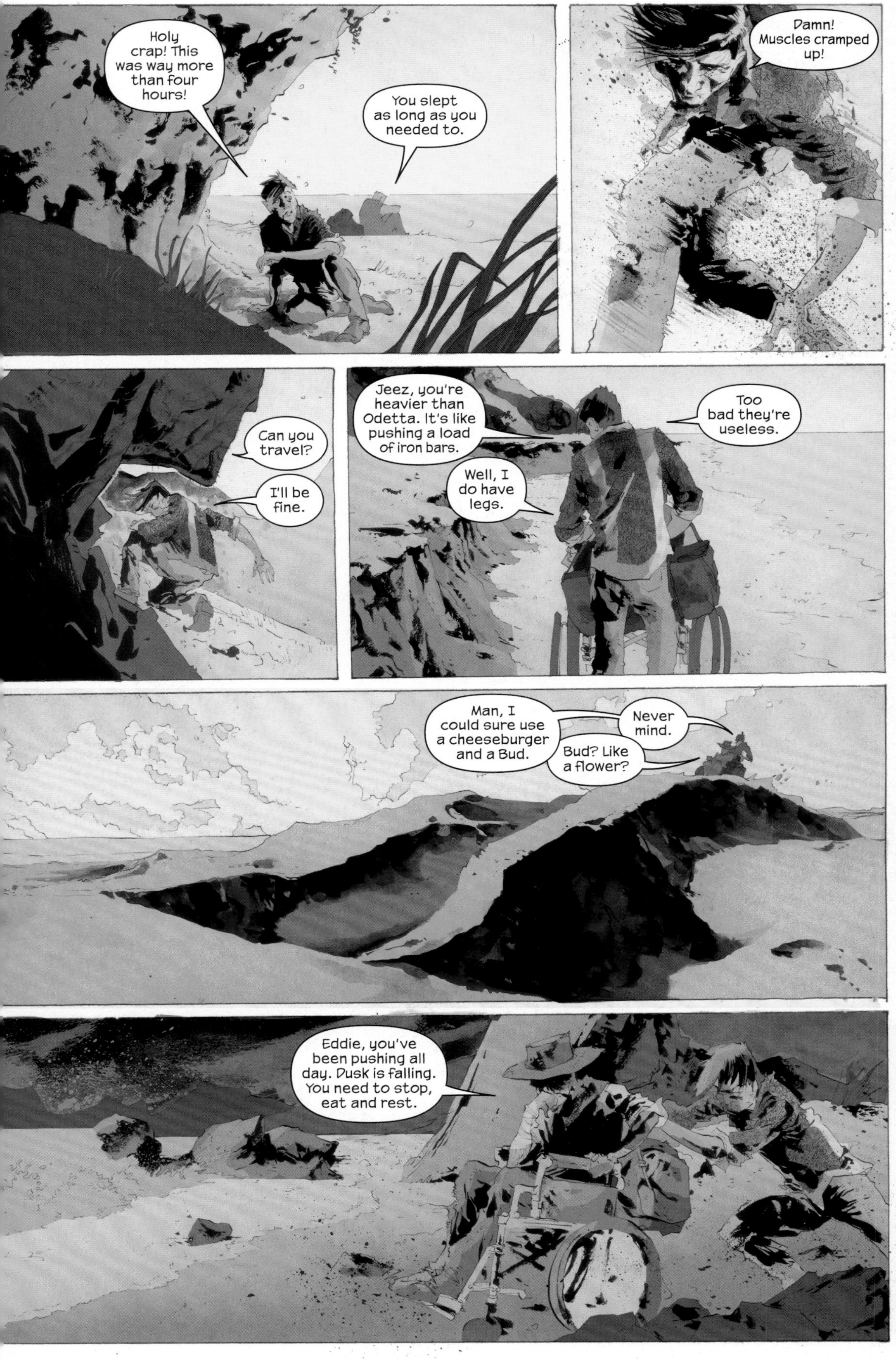
Holy crap! This was way more than four hours!
You slept as long as you needed to.
Damn! Muscles cramped up!
Can you travel?
I'll be fine.
Jeez, you're heavier than Odetta. It's like pushing a load of iron bars.
Well, I do have legs.
Too bad they're useless.
Man, I could sure use a cheeseburger and a Bud.
Bud? Like a flower?
Never mind.
Eddie, you've been pushing all day. Dusk is falling. You need to stop, eat and rest.

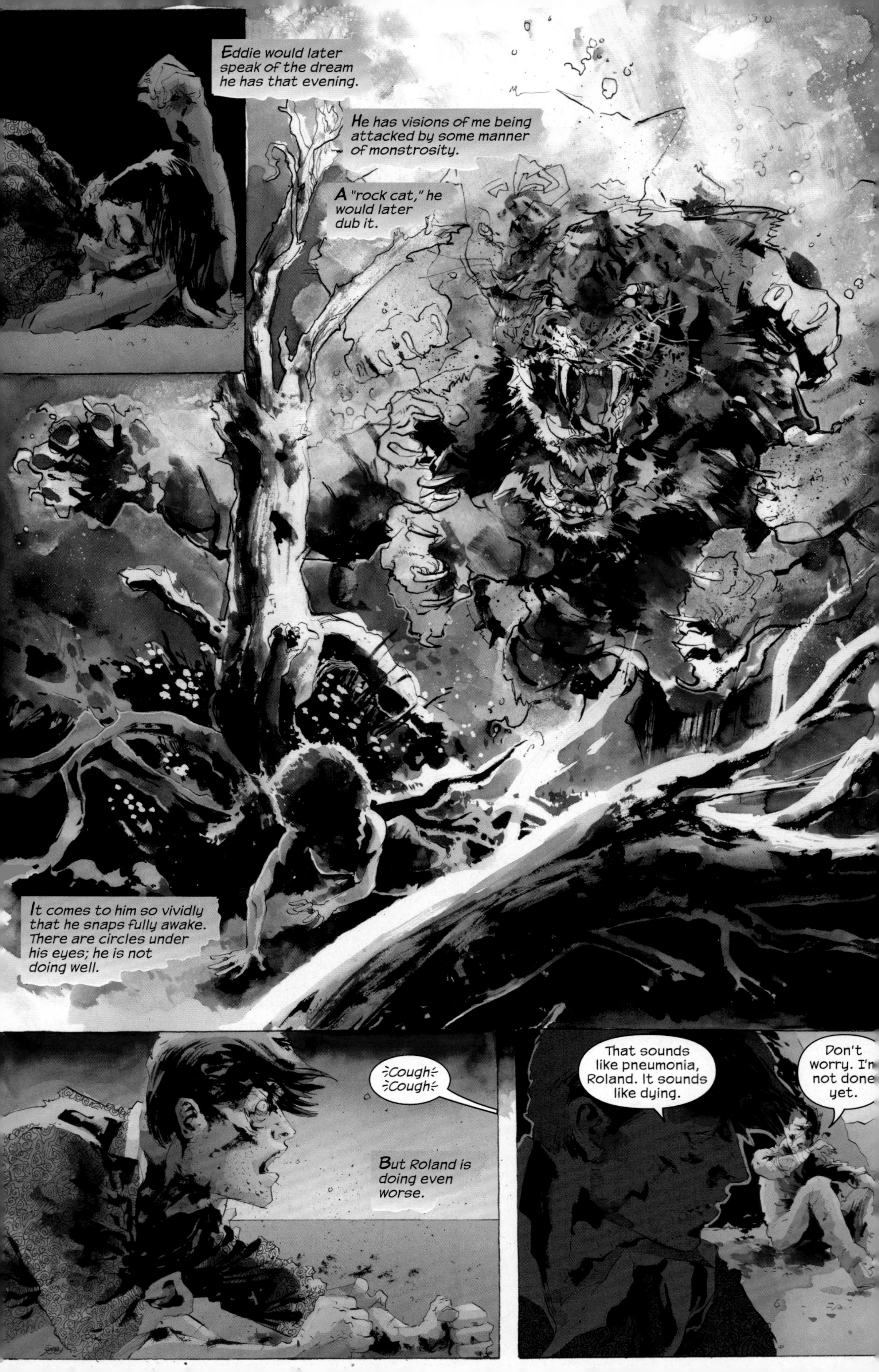

Eddie would later speak of the dream he has that evening.
He has visions of me being attacked by some manner of monstrosity.
A "rock cat," he would later dub it.
It comes to him so vividly that he snaps fully awake. There are circles under his eyes; he is not doing well.
Cough Cough
But Roland is doing even worse.
That sounds like pneumonia, Roland. It sounds like dying.
Don't worry. I'm not done yet.

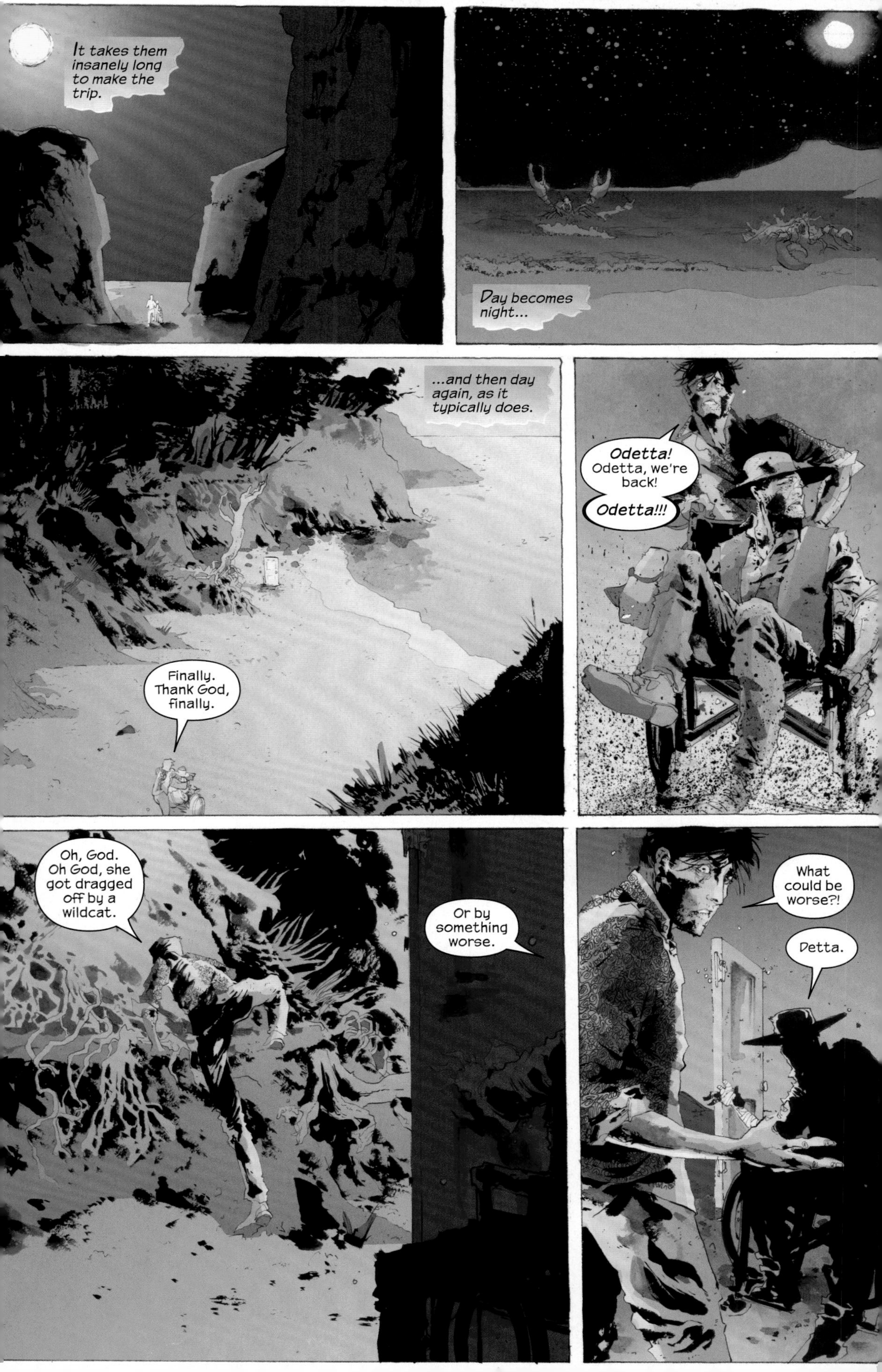
It takes them insanely long to make the trip.
Day becomes night...
...and then day again, as it typically does.
Finally. Thank God, finally.
Odetta! Odetta, we're back!
Odetta!!!
Oh, God. Oh God, she got dragged off by a wildcat.
Or by something worse.
What could be worse?!
Detta.

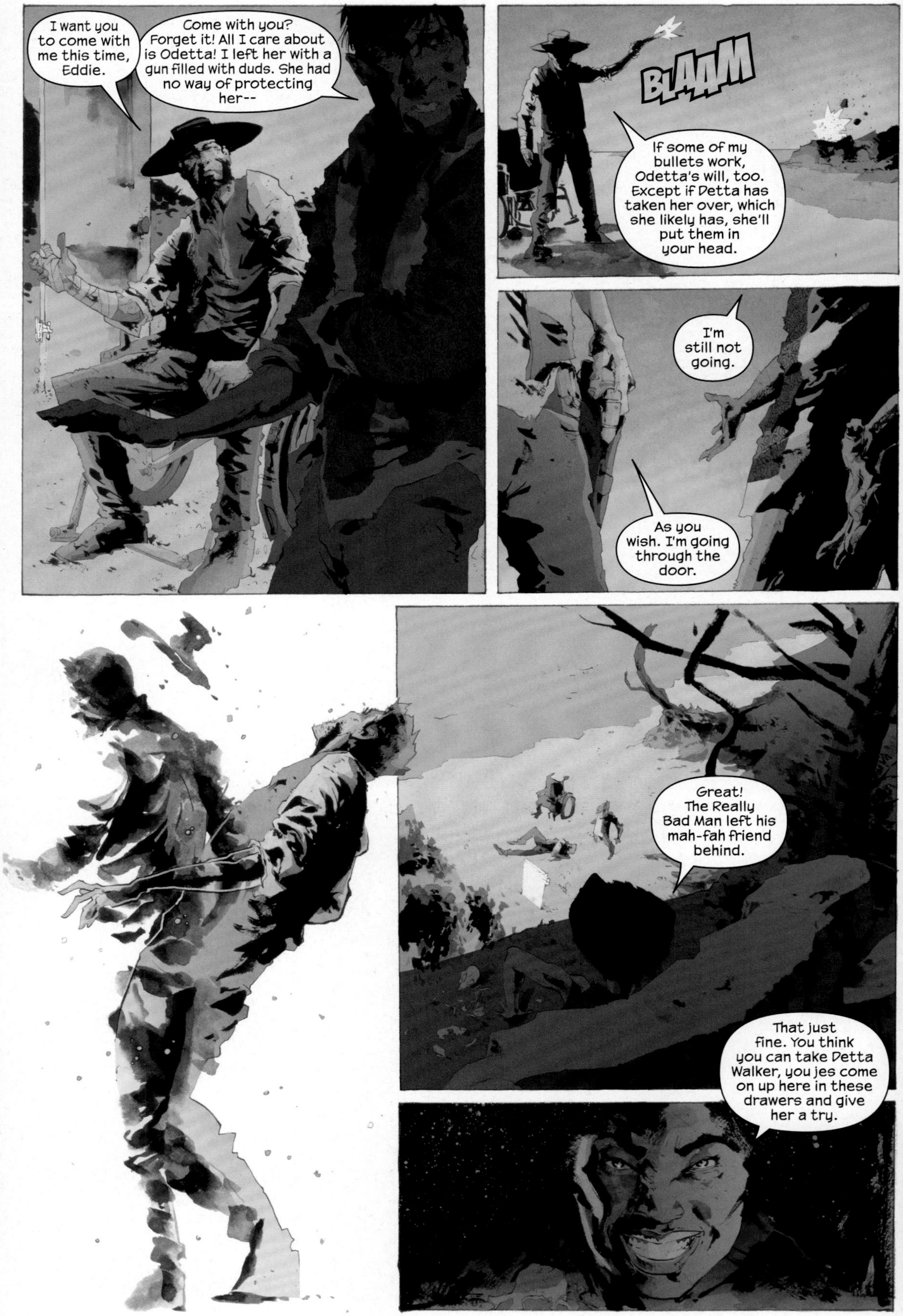
I want you to come with me this time, Eddie.
Come with you? Forget it! All I care about is Odetta! I left her with a gun filled with duds. She had no way of protecting her--
BLAAM
If some of my bullets work, Odetta's will, too. Except if Detta has taken her over, which she likely has, she'll put them in your head.
I'm still not going.
As you wish. I'm going through the door.
Great! The Really Bad Man left his mah-fah friend behind.
That just fine. You think you can take Detta Walker, you jes come on up here in these drawers and give her a try.

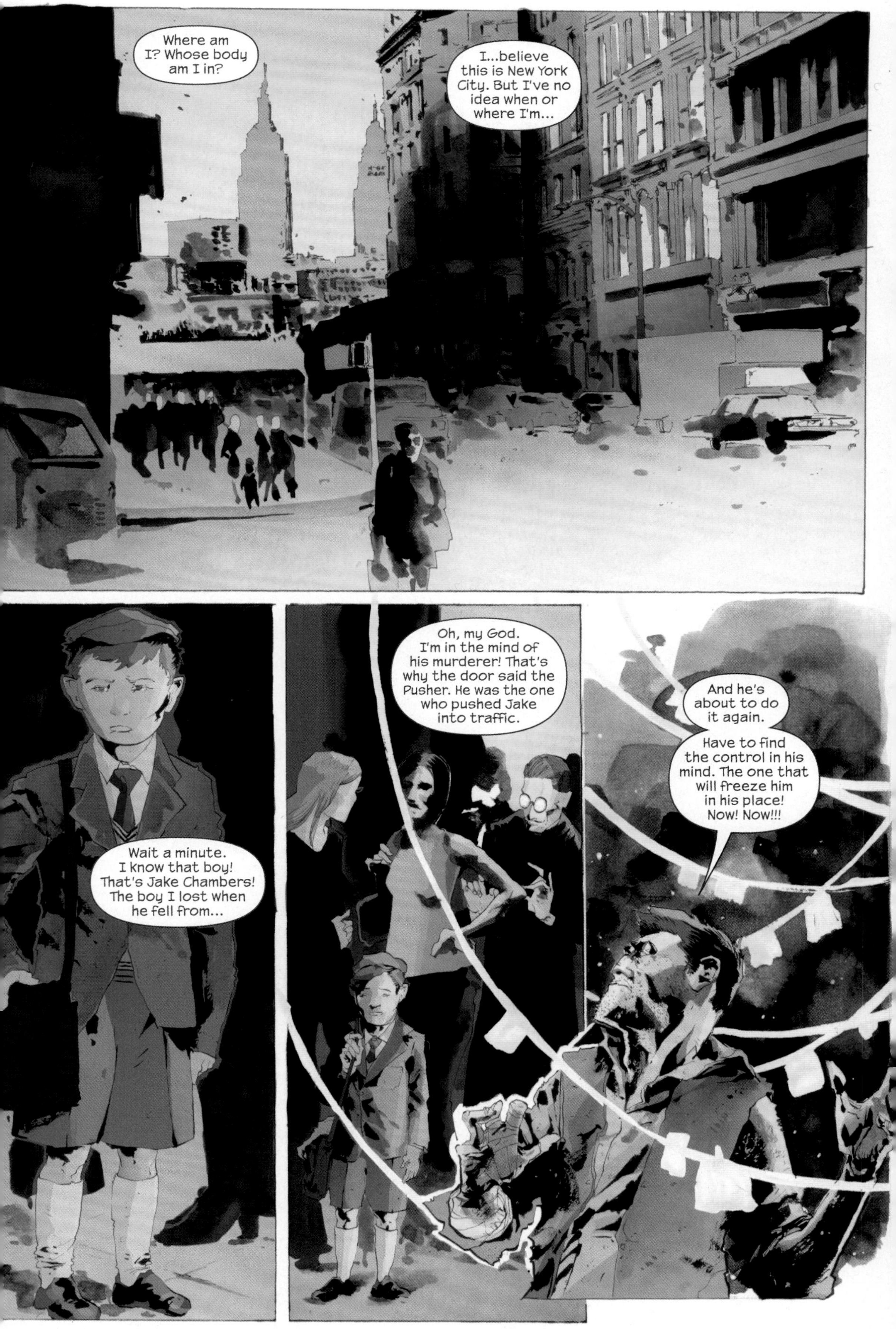
Where am I? Whose body am I in?
I...believe this is New York City. But I've no idea when or where I'm...
Wait a minute. I know that boy! That's Jake Chambers! The boy I lost when he fell from...
Oh, my God. I'm in the mind of his murderer! That's why the door said the Pusher. He was the one who pushed Jake into traffic.
And he's about to do it again.
Have to find the control in his mind. The one that will freeze him in his place! Now! Now!!!

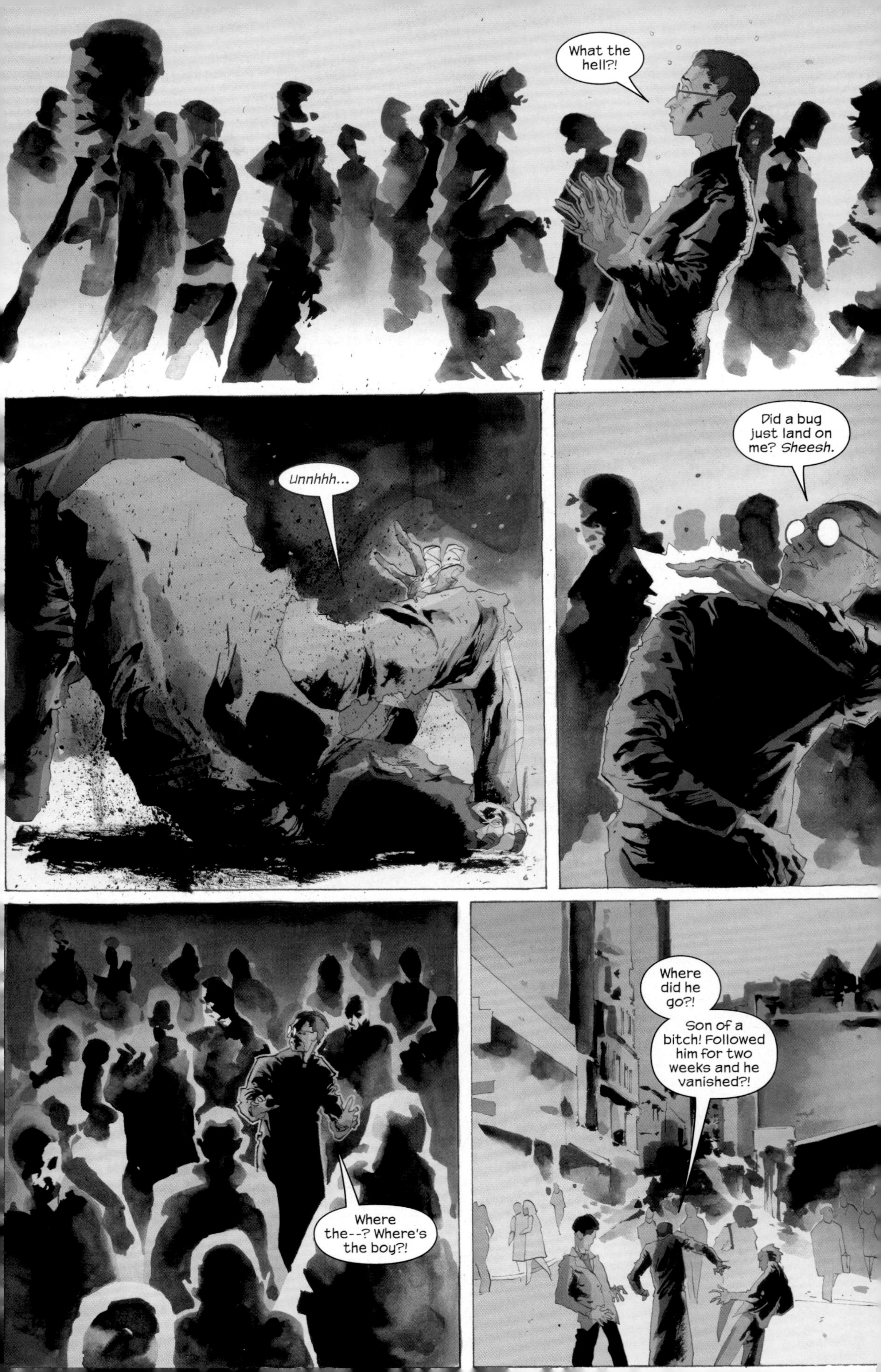
What the hell?!
Unnhhh...
Did a bug just land on me? Sheesh.
Where the--? Where's the boy?!
Where did he go?!
Son of a bitch! Followed him for two weeks and he vanished?!

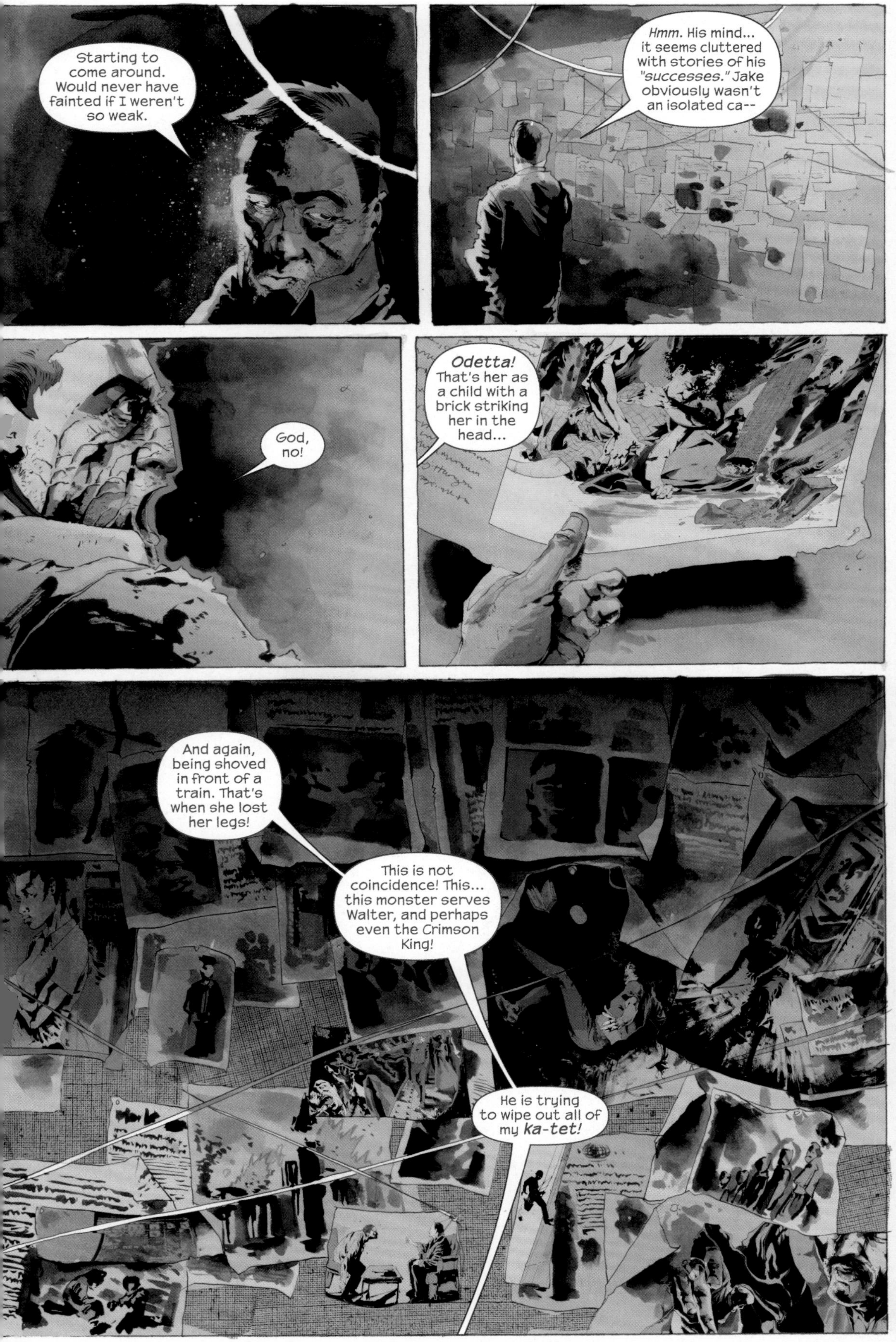
Starting to come around. Would never have fainted if I weren't so weak.
Hmm. His mind... it seems cluttered with stories of his "successes." Jake obviously wasn't an isolated ca--
God, no!
Odetta! That's her as a child with a brick striking her in the head...
And again, being shoved in front of a train. That's when she lost her legs!
This is not coincidence! This... this monster serves Walter, and perhaps even the Crimson King!
He is trying to wipe out all of my ka-tet!

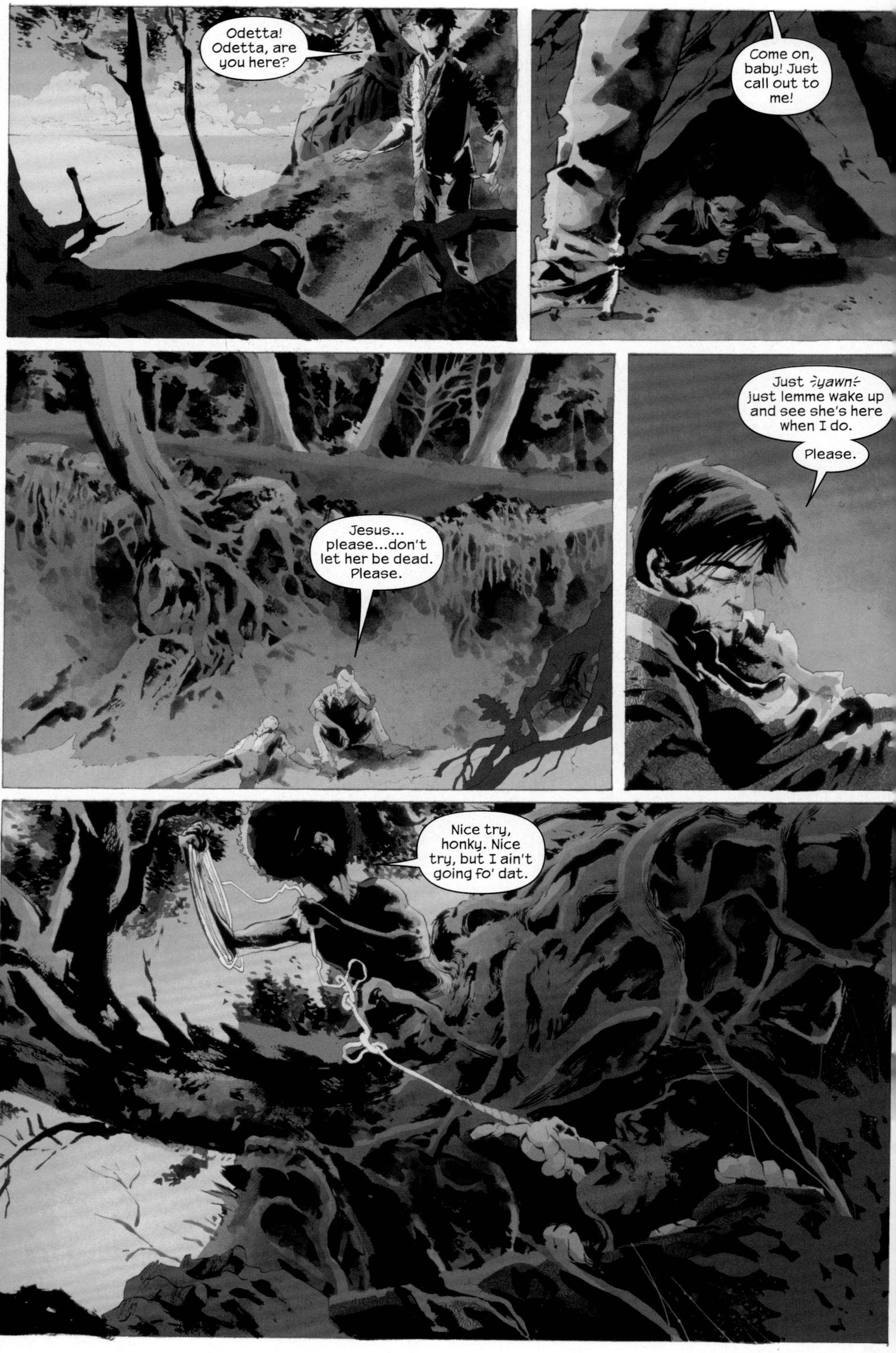
Odetta! Odetta, are you here?
Come on, baby! Just call out to me!
Jesus... please...don't let her be dead. Please.
Just ⁓yawn⁓ just lemme wake up and see she's here when I do.
Please.
Nice try, honky. Nice try, but I ain't going fo' dat.

THE DARK TOWER

THE DRAWING OF THE THREE

STEPHEN KING

BITTER MEDICINE
CHAPTER FOUR

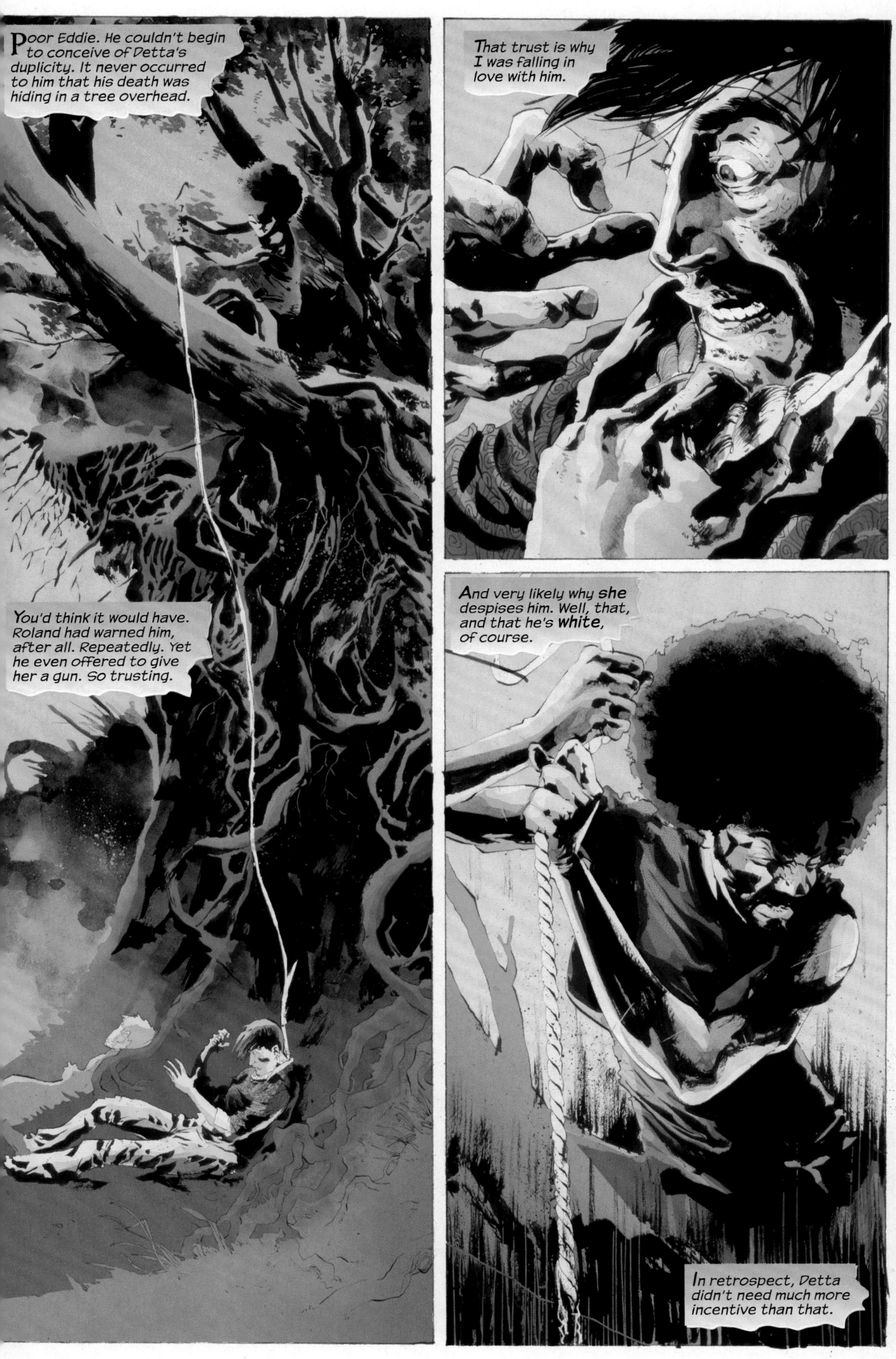
Poor Eddie. He couldn't begin to conceive of Detta's duplicity. It never occurred to him that his death was hiding in a tree overhead.
You'd think it would have. Roland had warned him, after all. Repeatedly. Yet he even offered to give her a gun. So trusting.
That trust is why I was falling in love with him.
And very likely why she despises him. Well, that, and that he's white, of course.
In retrospect, Detta didn't need much more incentive than that.

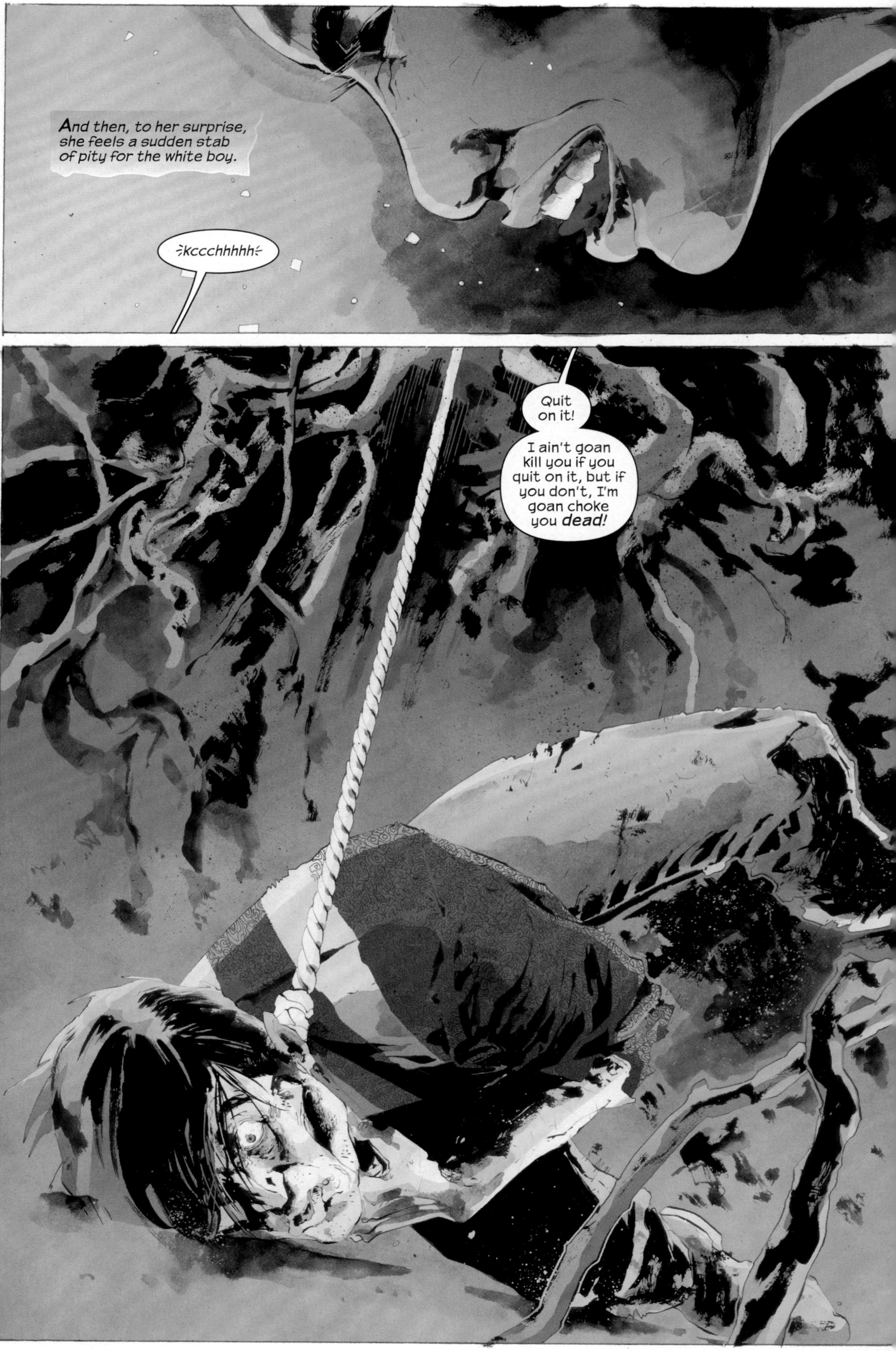
And then, to her surprise, she feels a sudden stab of pity for the white boy.
kccchhhhh
Quit on it!
I ain't goan kill you if you quit on it, but if you don't, I'm goan choke you dead!

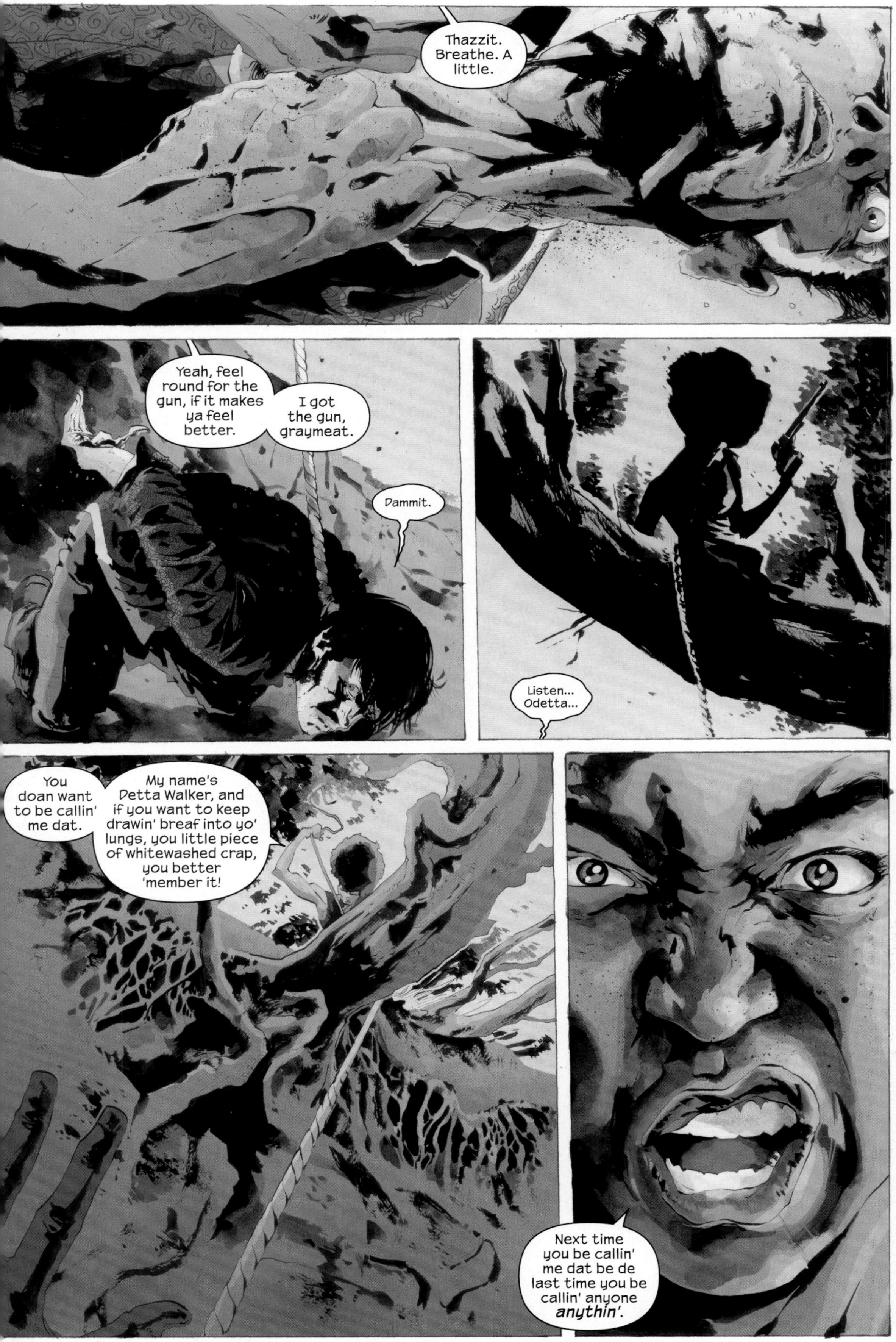
Thazzit. Breathe. A little.
Yeah, feel round for the gun, if it makes ya feel better.
I got the gun, graymeat.
Dammit.
Listen... Odetta...
You doan want to be callin' me dat.
My name's Detta Walker, and if you want to keep drawin' breaf into yo' lungs, you little piece of whitewashed crap, you better 'member it!
Next time you be callin' me dat be de last time you be callin' anyone *anythin'*.

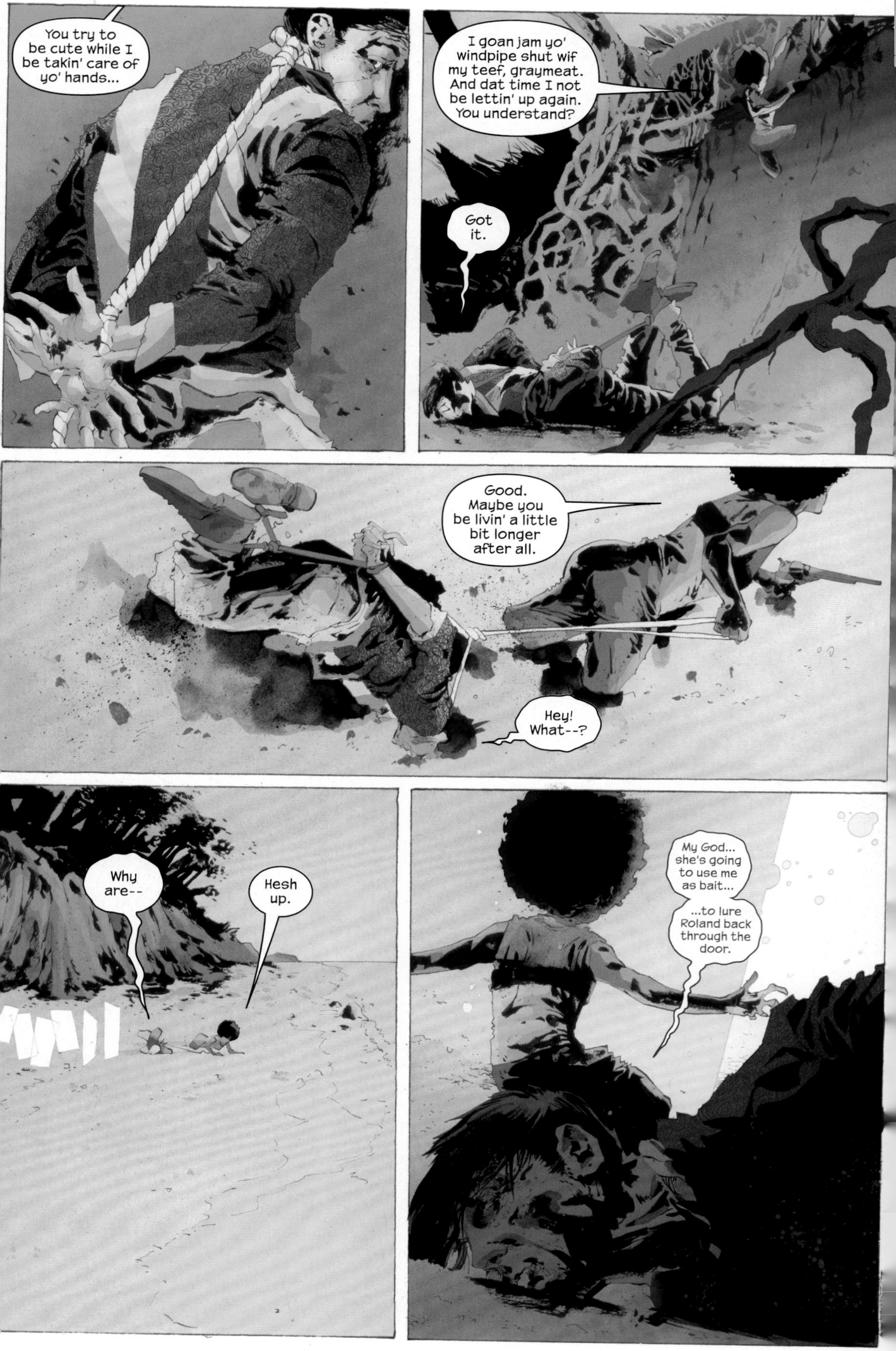
You try to be cute while I be takin' care of yo' hands...
I goan jam yo' windpipe shut wif my teef, graymeat. And dat time I not be lettin' up again. You understand?
Got it.
Good. Maybe you be livin' a little bit longer after all.
Hey! What--?
Why are--
Hesh up.
My God... she's going to use me as bait...
...to lure Roland back through the door.

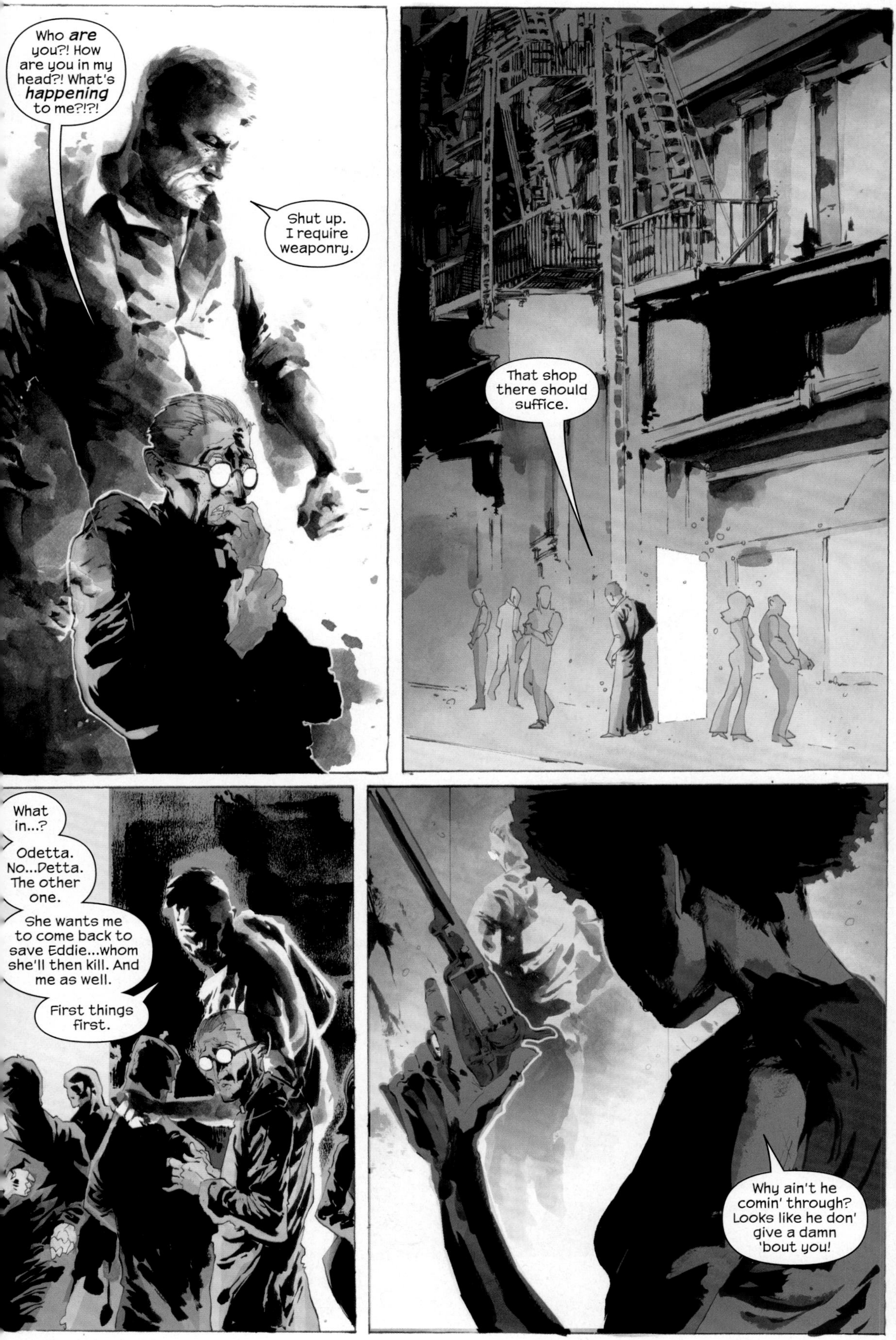
Who *are* you?! How are you in my head?! What's *happening* to me?!?!
Shut up. I require weaponry.
That shop there should suffice.
What in...?
Odetta. No...Detta. The other one.
She wants me to come back to save Eddie...whom she'll then kill. And me as well.
First things first.
Why ain't he comin' through? Looks like he don' give a damn 'bout you!

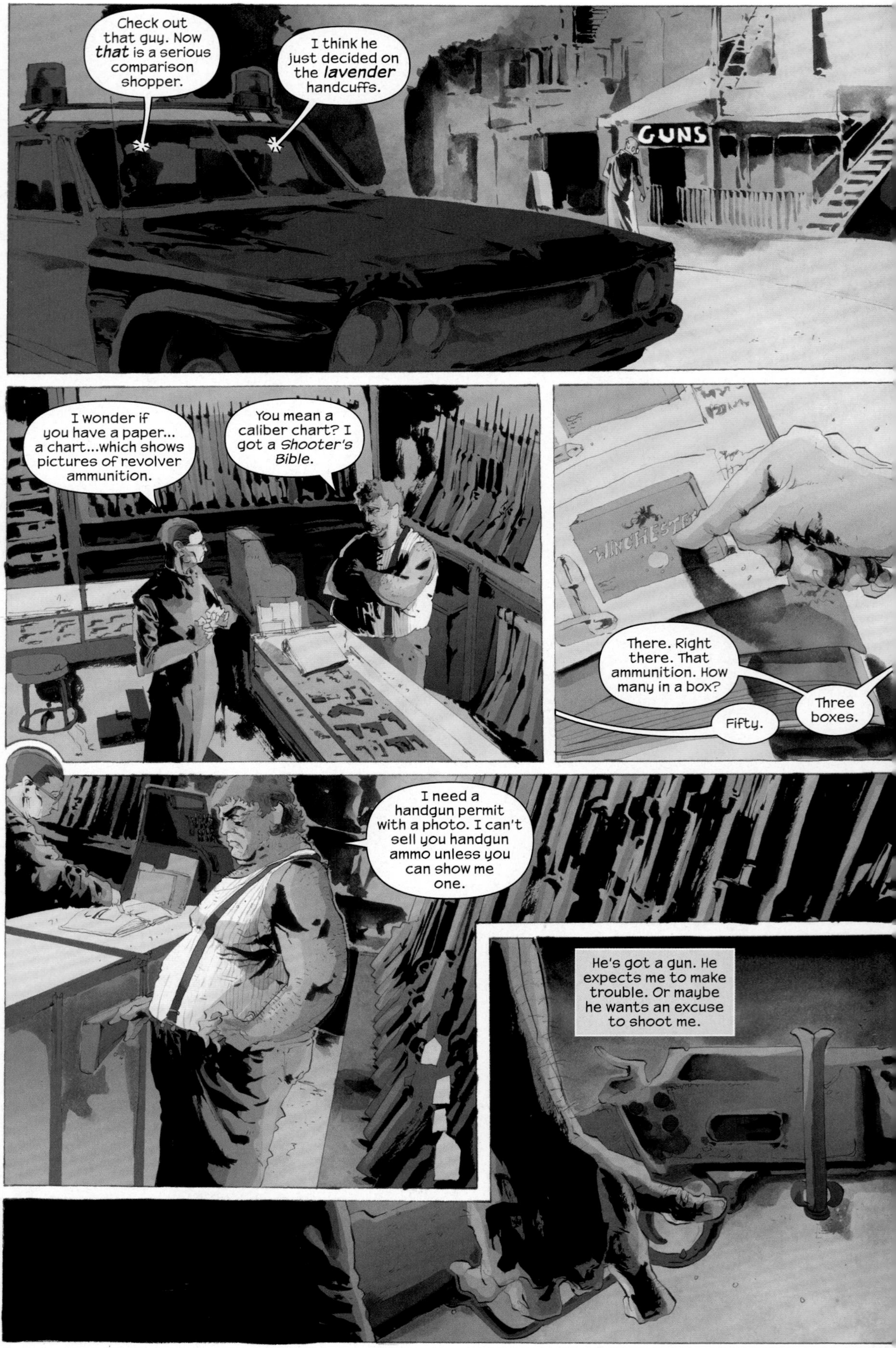

Check out that guy. Now *that* is a serious comparison shopper.
I think he just decided on the *lavender* handcuffs.
GUNS
I wonder if you have a paper... a chart...which shows pictures of revolver ammunition.
You mean a caliber chart? I got a *Shooter's Bible*.
WINCHESTER
There. Right there. That ammunition. How many in a box?
Fifty.
Three boxes.
I need a handgun permit with a photo. I can't sell you handgun ammo unless you can show me one.
He's got a gun. He expects me to make trouble. Or maybe he wants an excuse to shoot me.

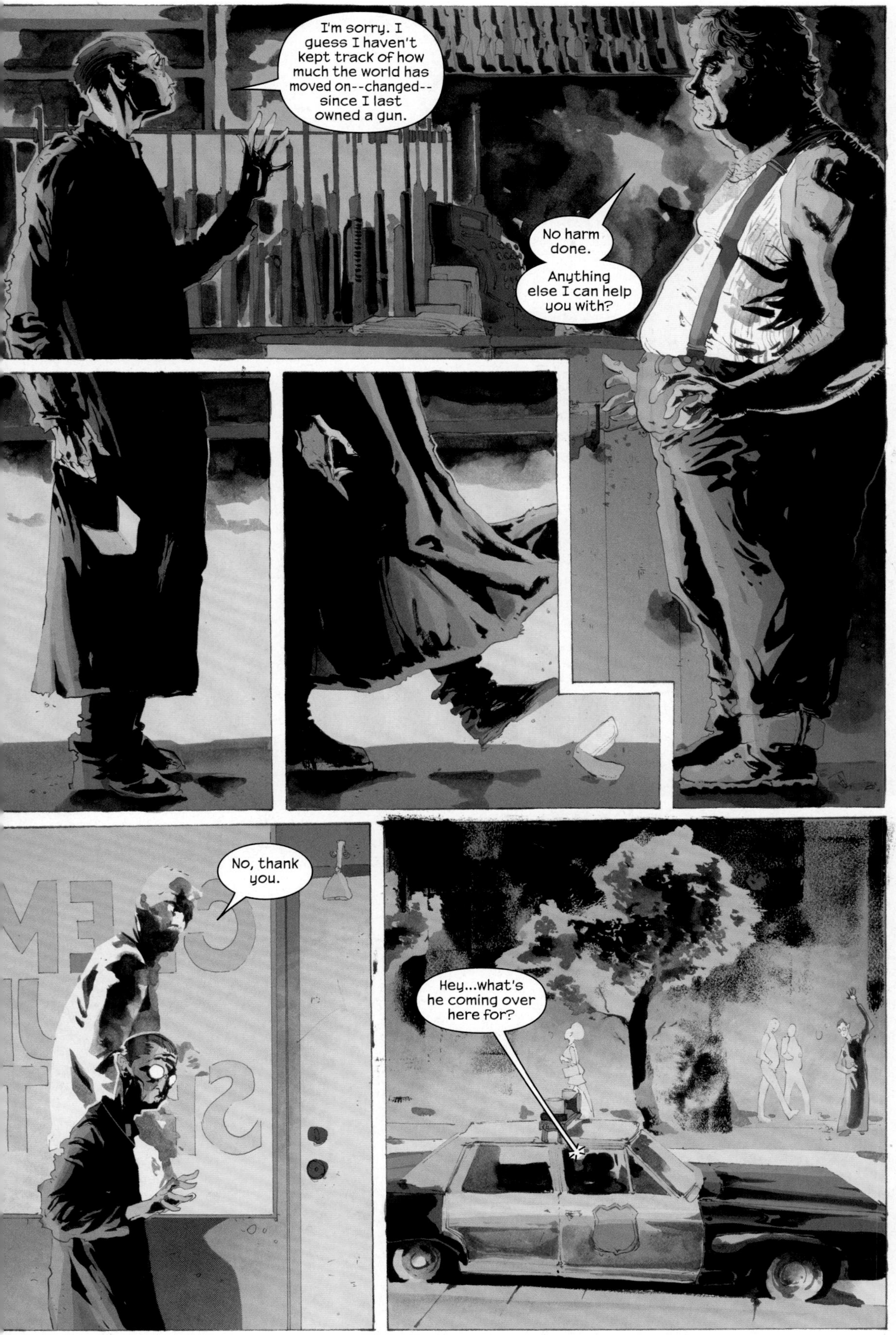
I'm sorry. I guess I haven't kept track of how much the world has moved on--changed--since I last owned a gun.
No harm done.
Anything else I can help you with?
No, thank you.
Hey...what's he coming over here for?

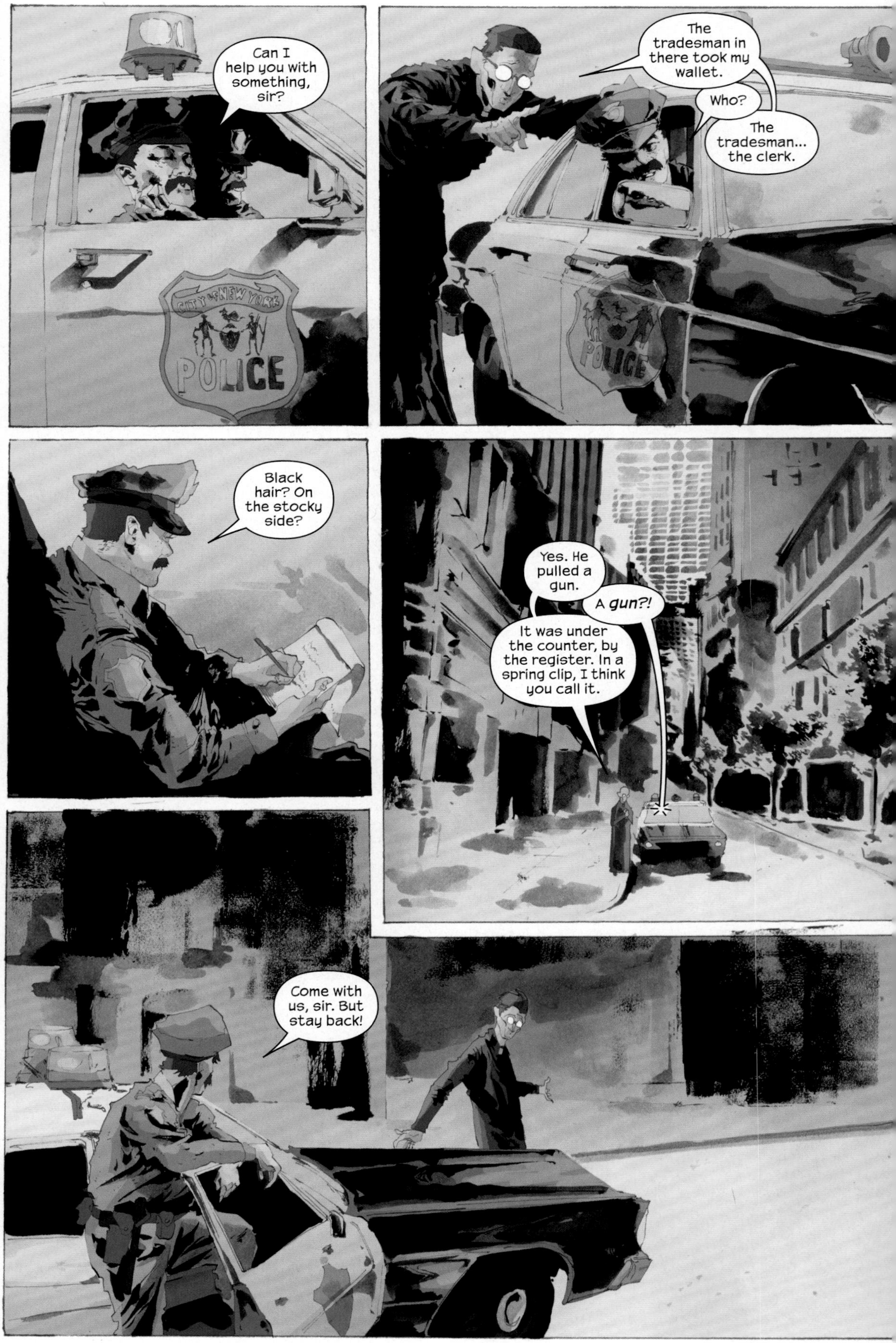
Can I help you with something, sir?
The tradesman in there took my wallet.
Who?
The tradesman... the clerk.
Black hair? On the stocky side?
Yes. He pulled a gun.
A gun?!
It was under the counter, by the register. In a spring clip, I think you call it.
Come with us, sir. But stay back!
CITY of NEW YORK
POLICE

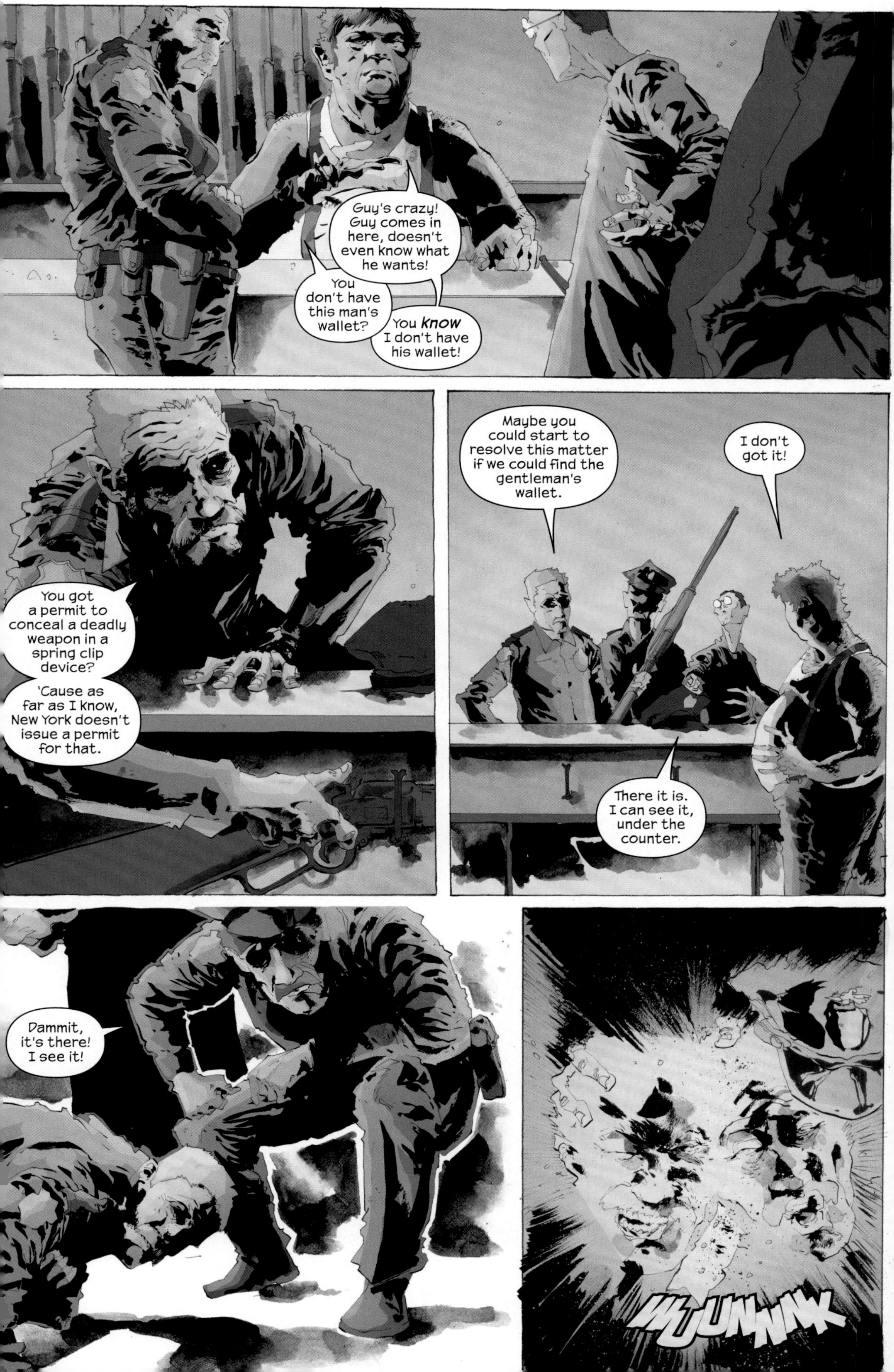
Guy's crazy! Guy comes in here, doesn't even know what he wants!
You don't have this man's wallet?
You *know* I don't have his wallet!
You got a permit to conceal a deadly weapon in a spring clip device?
'Cause as far as I know, New York doesn't issue a permit for that.
Maybe you could start to resolve this matter if we could find the gentleman's wallet.
I don't got it!
There it is. I can see it, under the counter.
Dammit, it's there! I see it!
WUNNNK

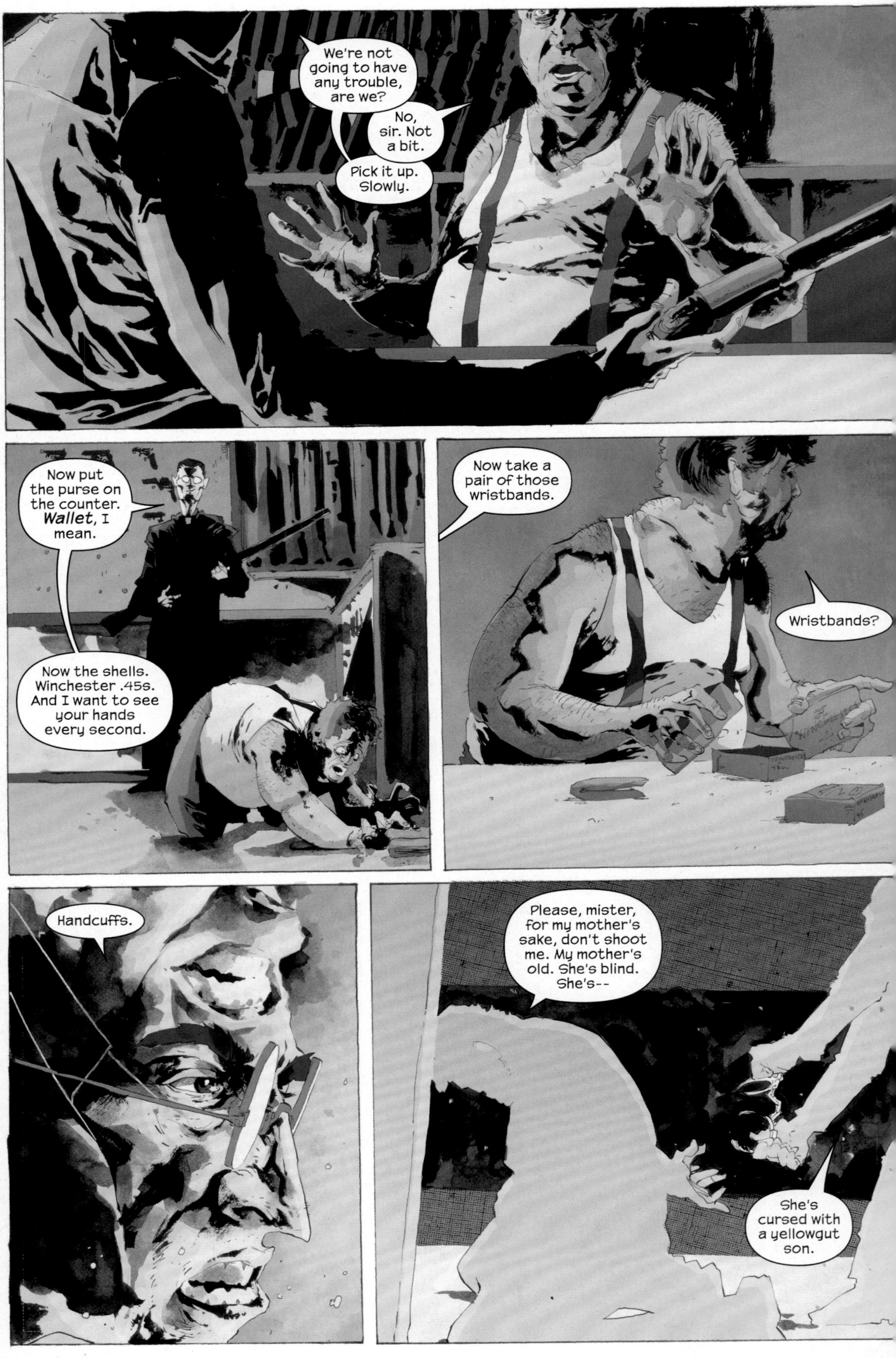

We're not going to have any trouble, are we?
No, sir. Not a bit.
Pick it up. Slowly.
Now put the purse on the counter. *Wallet*, I mean.
Now the shells. Winchester .45s. And I want to see your hands every second.
Now take a pair of those wristbands.
Wristbands?
Handcuffs.
Please, mister, for my mother's sake, don't shoot me. My mother's old. She's blind. She's--
She's cursed with a yellowgut son.

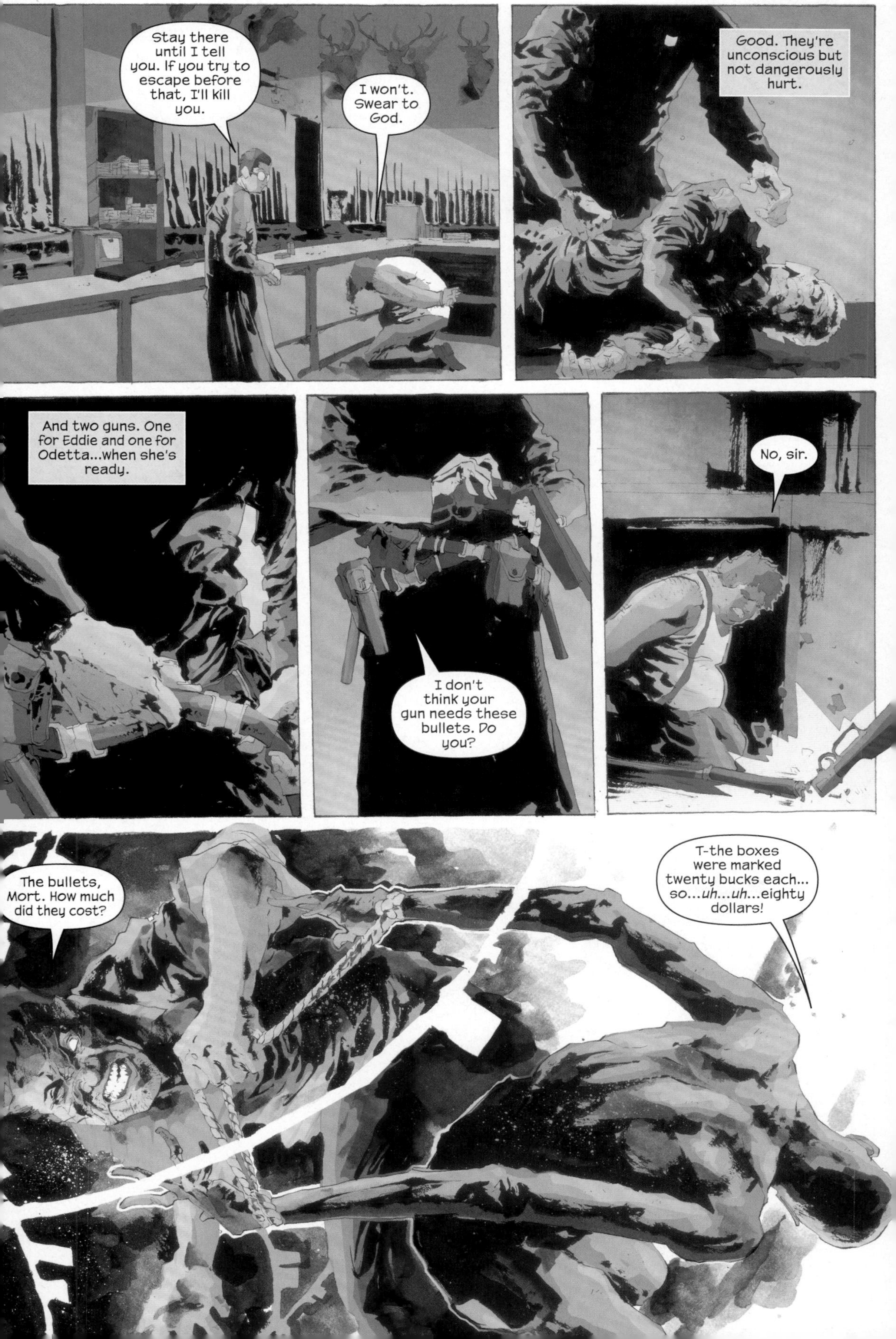

Stay there until I tell you. If you try to escape before that, I'll kill you.
I won't. Swear to God.
Good. They're unconscious but not dangerously hurt.
And two guns. One for Eddie and one for Odetta...when she's ready.
I don't think your gun needs these bullets. Do you?
No, sir.
The bullets, Mort. How much did they cost?
T-the boxes were marked twenty bucks each... so...*uh*...*uh*...eighty dollars!

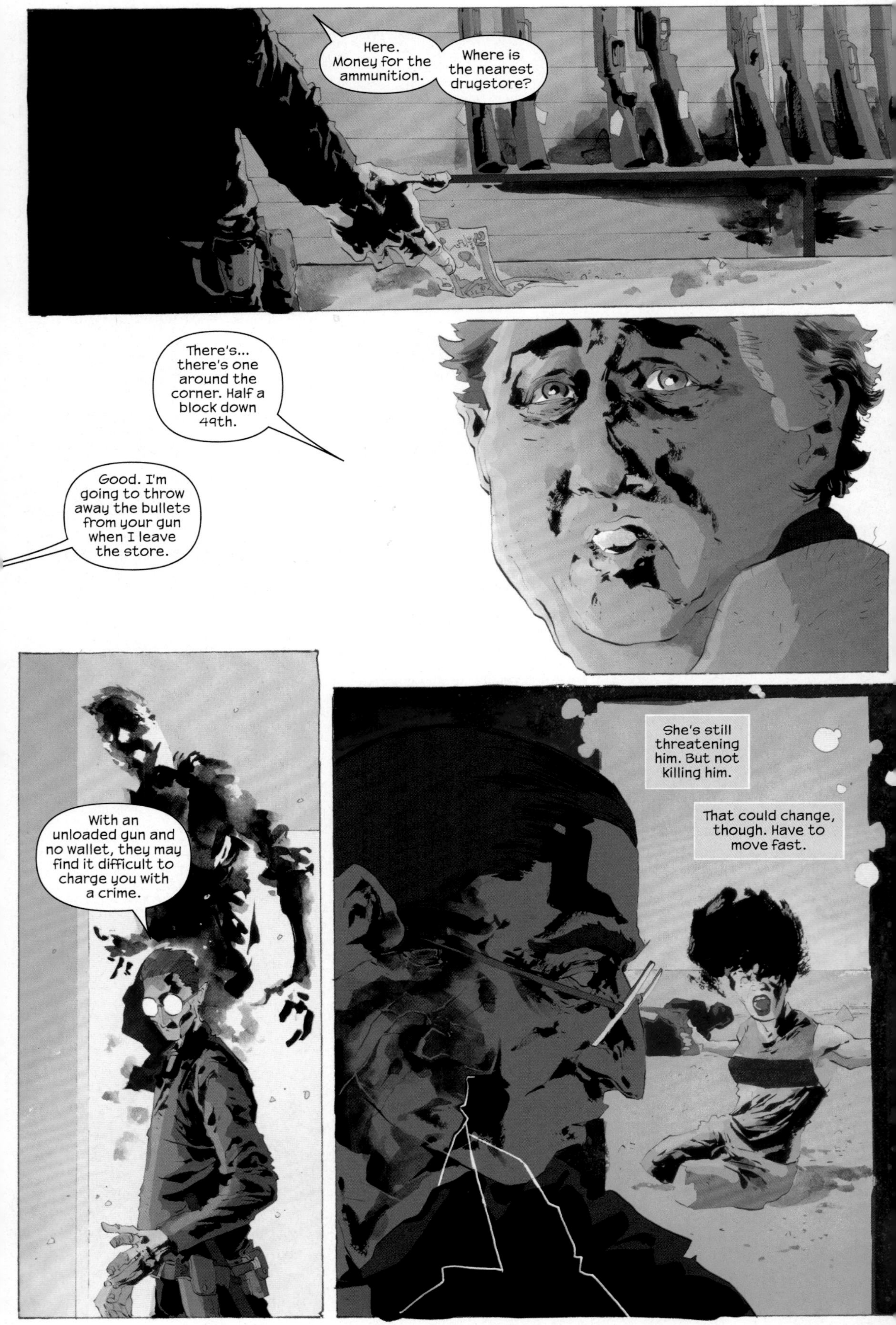

Here. Money for the ammunition.
Where is the nearest drugstore?
There's... there's one around the corner. Half a block down 49th.
Good. I'm going to throw away the bullets from your gun when I leave the store.
With an unloaded gun and no wallet, they may find it difficult to charge you with a crime.
She's still threatening him. But not killing him.
That could change, though. Have to move fast.

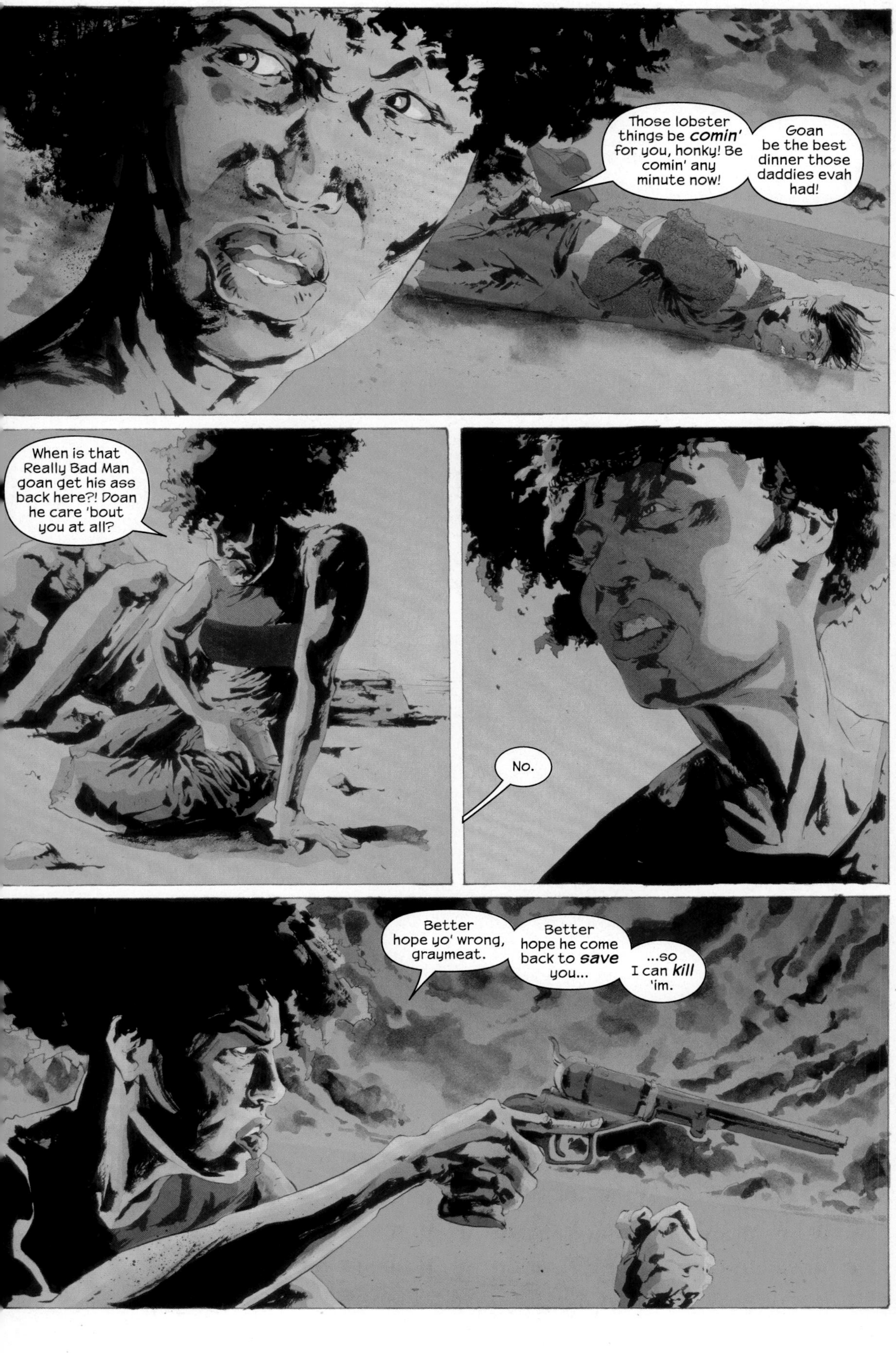
Those lobster things be *comin'* for you, honky! Be comin' any minute now!
Goan be the best dinner those daddies evah had!
When is that Really Bad Man goan get his ass back here?! Doan he care 'bout you at all?
No.
Better hope yo' wrong, graymeat.
Better hope he come back to *save* you...
...so I can *kill* 'im.

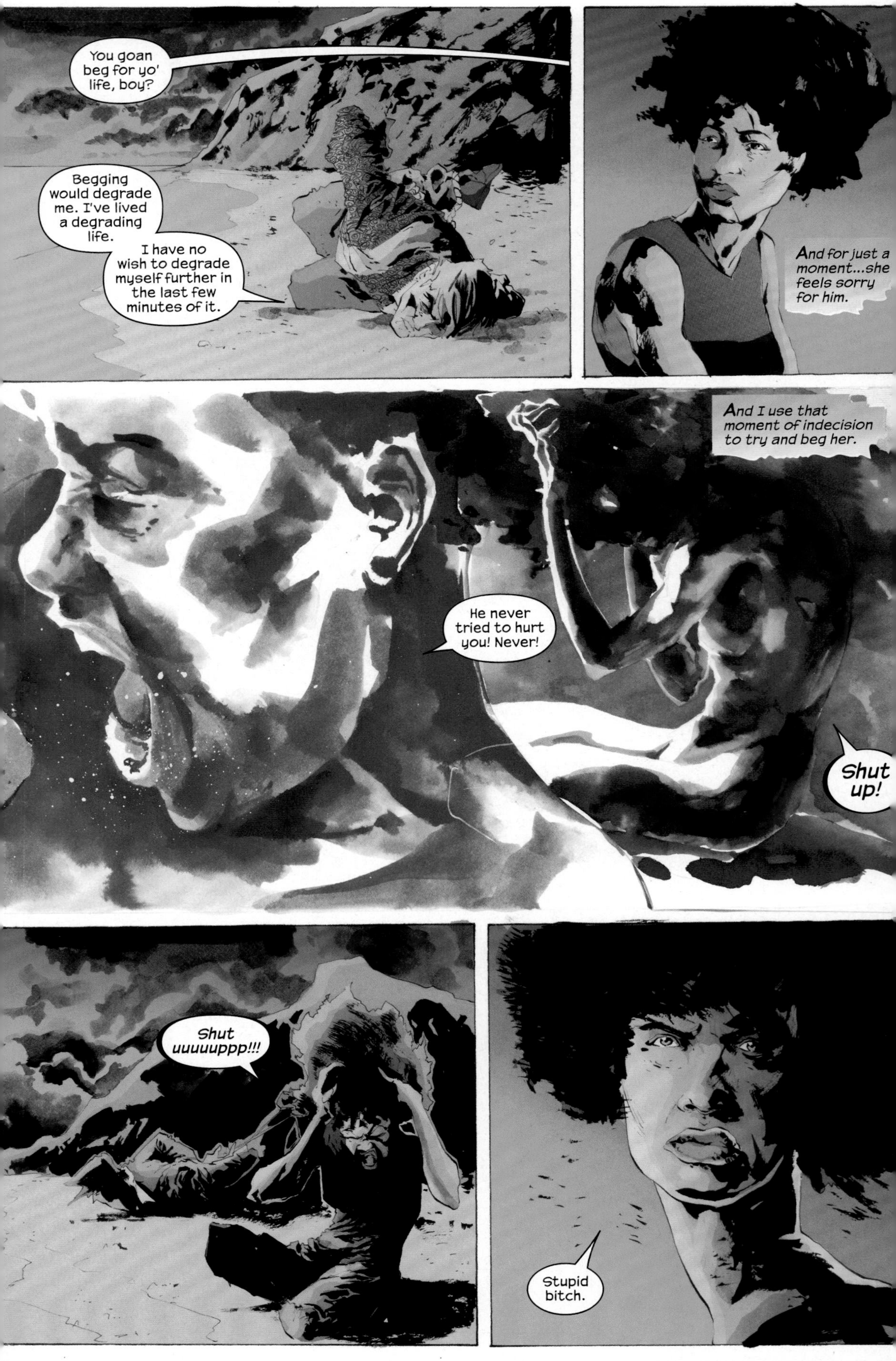
You goan beg for yo' life, boy?
Begging would degrade me. I've lived a degrading life.
I have no wish to degrade myself further in the last few minutes of it.
And for just a moment...she feels sorry for him.
And I use that moment of indecision to try and beg her.
He never tried to hurt you! Never!
Shut up!
Shut uuuuuppp!!!
Stupid bitch.

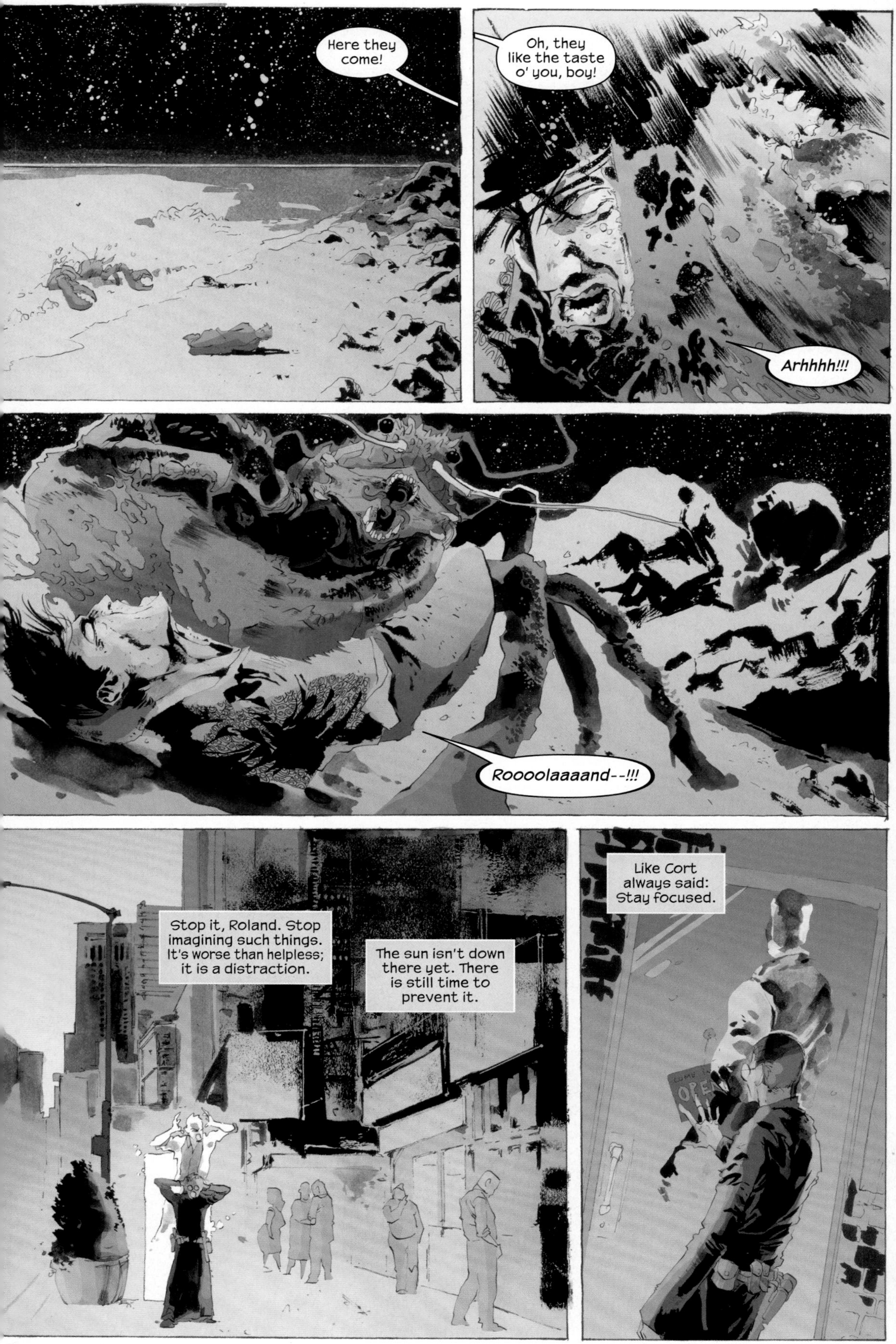
Here they come!
Oh, they like the taste o' you, boy!
Arhhhh!!!
Roooolaaaand--!!!
Stop it, Roland. Stop imagining such things. It's worse than helpless; it is a distraction.
The sun isn't down there yet. There is still time to prevent it.
Like Cort always said: Stay focused.
OPE

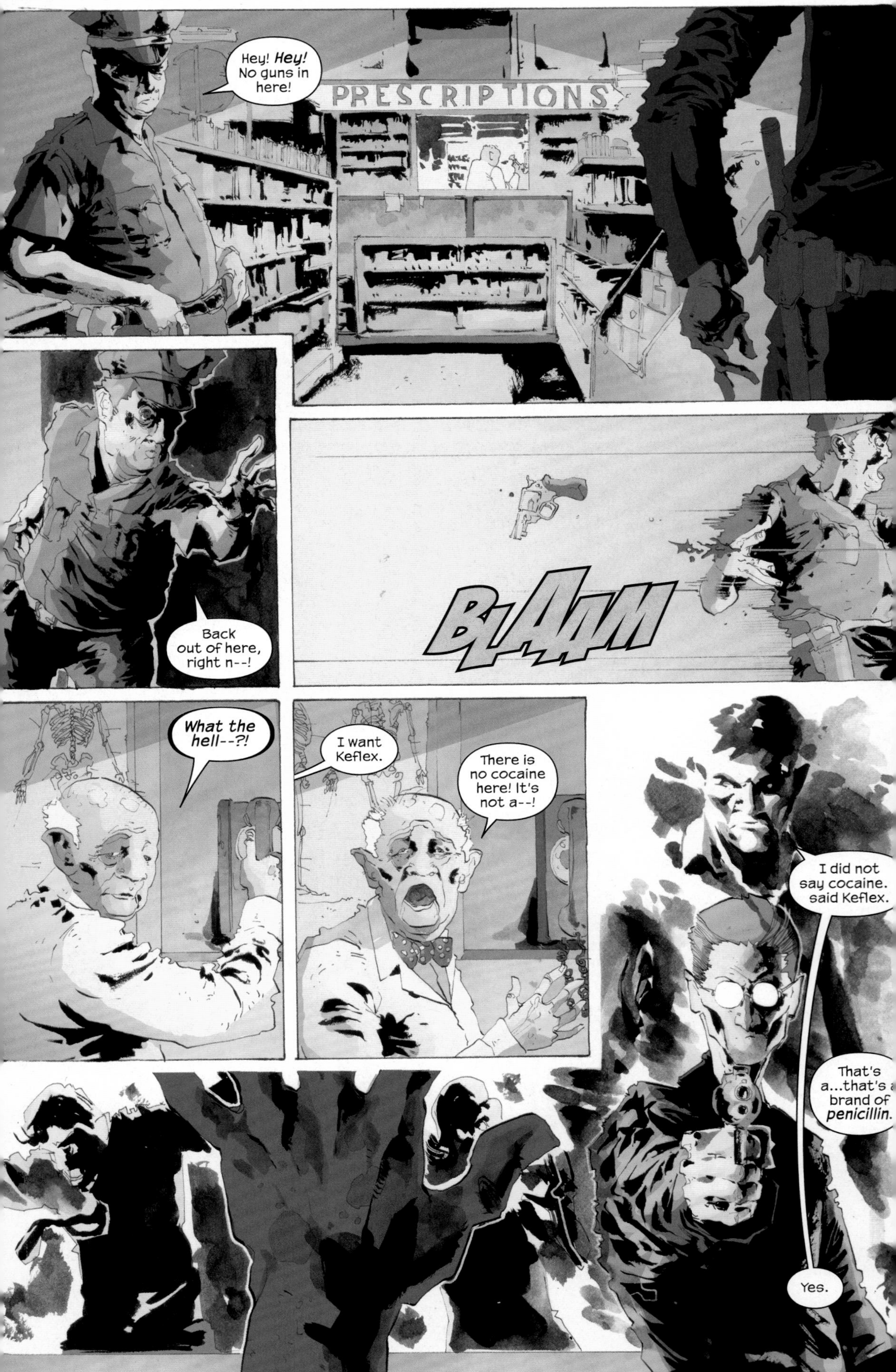
Hey! *Hey!* No guns in here!
PRESCRIPTIONS
Back out of here, right n--!
BLAAM
What the hell--?!
I want Keflex.
There is no cocaine here! It's not a--!
I did not say cocaine. said Keflex.
That's a...that's a brand of *penicillin.*
Yes.

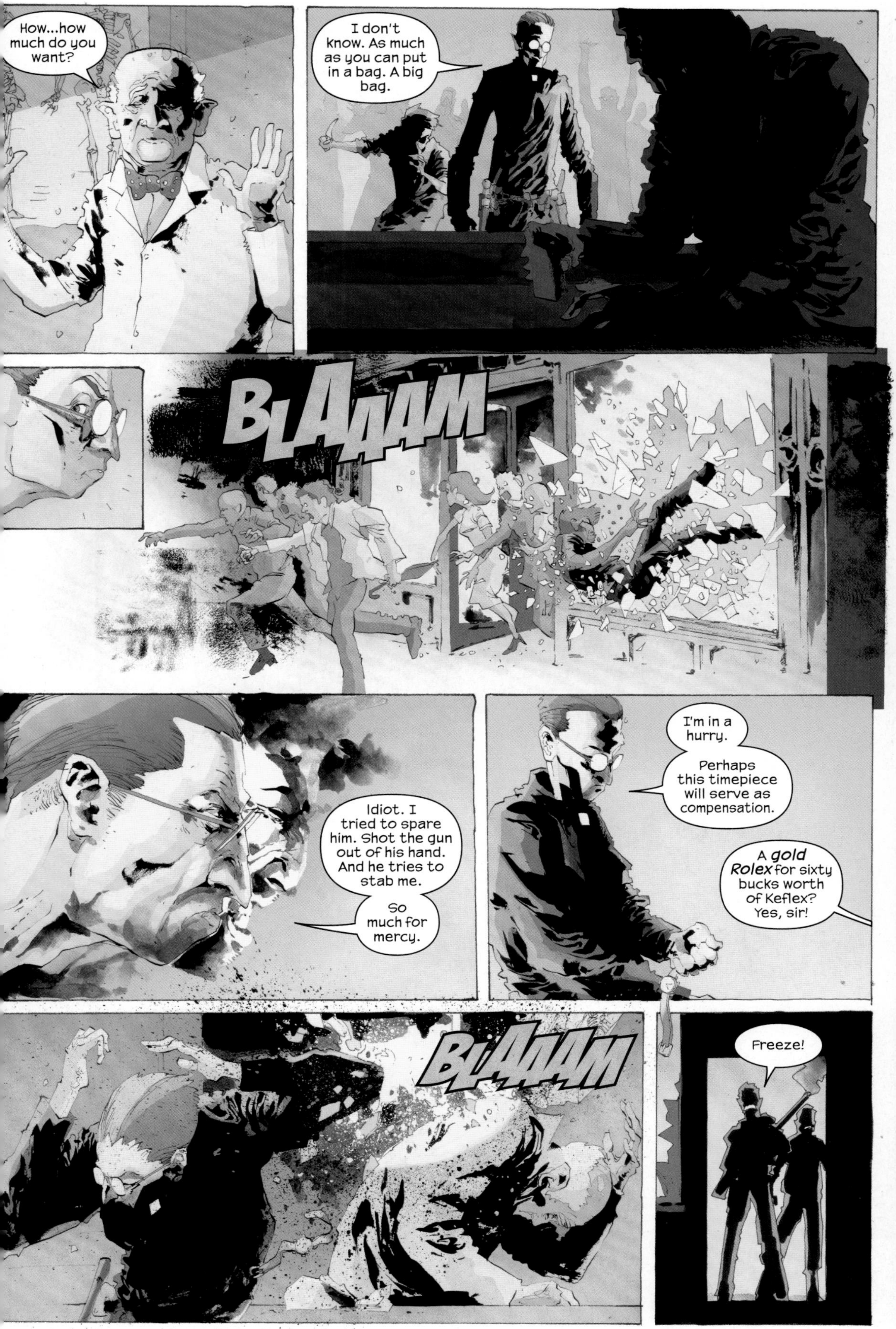
How...how much do you want?
I don't know. As much as you can put in a bag. A big bag.
BLAAAM
Idiot. I tried to spare him. Shot the gun out of his hand. And he tries to stab me.
So much for mercy.
I'm in a hurry.
Perhaps this timepiece will serve as compensation.
A gold Rolex for sixty bucks worth of Keflex? Yes, sir!
BLAAAM
Freeze!

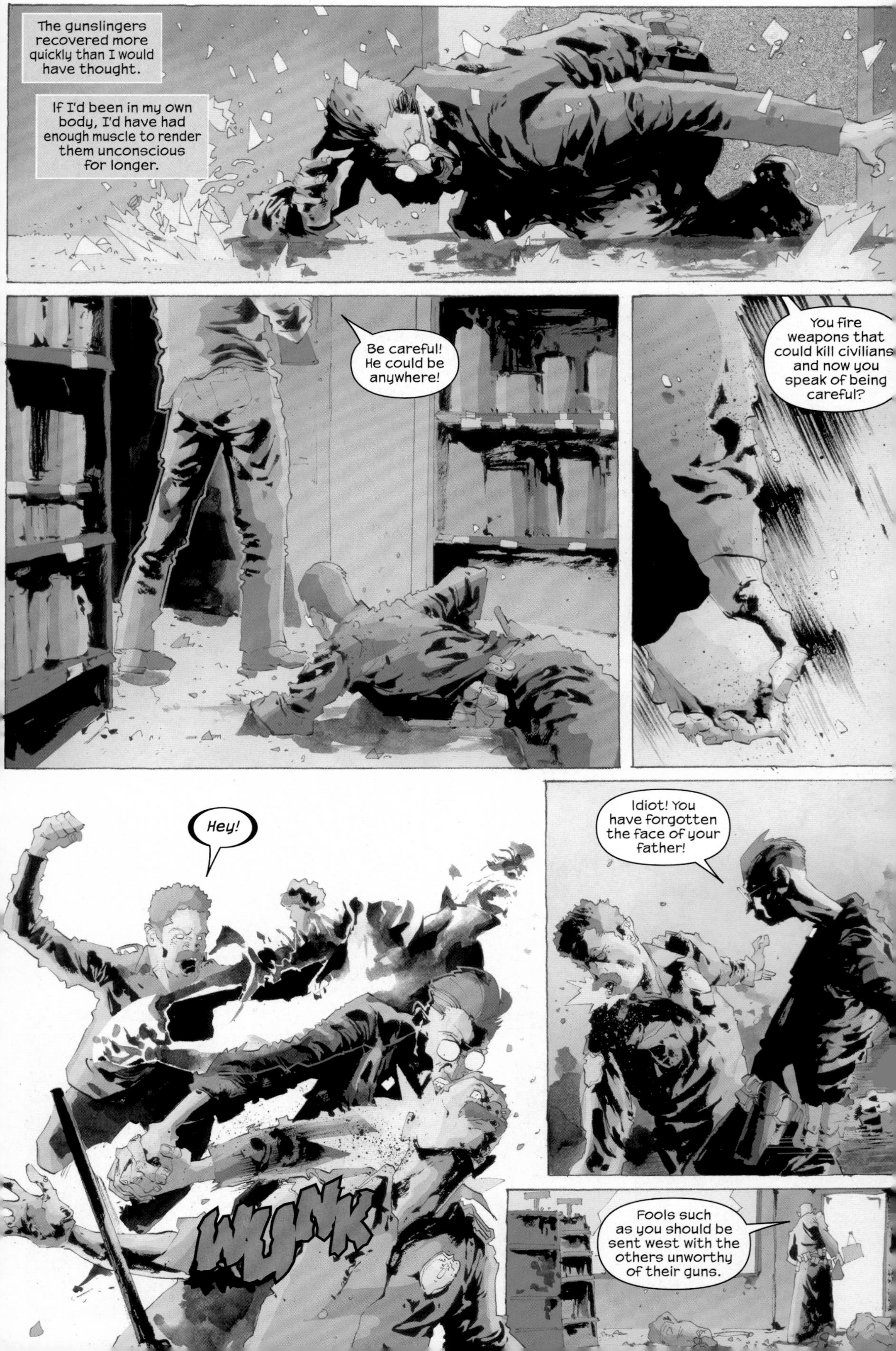

The gunslingers recovered more quickly than I would have thought.
If I'd been in my own body, I'd have had enough muscle to render them unconscious for longer.
Be careful! He could be anywhere!
You fire weapons that could kill civilians and now you speak of being careful?
Hey!
WUNK
Idiot! You have forgotten the face of your father!
Fools such as you should be sent west with the others unworthy of their guns.

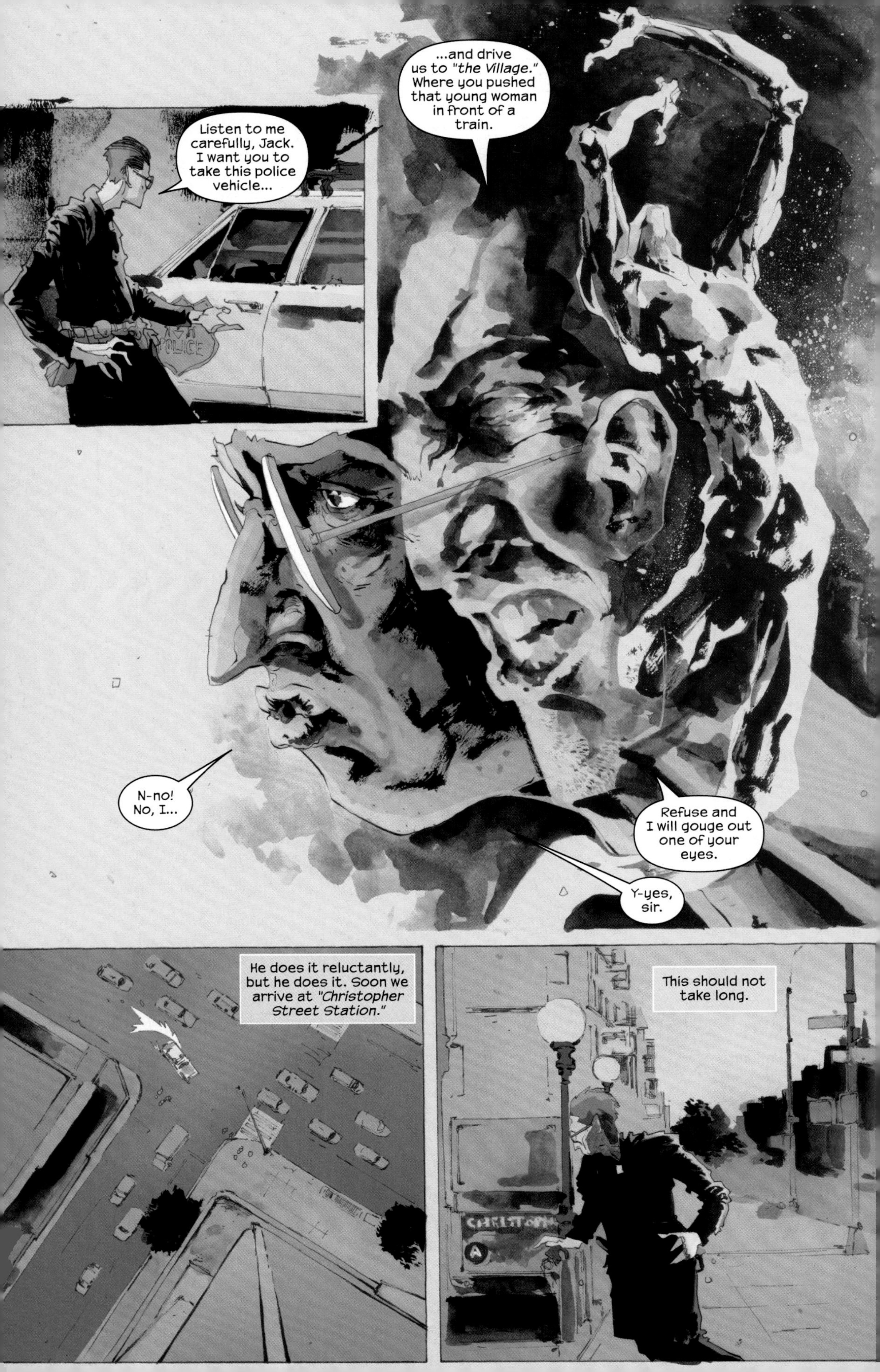
Listen to me carefully, Jack. I want you to take this police vehicle...
...and drive us to "the Village." Where you pushed that young woman in front of a train.
POLICE
N-no! No, I...
Refuse and I will gouge out one of your eyes.
Y-yes, sir.
He does it reluctantly, but he does it. Soon we arrive at "Christopher Street Station."
This should not take long.

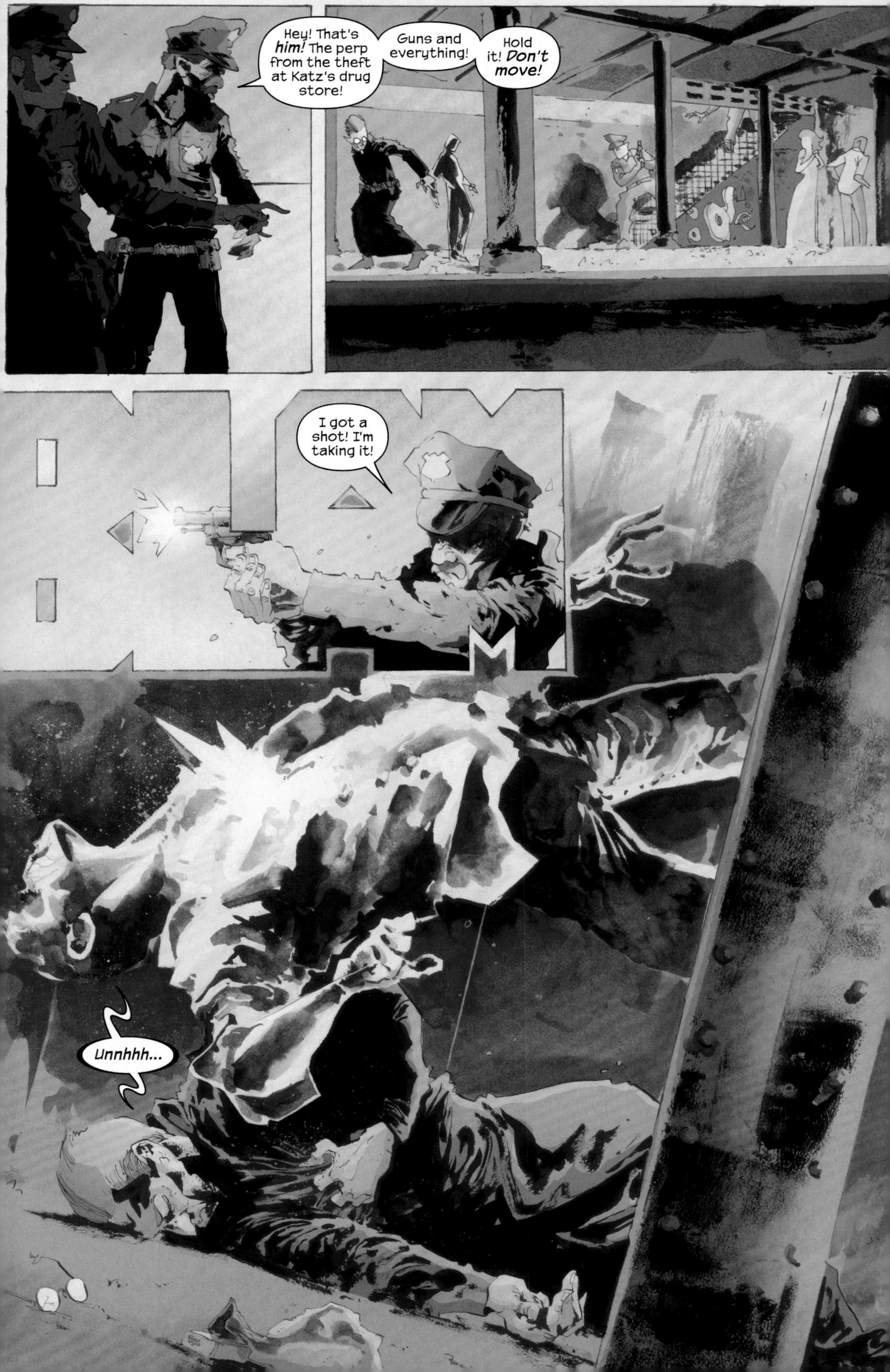
Hey! That's *him!* The perp from the theft at Katz's drug store!
Guns and everything!
Hold it! *Don't move!*
I got a shot! I'm taking it!
Unnhhh...

THE DARK TOWER

THE DRAWING OF THE THREE

STEPHEN KING

BITTER MEDICINE
CHAPTER FIVE

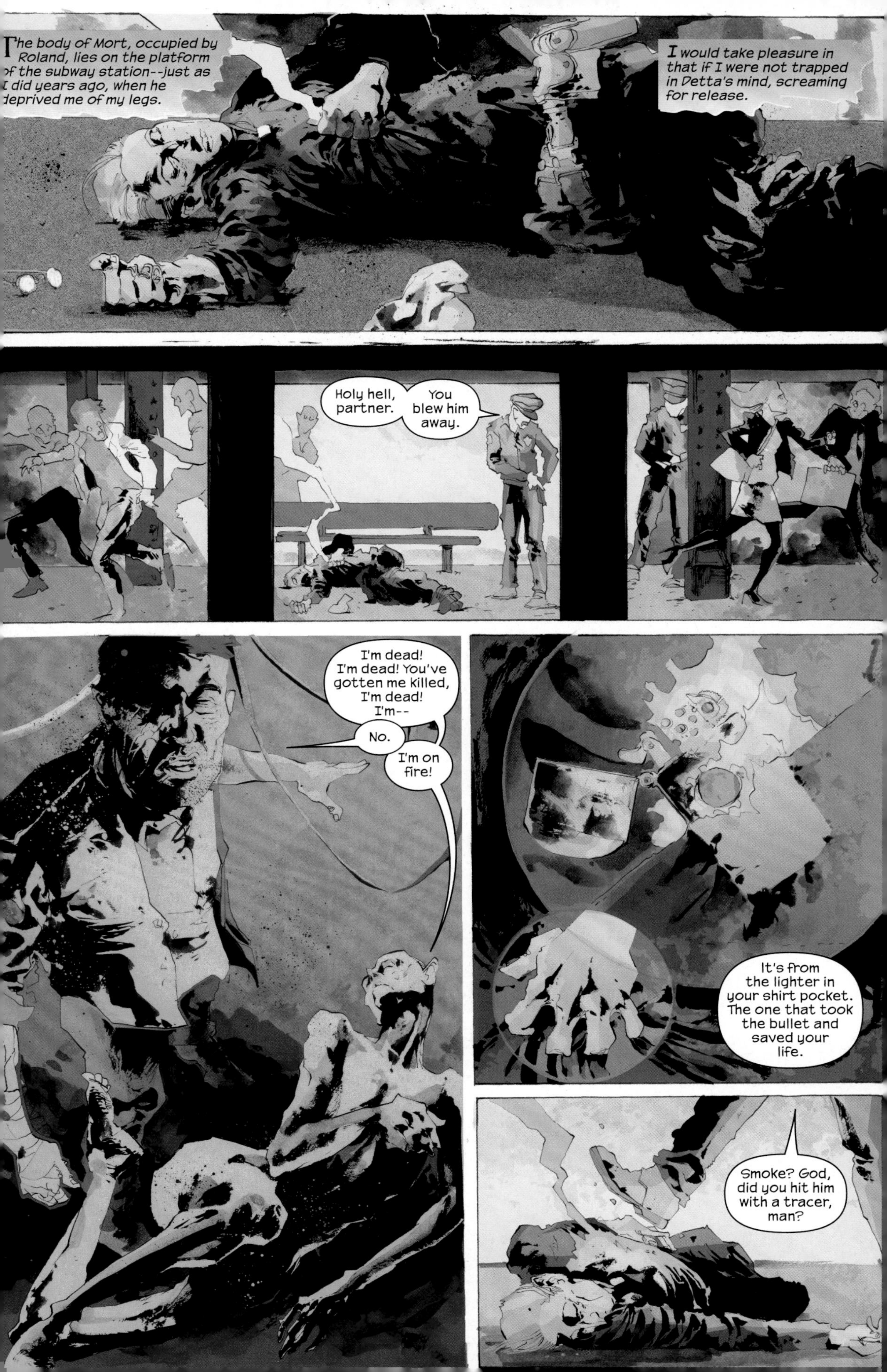
The body of Mort, occupied by Roland, lies on the platform of the subway station--just as I did years ago, when he deprived me of my legs.
I would take pleasure in that if I were not trapped in Detta's mind, screaming for release.
Holy hell, partner.
You blew him away.
I'm dead! I'm dead! You've gotten me killed, I'm dead! I'm--
No.
I'm on fire!
It's from the lighter in your shirt pocket. The one that took the bullet and saved your life.
Smoke? God, did you hit him with a tracer, man?

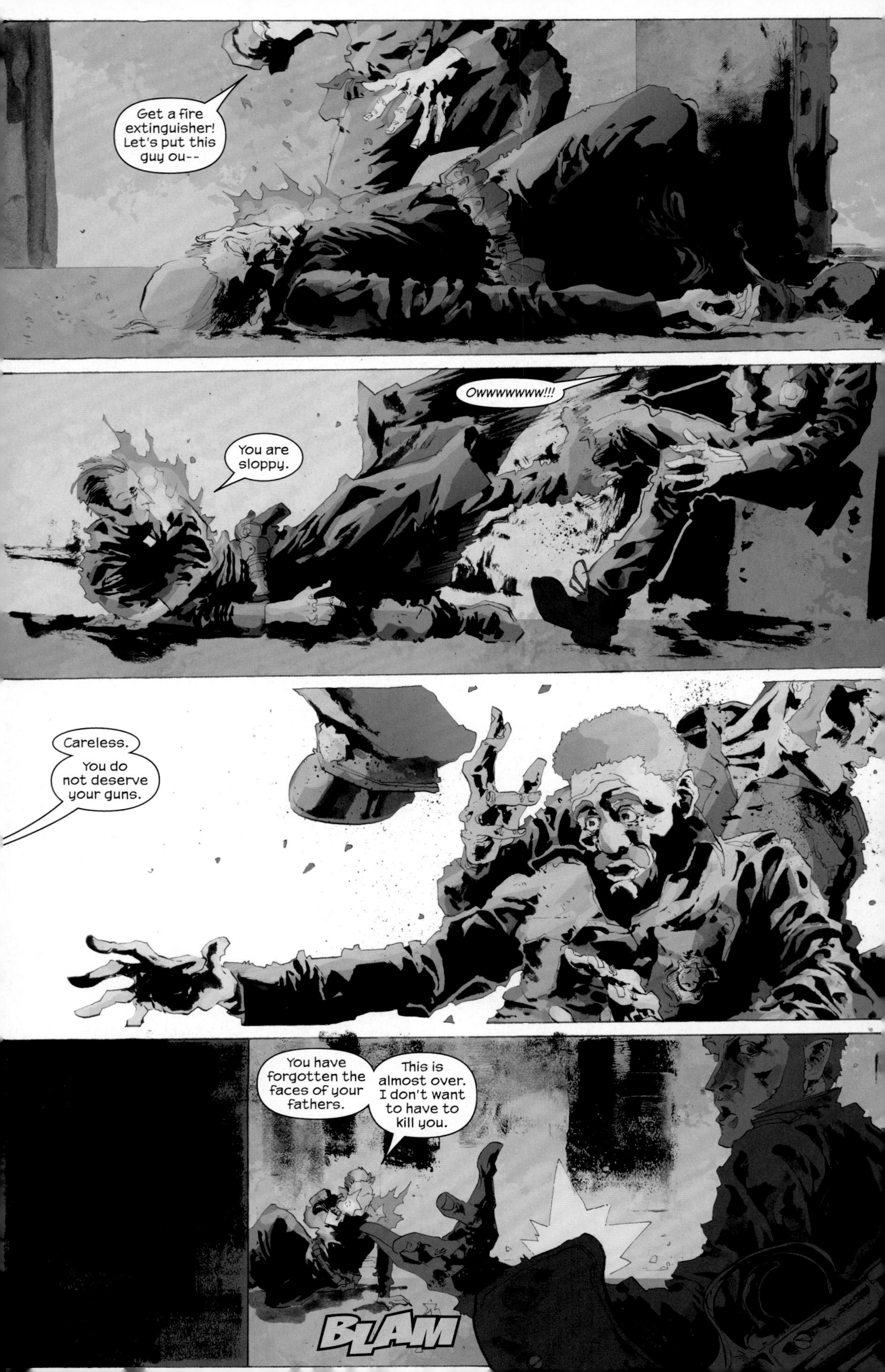

Get a fire extinguisher! Let's put this guy ou--
Owwwwwww!!!
You are sloppy.
Careless.
You do not deserve your guns.
You have forgotten the faces of your fathers.
This is almost over. I don't want to have to kill you.
BLAM

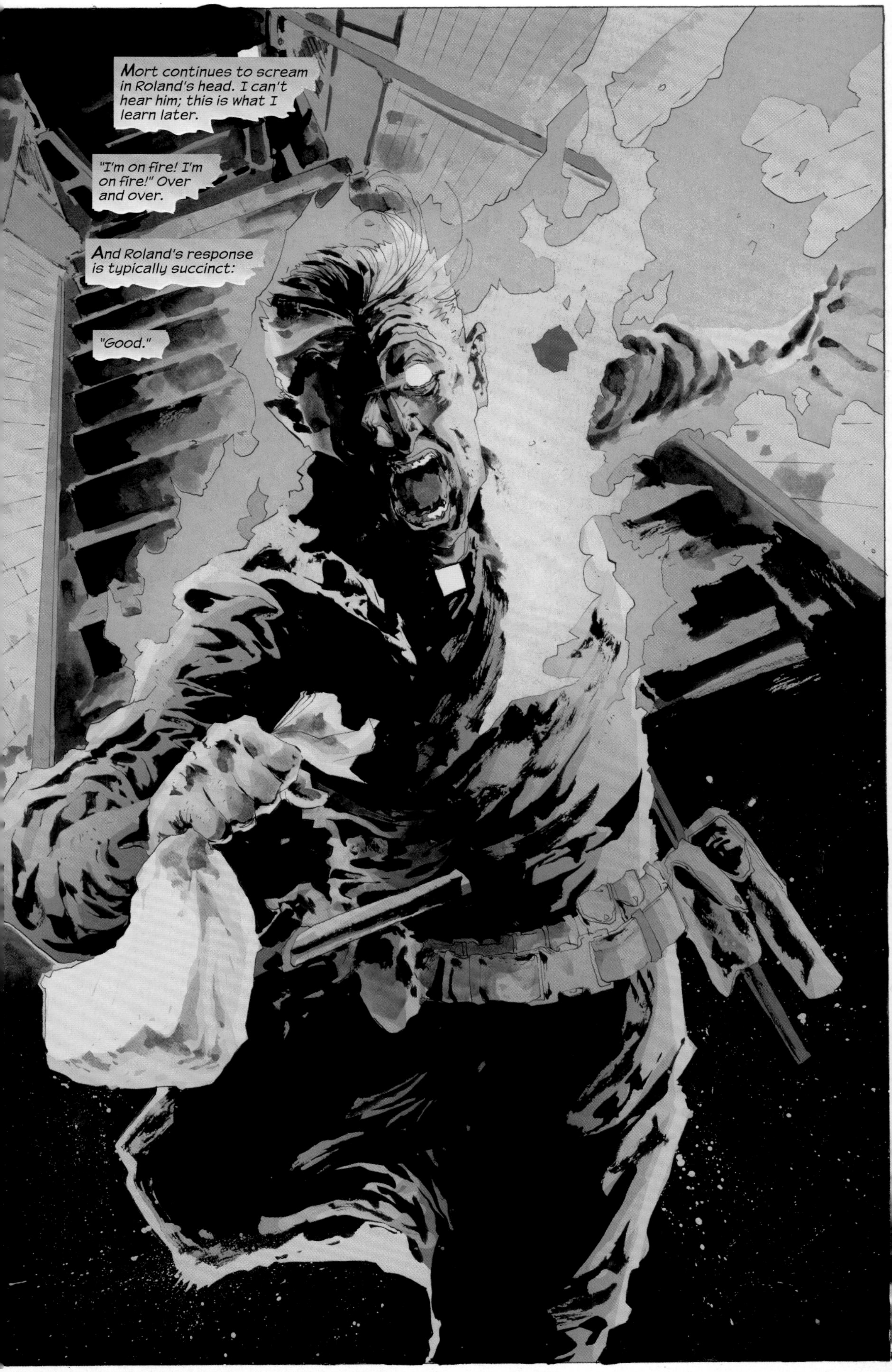
Mort continues to scream in Roland's head. I can't hear him; this is what I learn later.
"I'm on fire! I'm on fire!" Over and over.
And Roland's response is typically succinct:
"Good."

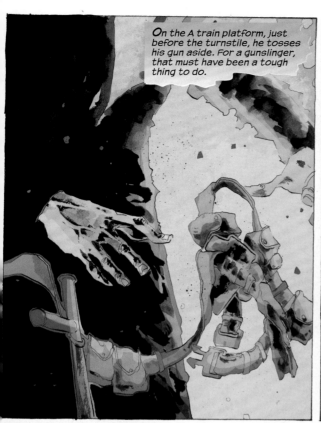

On the A train platform, just before the turnstile, he tosses his gun aside. For a gunslinger, that must have been a tough thing to do.

He feels the rush of air, sees the distant light of an oncoming train.

He removes and tosses aside the flaming jacket, and then quickly he undoes his pants.

Very frilly underwear. On the other hand, commando would have been worse, so I guess we should be grateful.

He stuffs bullet boxes and penicillin in the underwear. Or panties. Whatever.

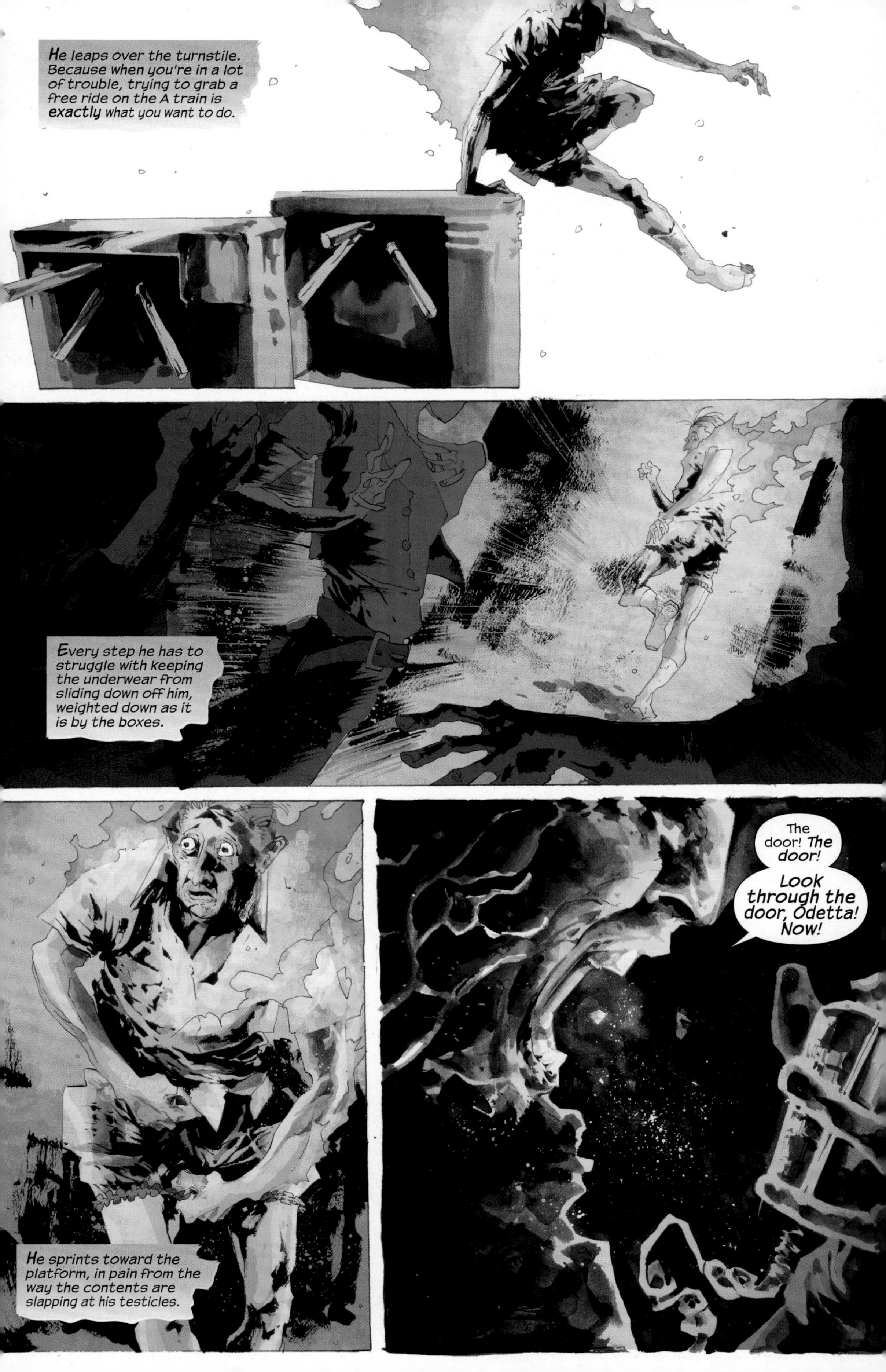
He leaps over the turnstile. Because when you're in a lot of trouble, trying to grab a free ride on the A train is exactly what you want to do.
Every step he has to struggle with keeping the underwear from sliding down off him, weighted down as it is by the boxes.
He sprints toward the platform, in pain from the way the contents are slapping at his testicles.
The door! The door!
Look through the door, Odetta! Now!

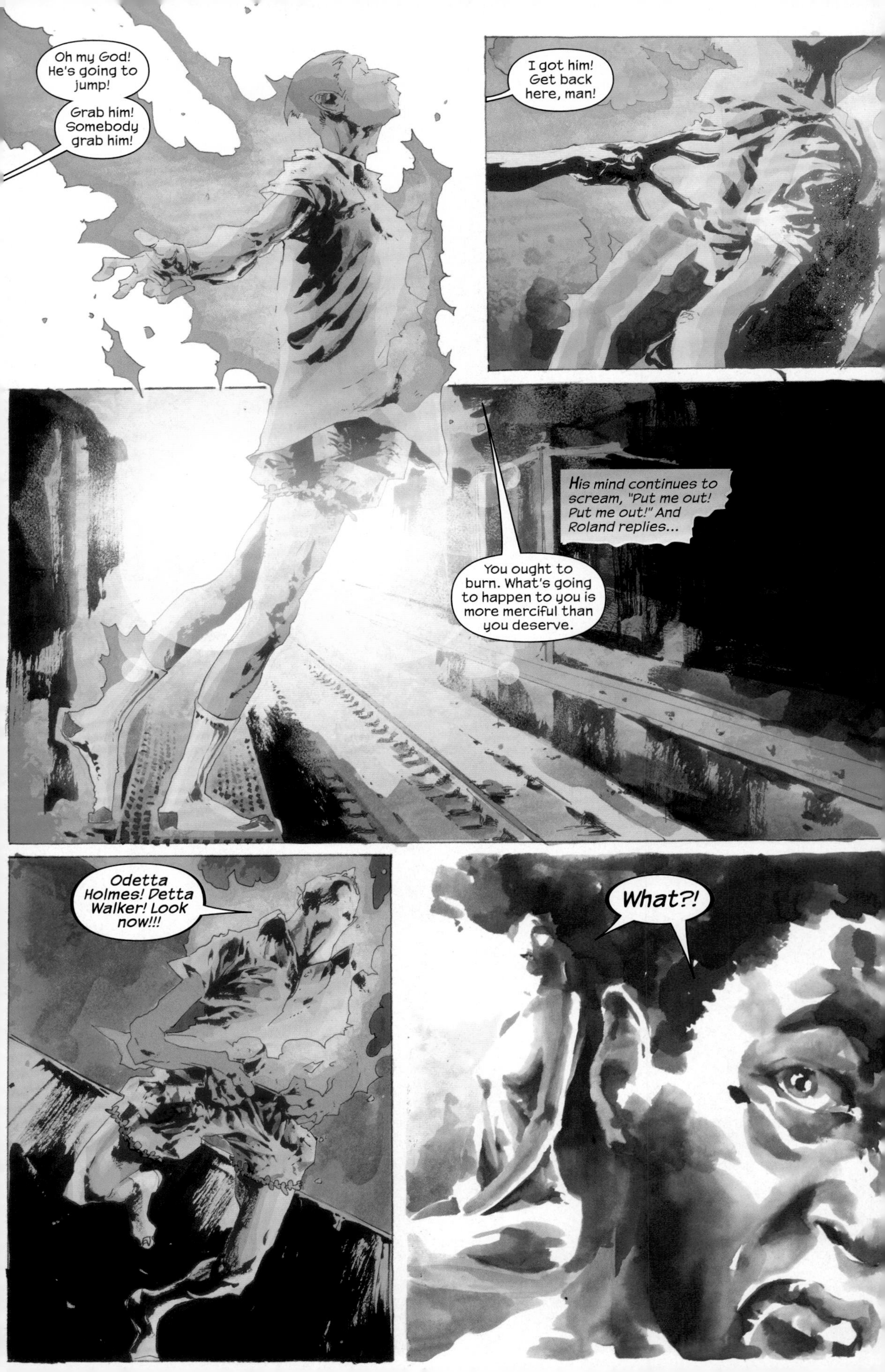
Oh my God! He's going to jump!
Grab him! Somebody grab him!
I got him! Get back here, man!
His mind continues to scream, "Put me out! Put me out!" And Roland replies...
You ought to burn. What's going to happen to you is more merciful than you deserve.
Odetta Holmes! Detta Walker! Look now!!!
What?!

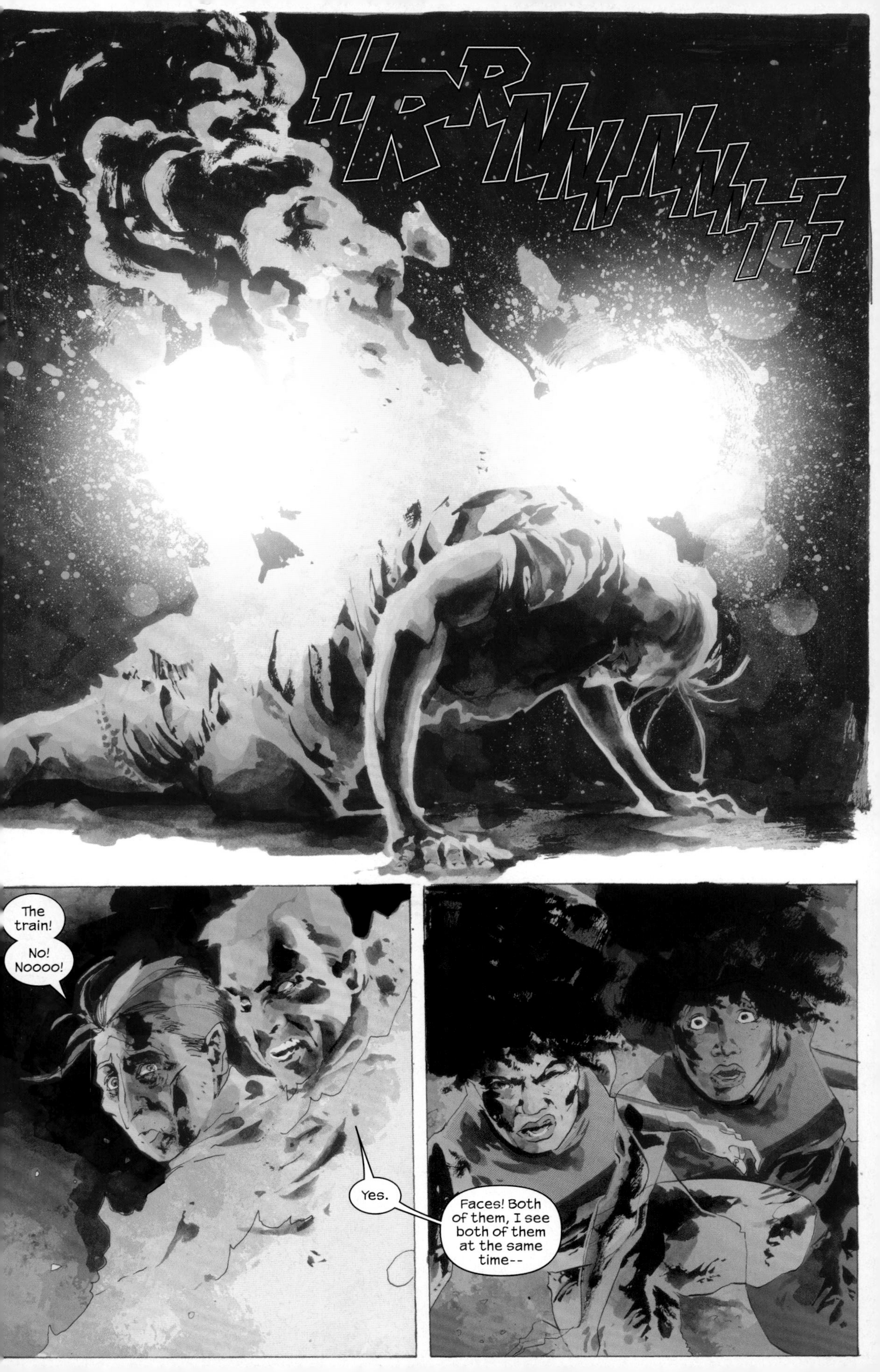
HRNNNNNNNT
The train!
No! Noooo!
Yes.
Faces! Both of them, I see both of them at the same time--

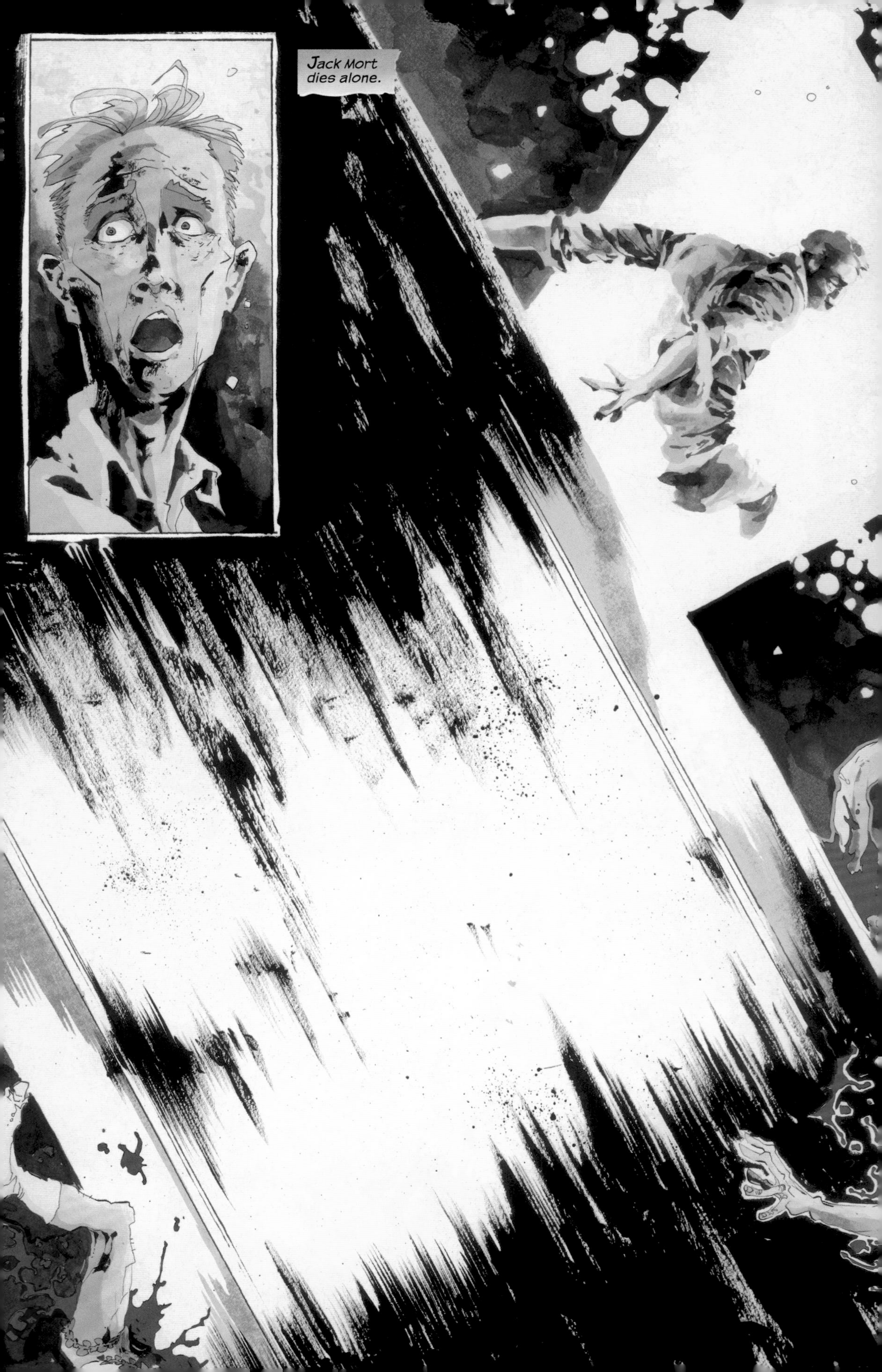
Jack Mort
dies alone.

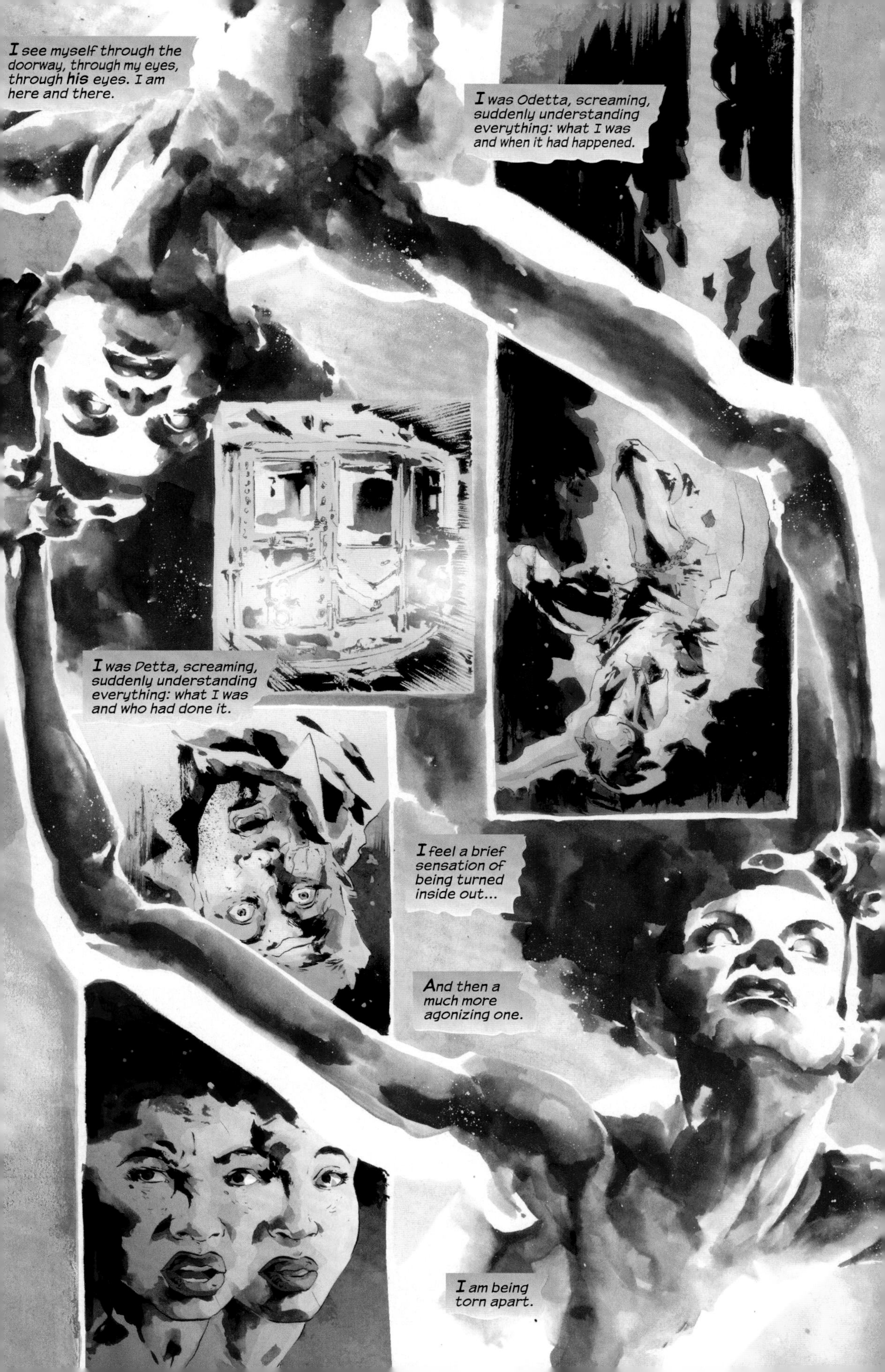
I see myself through the doorway, through my eyes, through his eyes. I am here and there.
I was Odetta, screaming, suddenly understanding everything: what I was and when it had happened.
I was Detta, screaming, suddenly understanding everything: what I was and who had done it.
I feel a brief sensation of being turned inside out...
And then a much more agonizing one.
I am being torn apart.

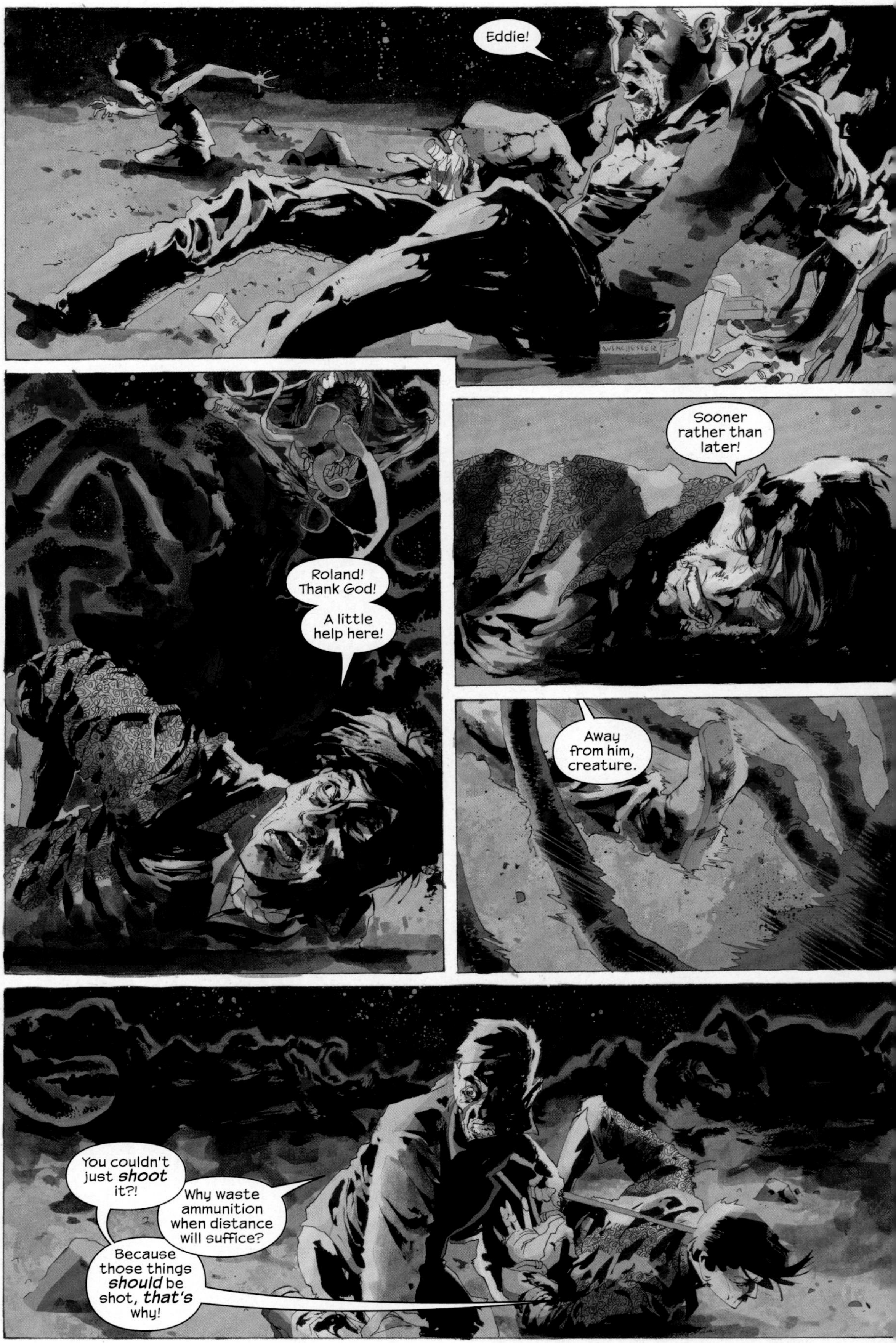
Eddie!
Roland! Thank God!
A little help here!
Sooner rather than later!
Away from him, creature.
You couldn't just *shoot* it?!
Why waste ammunition when distance will suffice?
Because those things *should* be shot, *that's* why!

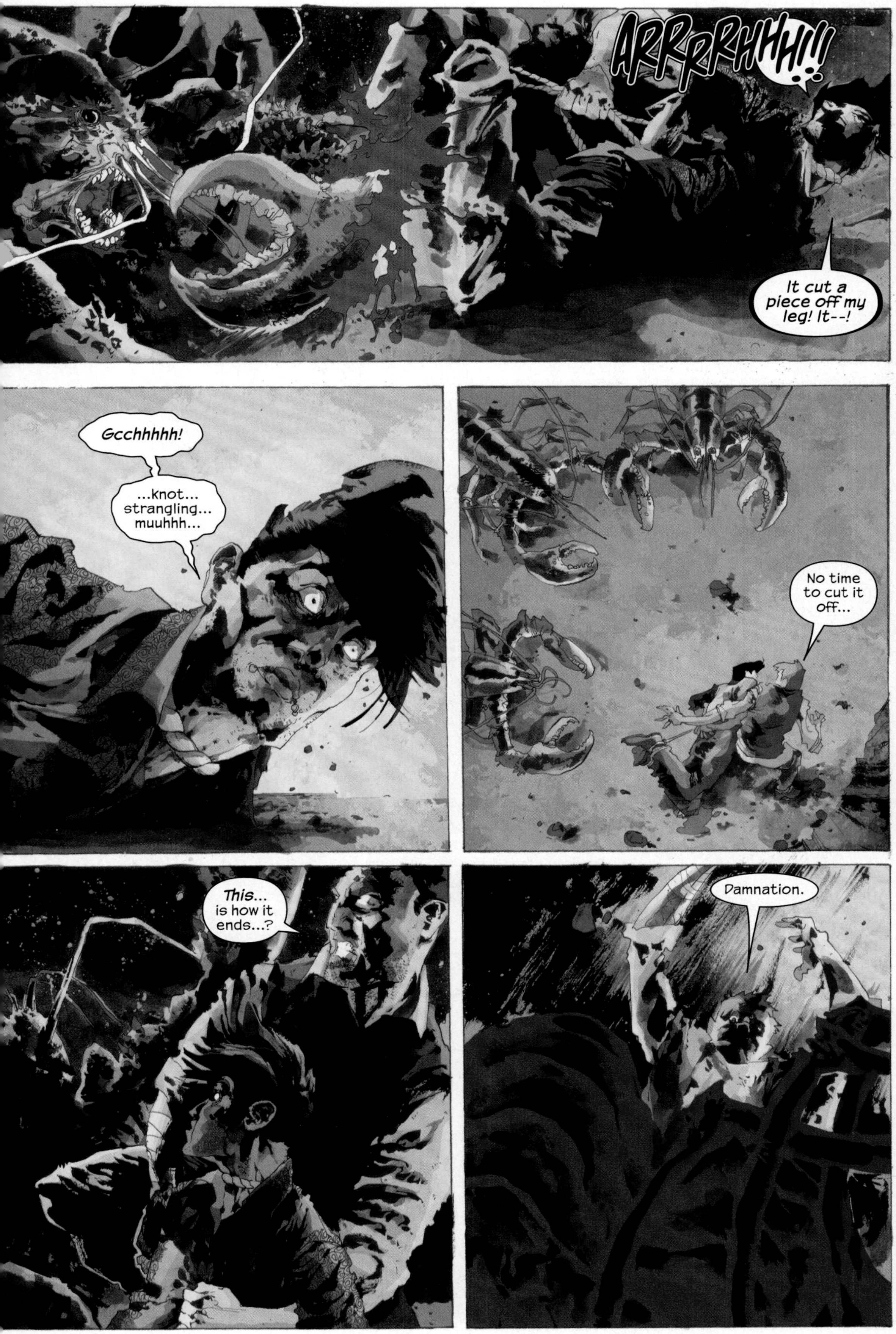
ARRRRHHH!!!
It cut a piece off my leg! It--!
Gcchhhhh!
...knot... strangling... muuhhh...
No time to cut it off...
This... is how it ends...?
Damnation.

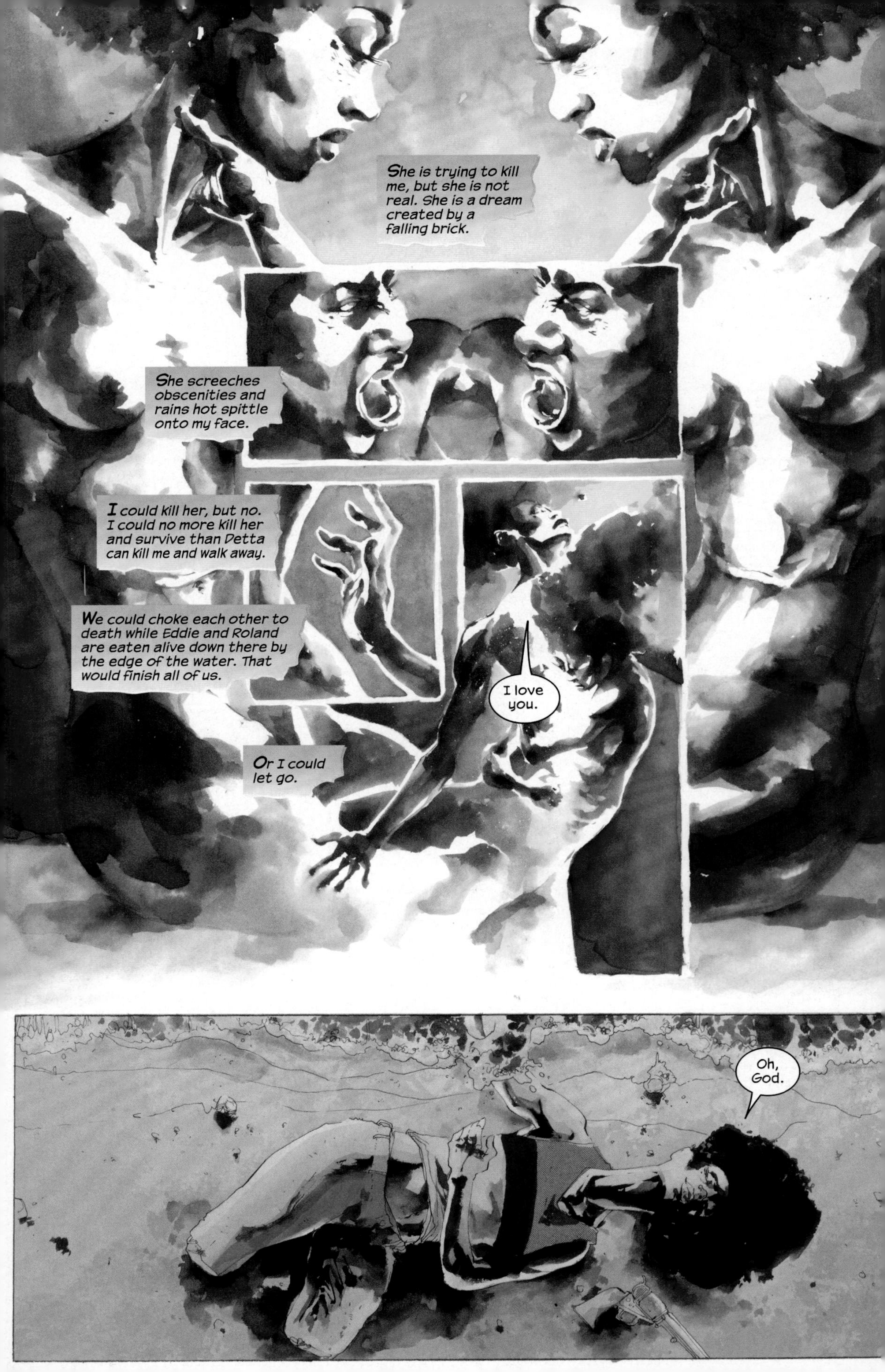
She is trying to kill me, but she is not real. She is a dream created by a falling brick.
She screeches obscenities and rains hot spittle onto my face.
I could kill her, but no. I could no more kill her and survive than Detta can kill me and walk away.
We could choke each other to death while Eddie and Roland are eaten alive down there by the edge of the water. That would finish all of us.
I love you.
Or I could let go.
Oh, God.

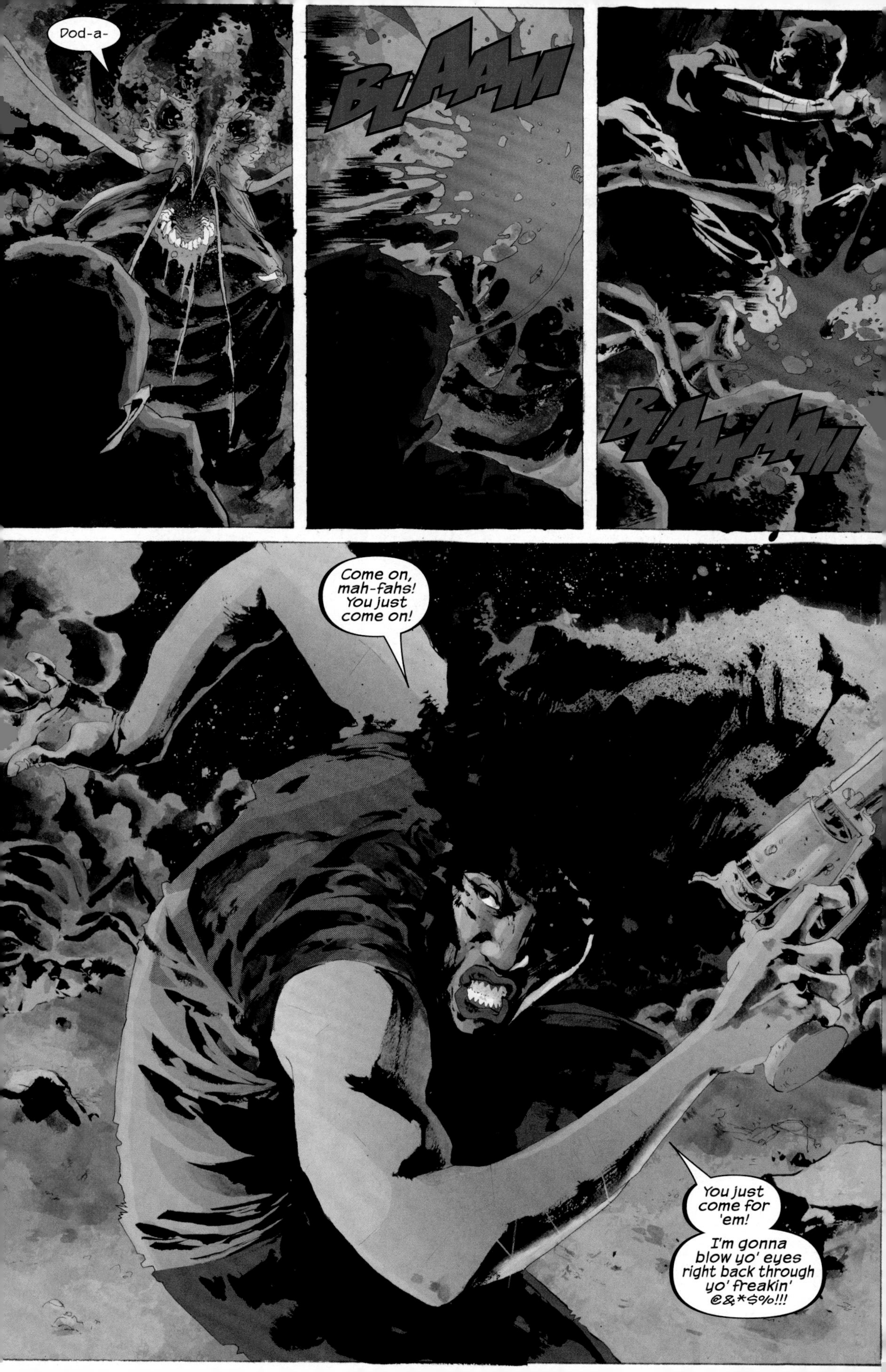
Dod-a-
BLAAM
BLAAAAAM
Come on, mah-fahs! You just come on!
You just come for 'em!
I'm gonna blow yo' eyes right back through yo' freakin' @&*$%!!!

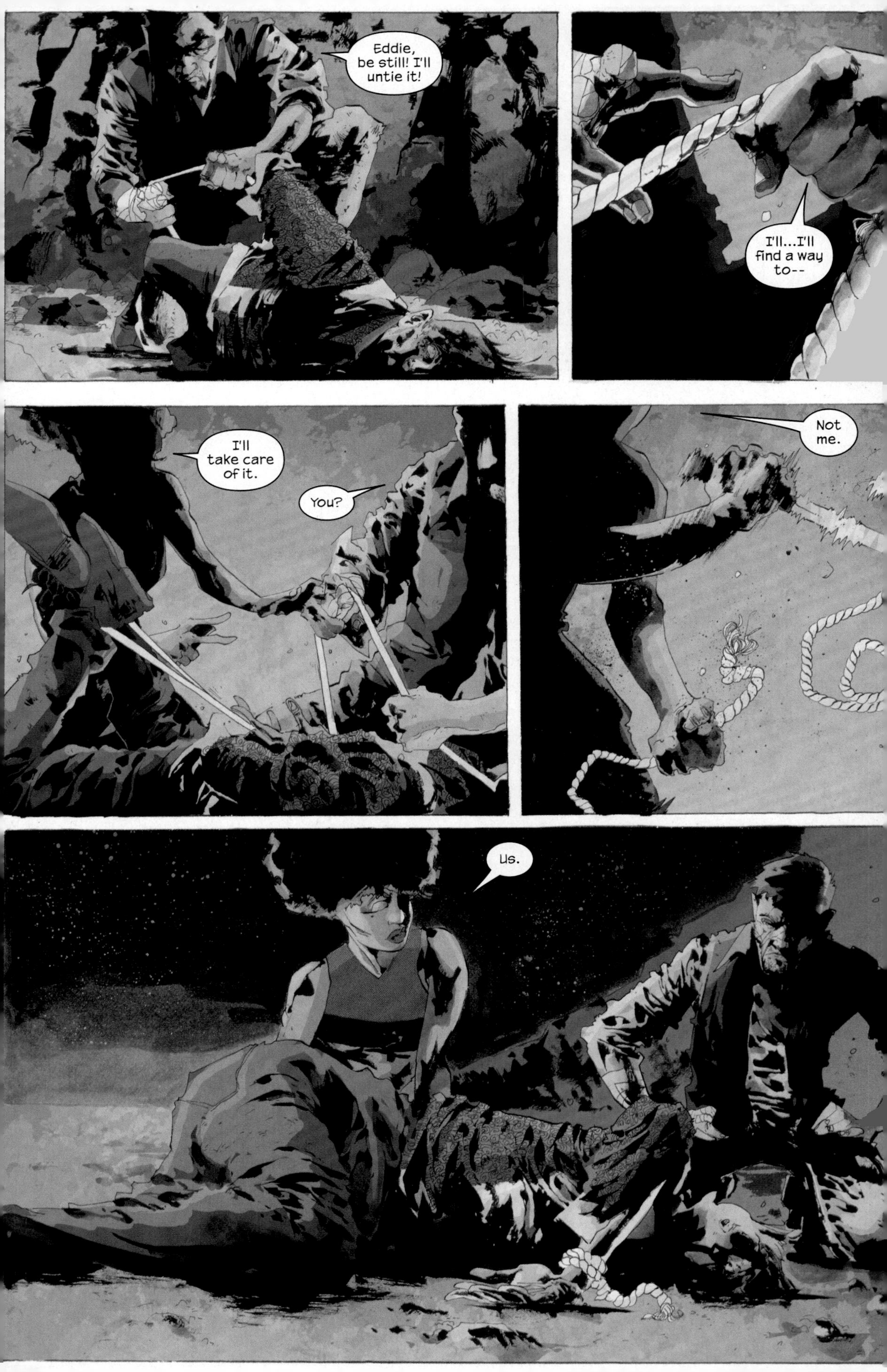
Eddie, be still! I'll untie it!
I'll...I'll find a way to--
I'll take care of it.
You?
Not me.
Us.

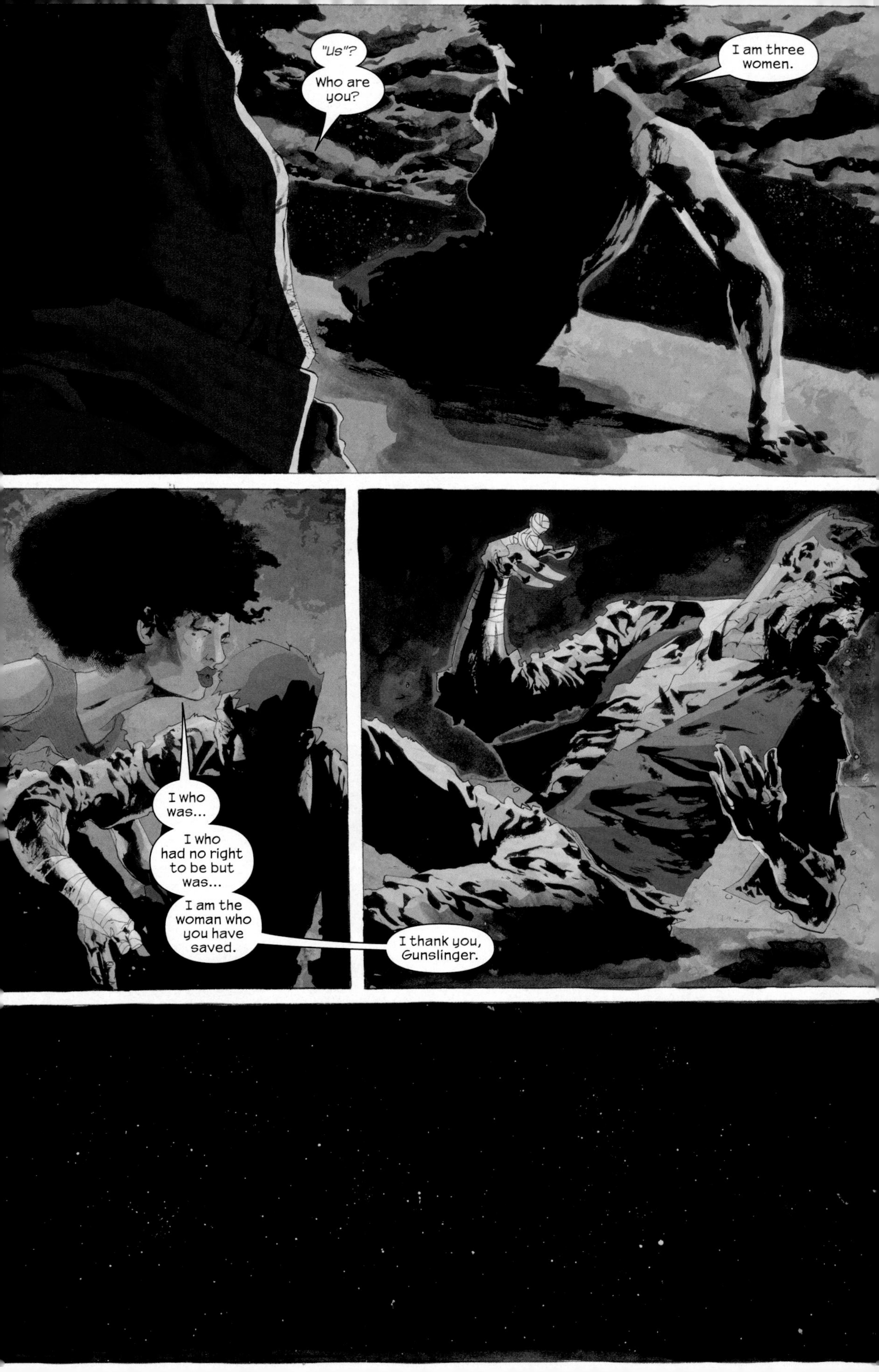
"Us"?
Who are you?
I am three women.
I who was...
I who had no right to be but was...
I am the woman who you have saved.
I thank you, Gunslinger.

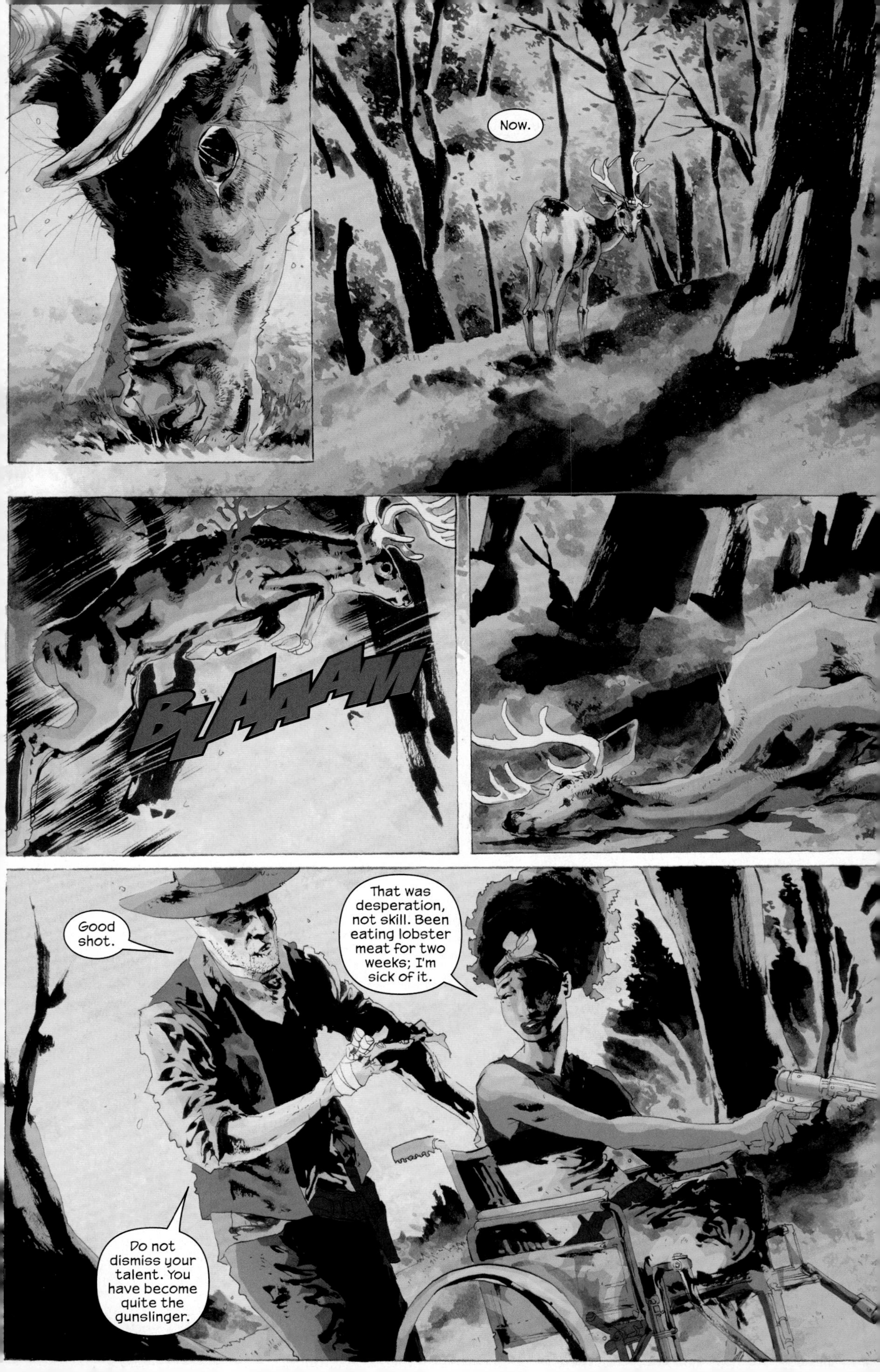
Now.
BLAAAAM
Good shot.
That was desperation, not skill. Been eating lobster meat for two weeks; I'm sick of it.
Do not dismiss your talent. You have become quite the gunslinger.

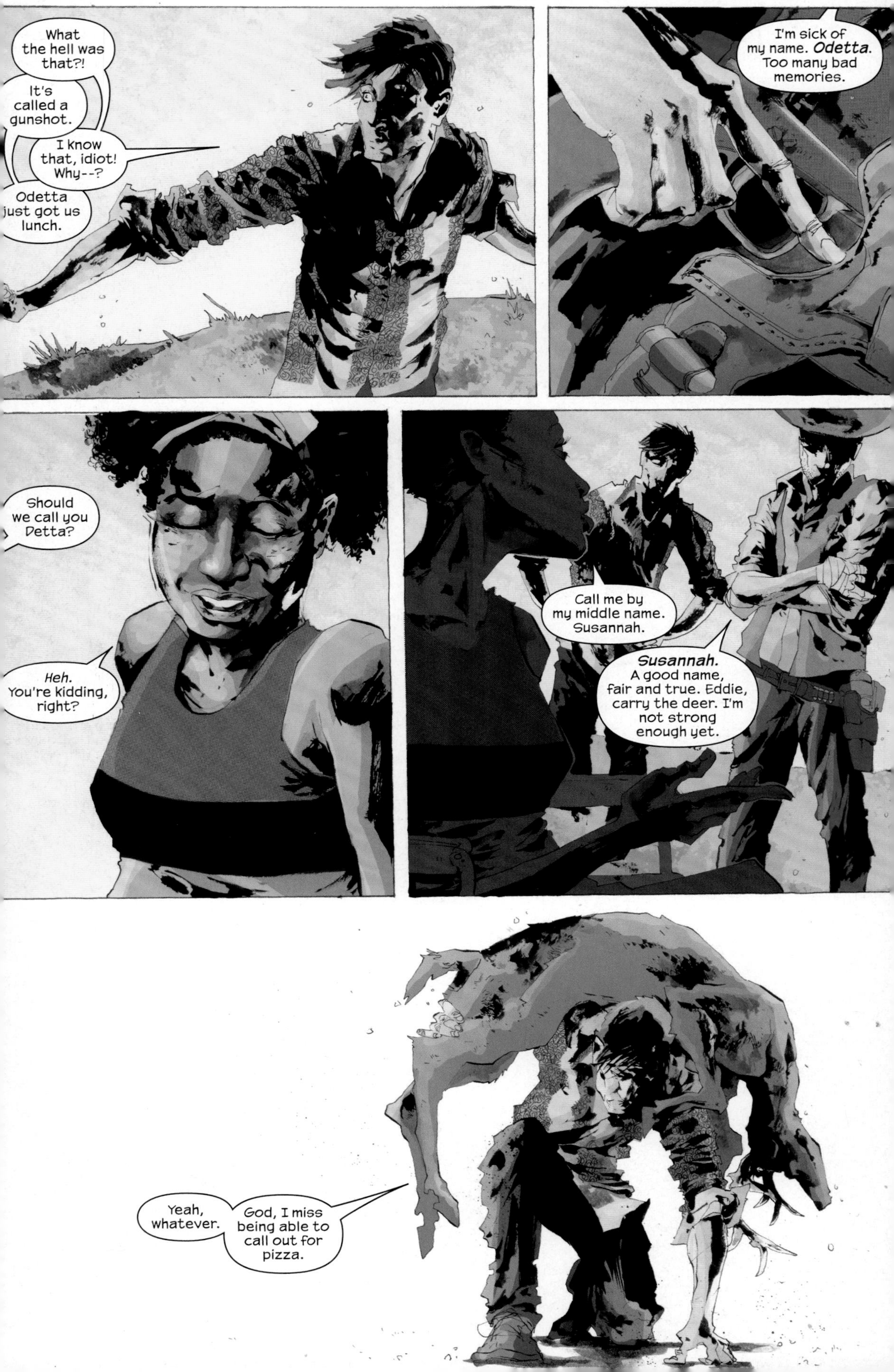
What the hell was that?!
It's called a gunshot.
I know that, idiot! Why--?
Odetta just got us lunch.
I'm sick of my name. *Odetta.* Too many bad memories.
Should we call you Detta?
Heh. You're kidding, right?
Call me by my middle name. Susannah.
Susannah. A good name, fair and true. Eddie, carry the deer. I'm not strong enough yet.
Yeah, whatever.
God, I miss being able to call out for pizza.

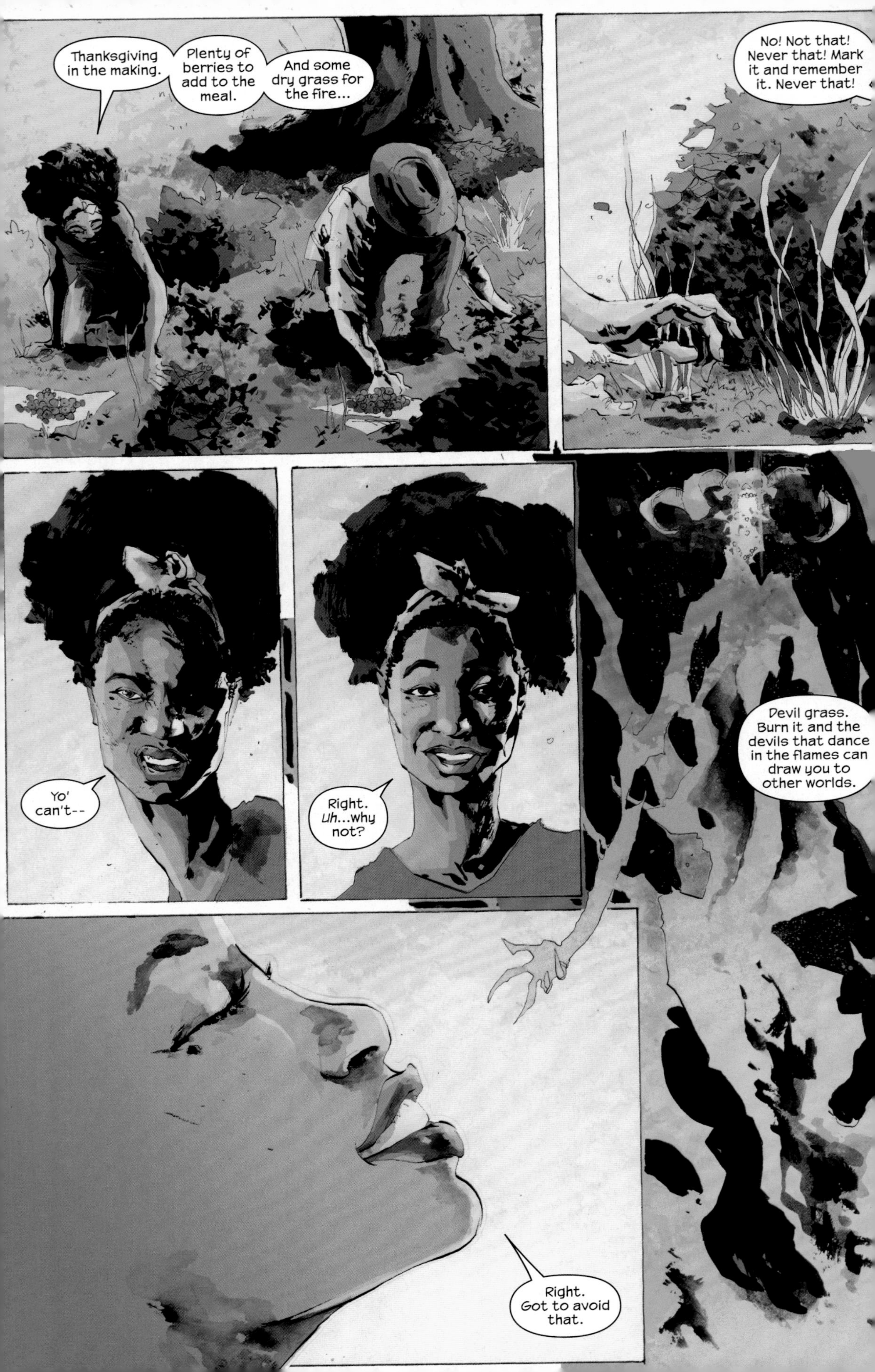
Thanksgiving in the making.
Plenty of berries to add to the meal.
And some dry grass for the fire...
No! Not that! Never that! Mark it and remember it. Never that!
Yo' can't--
Right. Uh...why not?
Devil grass. Burn it and the devils that dance in the flames can draw you to other worlds.
Right. Got to avoid that.

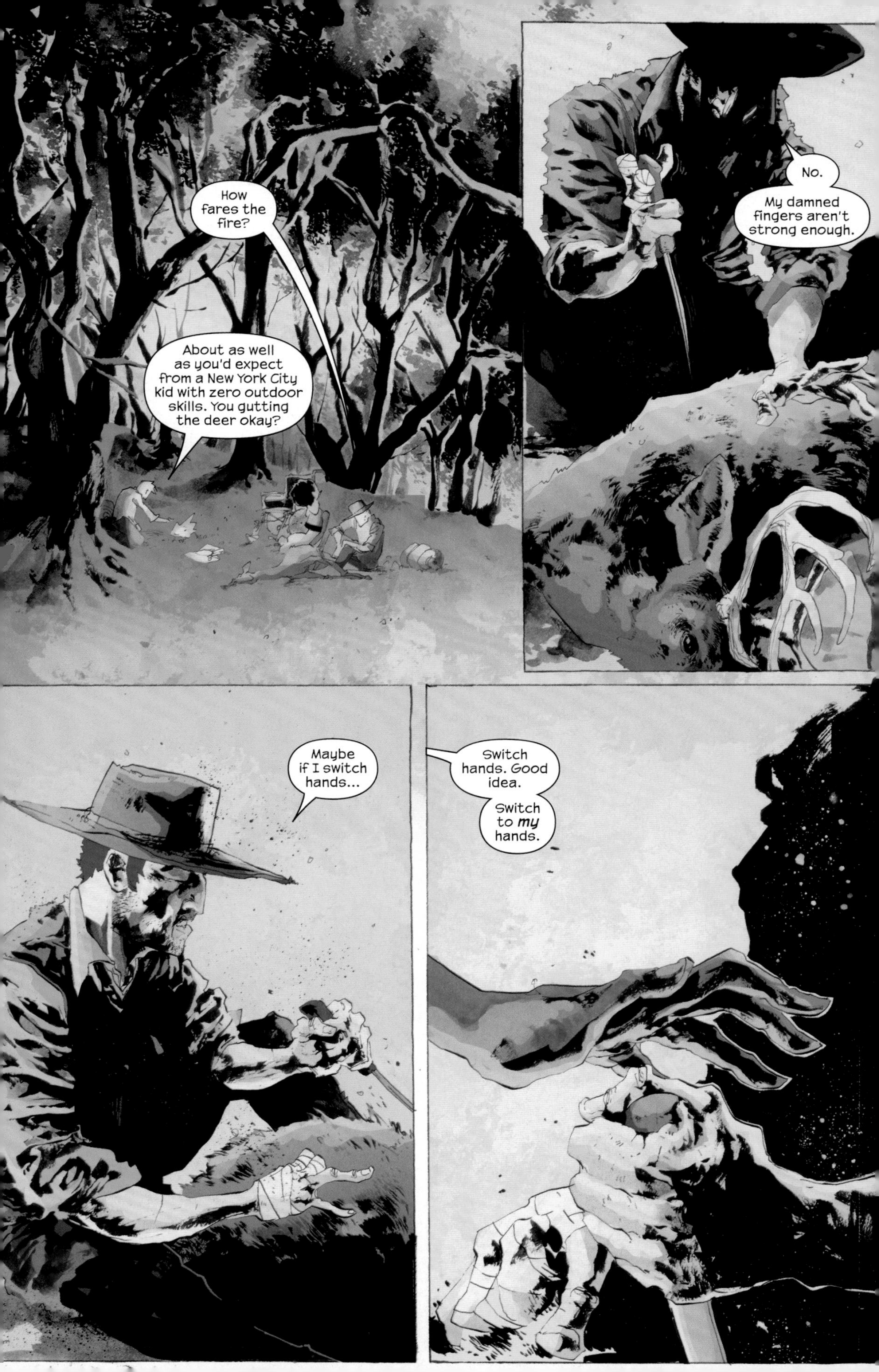
How fares the fire?
About as well as you'd expect from a New York City kid with zero outdoor skills. You gutting the deer okay?
No.
My damned fingers aren't strong enough.
Maybe if I switch hands...
Switch hands. Good idea.
Switch to *my* hands.

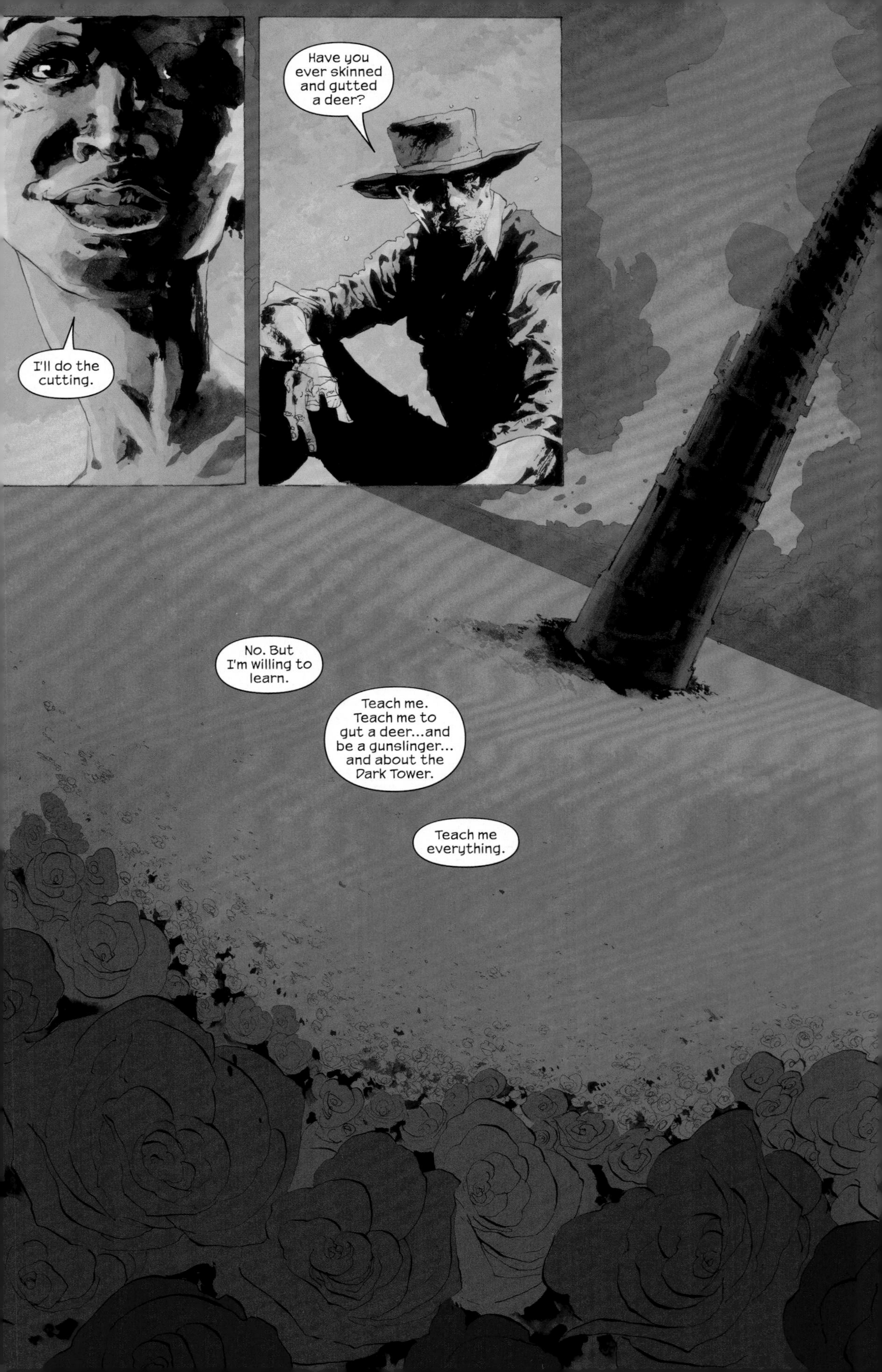
I'll do the cutting.
Have you ever skinned and gutted a deer?
No. But I'm willing to learn.
Teach me. Teach me to gut a deer...and be a gunslinger... and about the Dark Tower.
Teach me everything.

The story continues in *The Dark Tower: The Drawing of the Three — The Sailor*

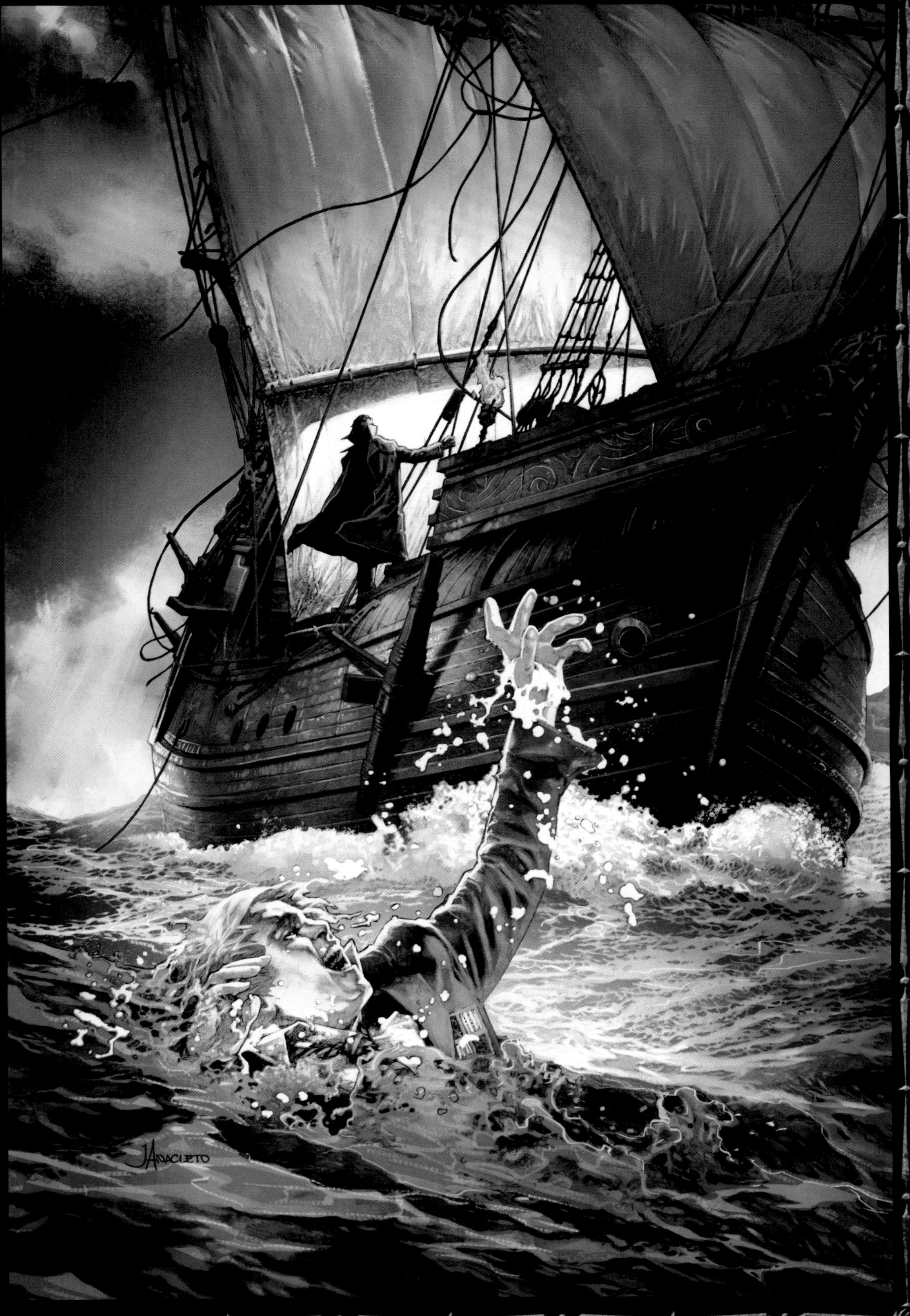
J Anacleto

The Dark Tower: The Drawing of the Three — Bitter Medicine #1 **Cover by Nimit Malavia**

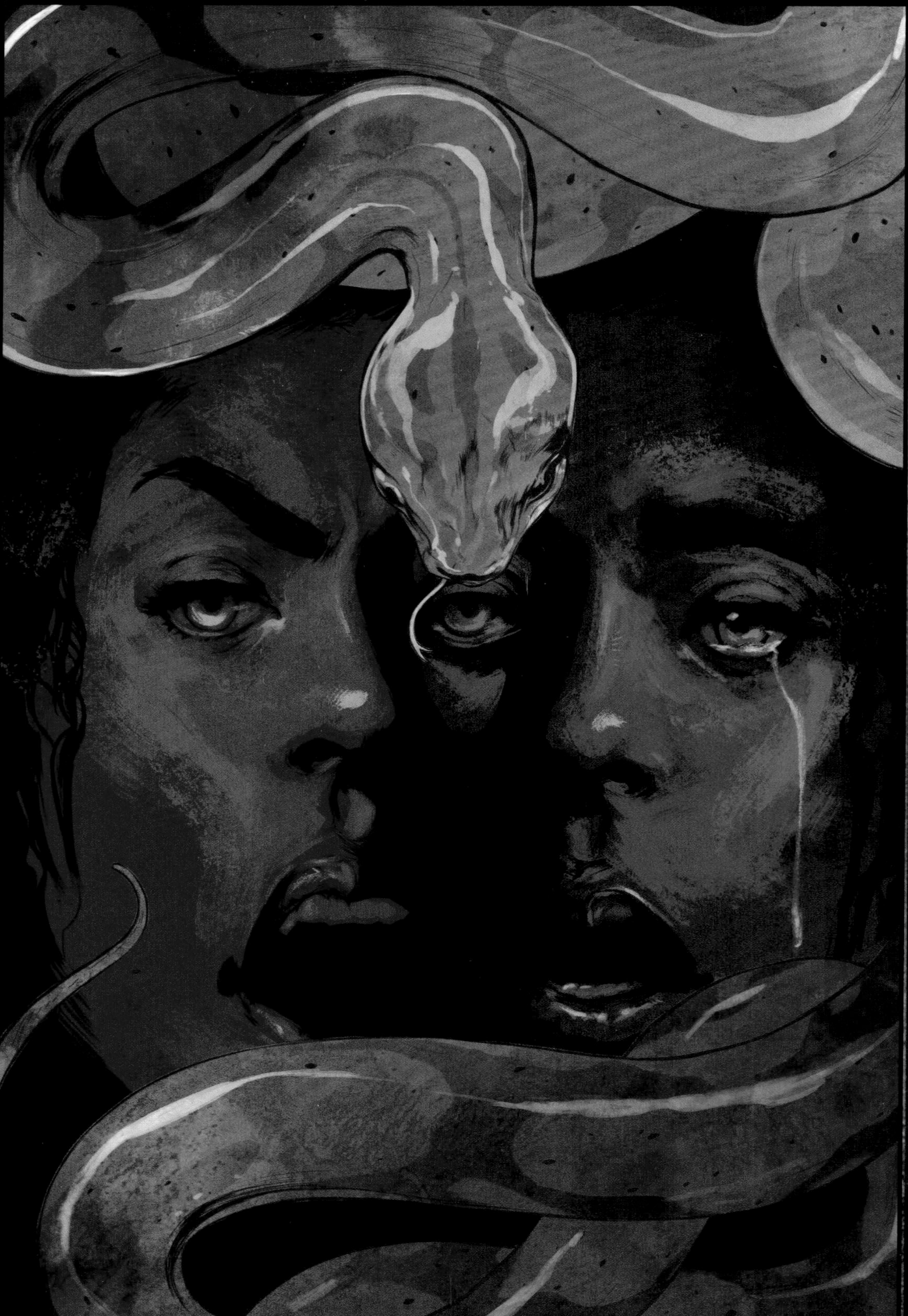

The Dark Tower: The Drawing of the Three — Bitter Medicine #2 **Cover by Nimit Malavia**

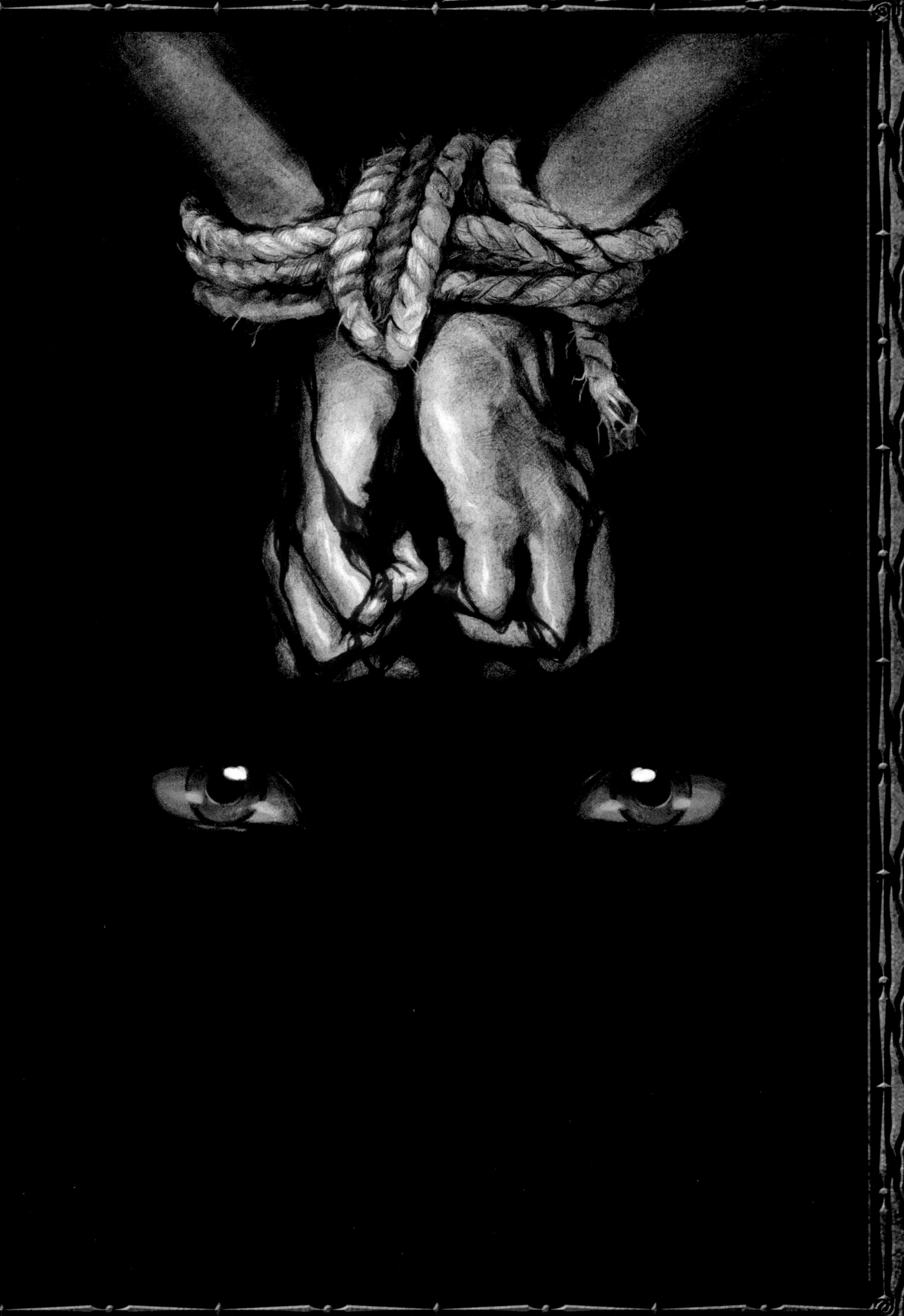

The Dark Tower: The Drawing of the Three — Bitter Medicine #3 **Cover by Nimit Malavia**

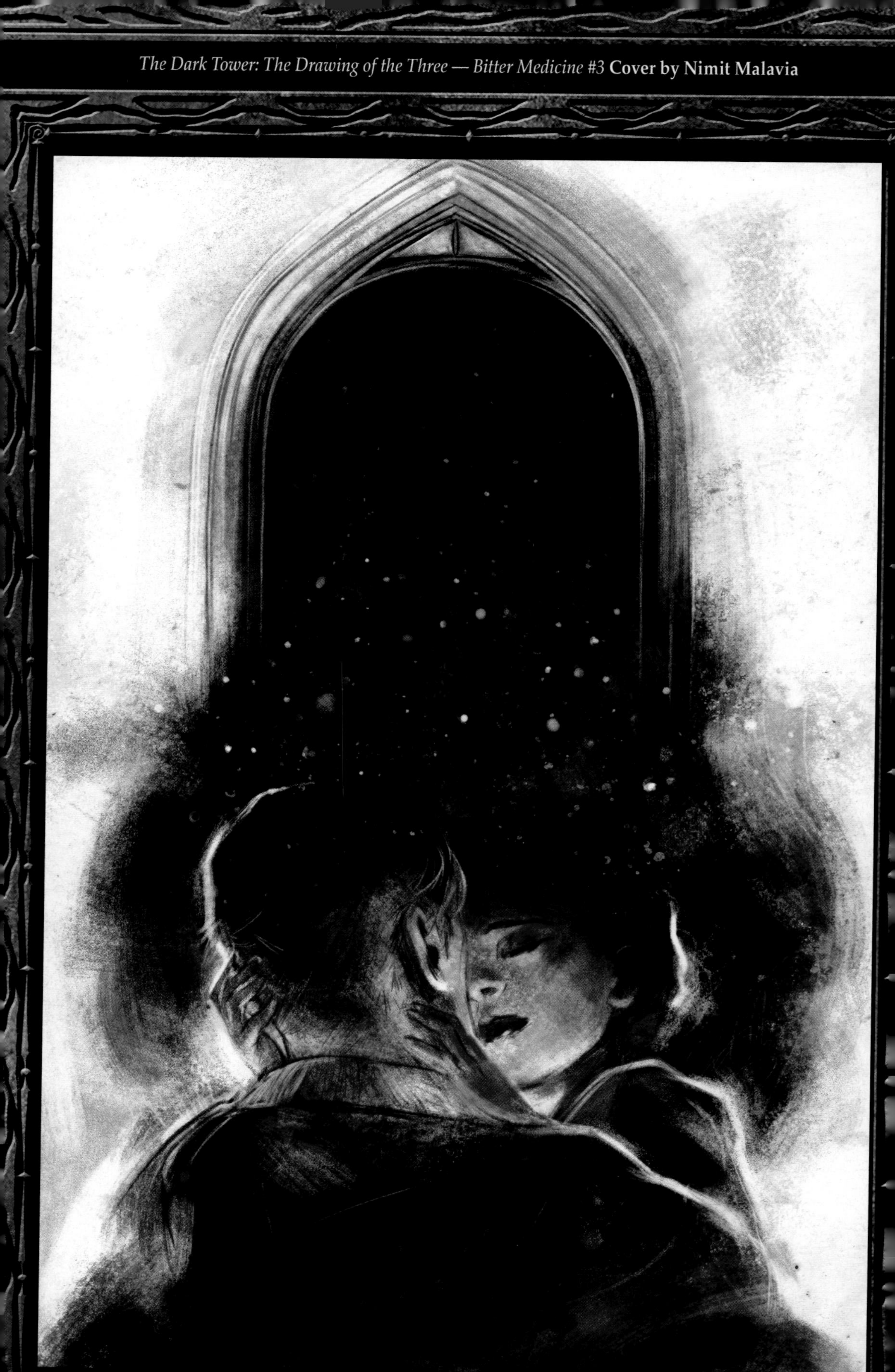

The Dark Tower: The Drawing of the Three — Bitter Medicine #4 **Cover by Nimit Malavia**

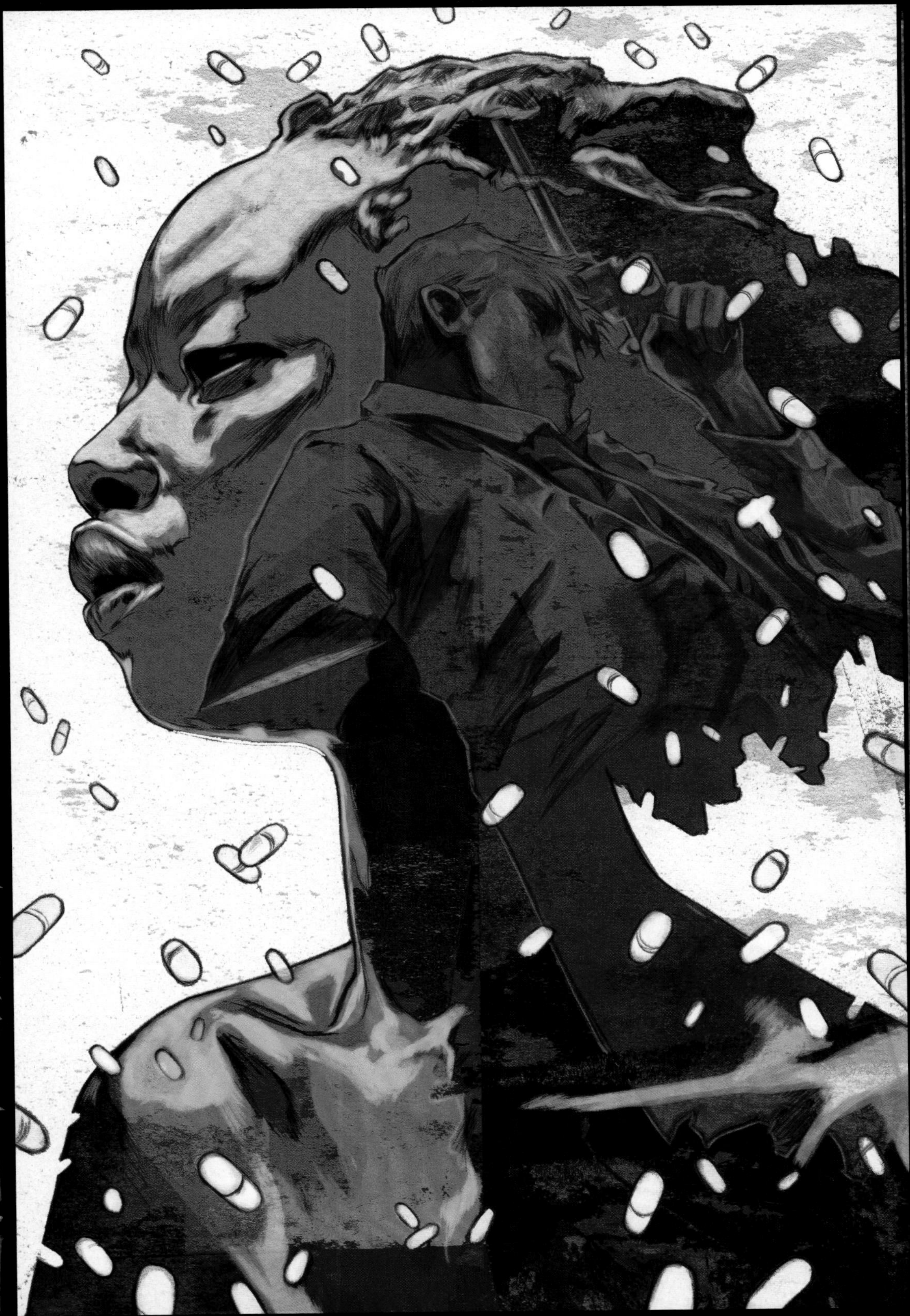

The Dark Tower: The Drawing of the Three — Bitter Medicine #5 **Cover by Nimit Malavia**

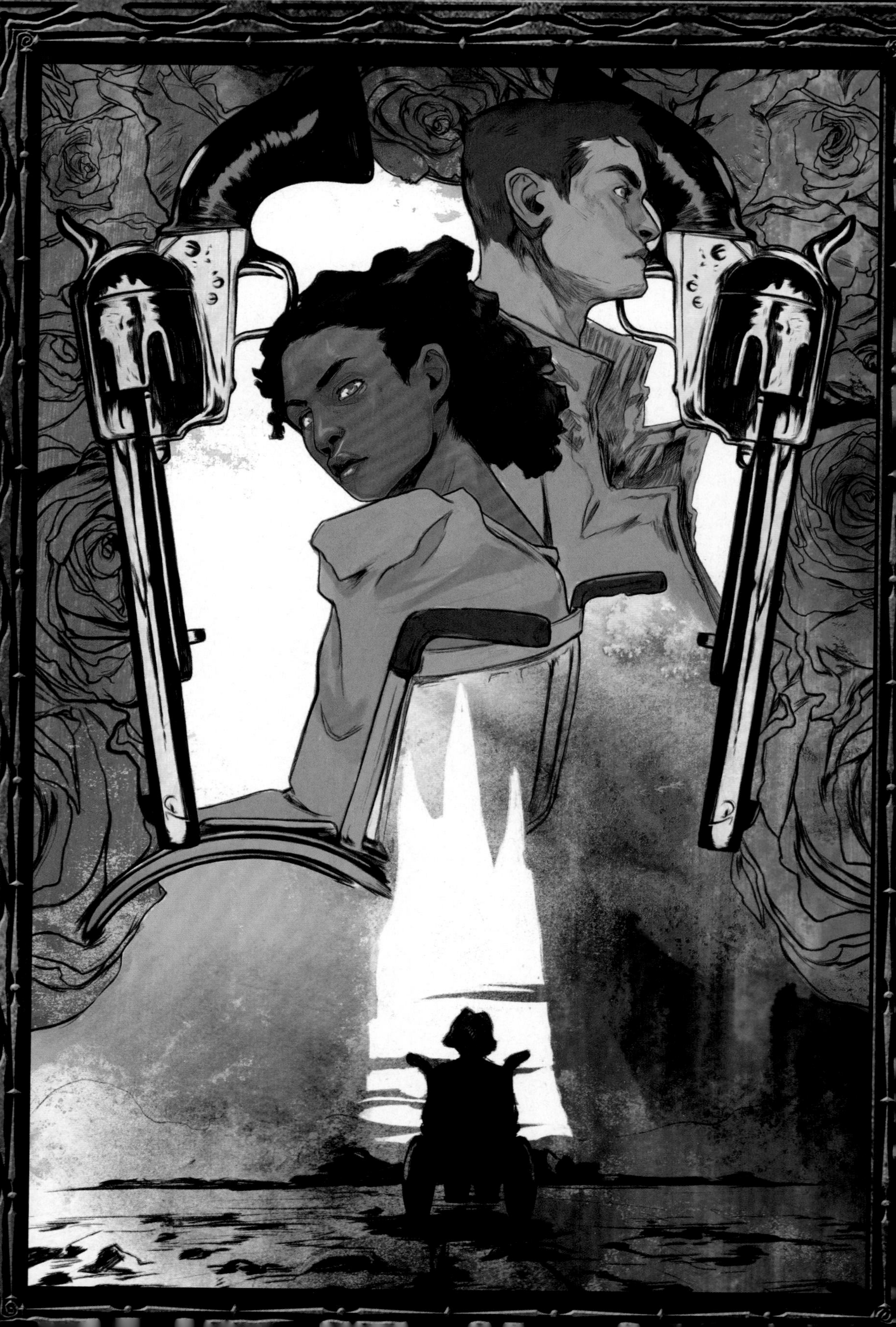

Bitter Medicine #2, page 19 **art by Jonathan Marks**

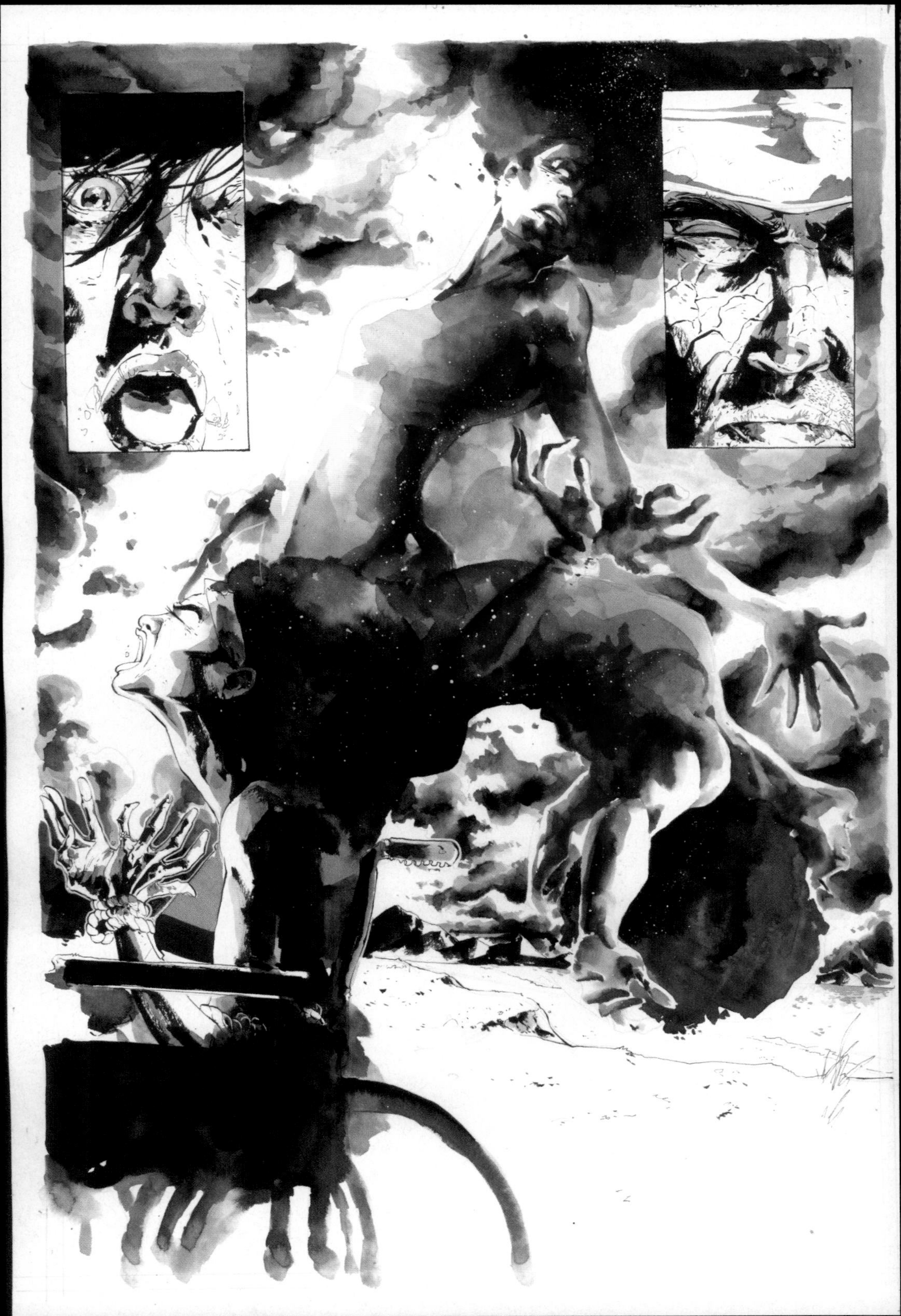

Page 1

1. Let's begin with an image of the magic door marked THE LADY OF SHADOWS. This is the doorway that will bring Odetta/ Detta into Mid-World.

2. We pull back. Eddie Dean and Roland Deschain are camped near the door. They are sleeping and their fire has burned down to embers. In the distance we see a grey sea crashing onto a grey beach, and in those crashing waves we see the monstrous lobstrosities which call "da-da-chum, da-da-chick" to the night sky. Overhead, we see the full moon and a shooting star.

3. The camera pulls back farther. Two ghostly figures sit by Roland and Eddie's campfire. (This is Eddie's dream, or perhaps it is a vision?) The two figures are Eddie's childhood gunslinger toys, Johnny Bronco and Sam Sidewinder. Sam Sidewinder holds a deck of tarot cards.

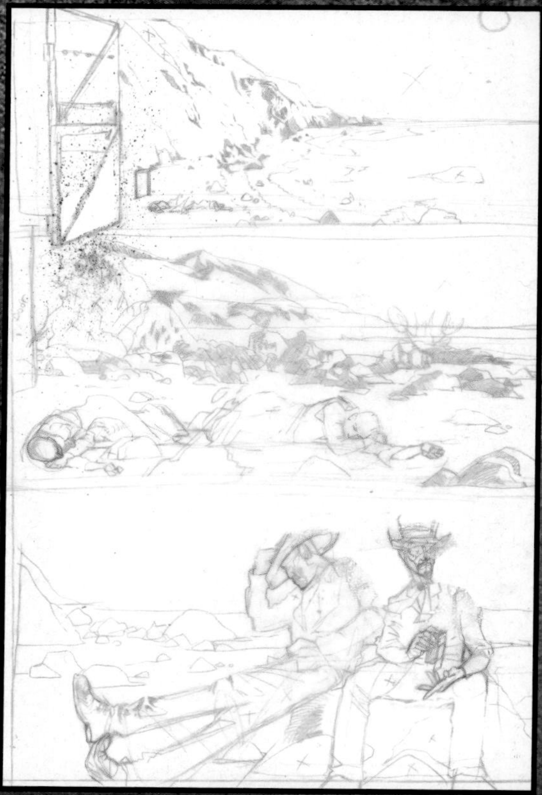

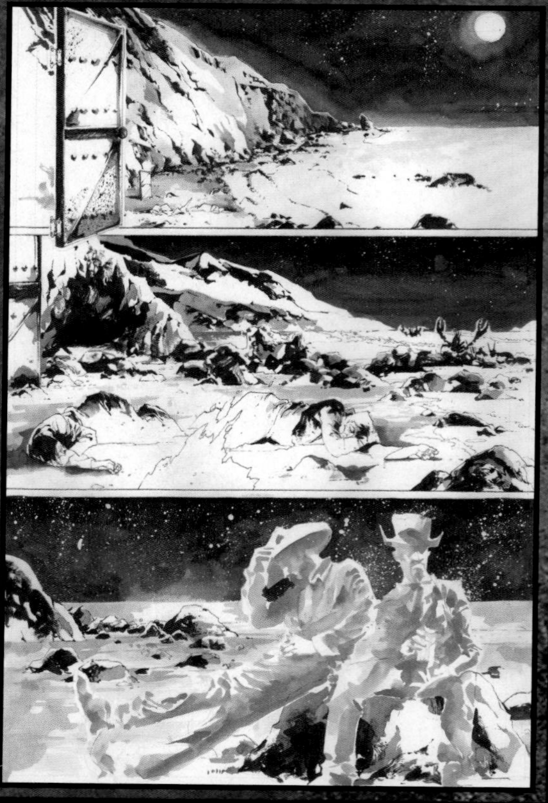

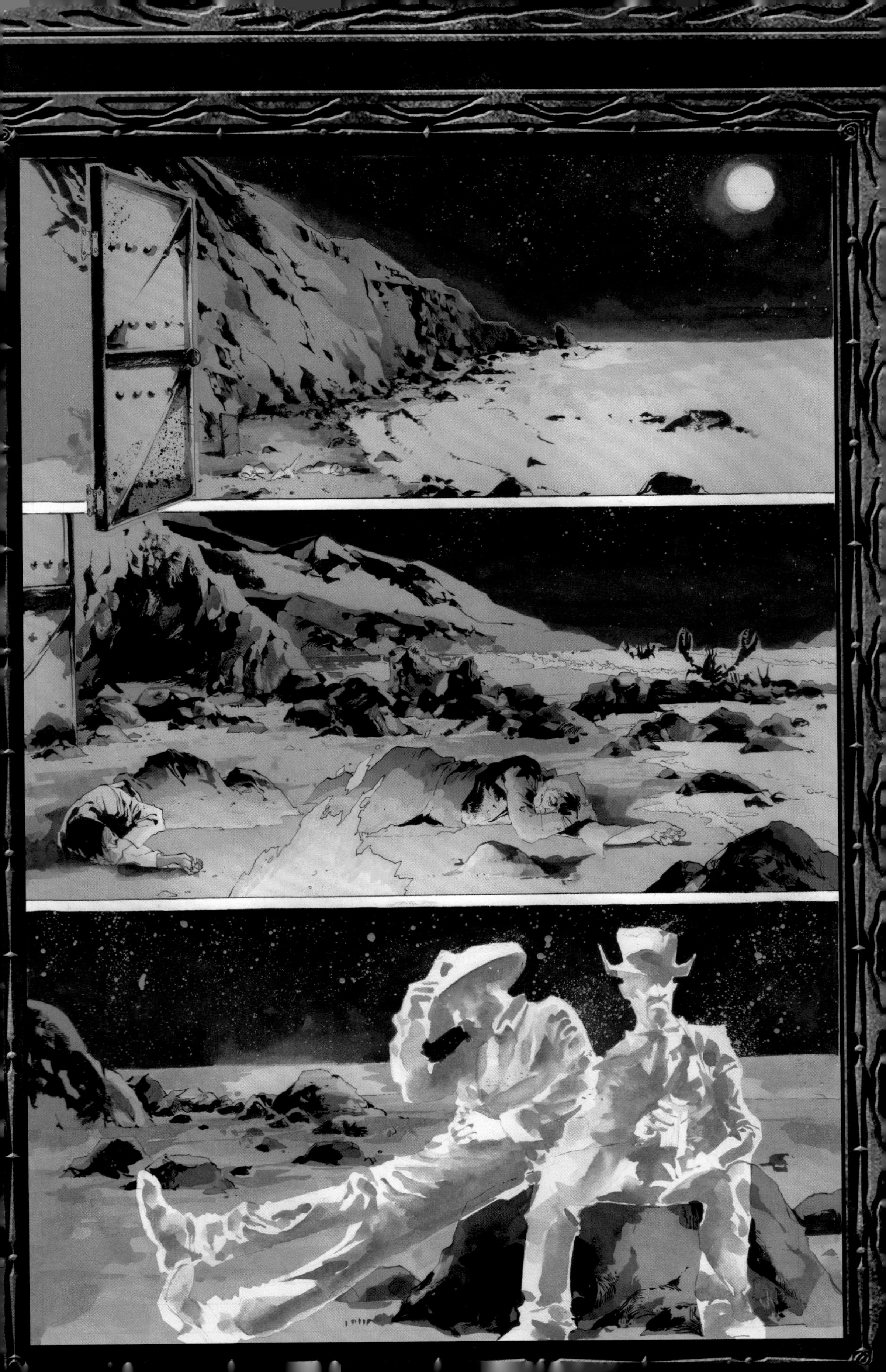

Page 2

1. Sam Sidewinder has laid three cards upon the ground. The first card has already been turned over. It is the card representing Eddie Dean in his former junkie incarnation! It is called THE PRISONER. (For visual references, see The Prisoner, Issue 4, and The Man in Black, final issue).

2. We still focus on the cards. The Man in Black/Sam Sidewinder/Walter O'Dim has just turned over a second card. This card is of a dark-skinned woman sitting at a spinning wheel. It is called THE LADY OF SHADOWS. The woman on the card has a shawl over her head, and she appears to have two faces. One is smiling craftily and one is sobbing. (We can either make her literally have two faces, or somehow we can combine the two expressions on one face.)

3. Let's focus on the third card, which Sam Sidewinder has just turned over. It is the card of DEATH.

4. Eddie has woken up from his dream. He is sweating and terrified. The two ghostly figures are gone, but the scene feels haunted. Looming over Eddie is the doorway marked THE LADY OF SHADOWS.

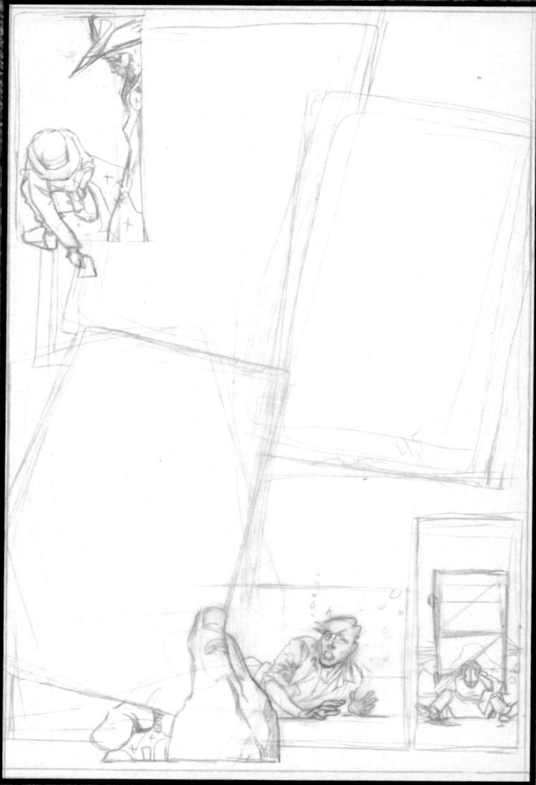

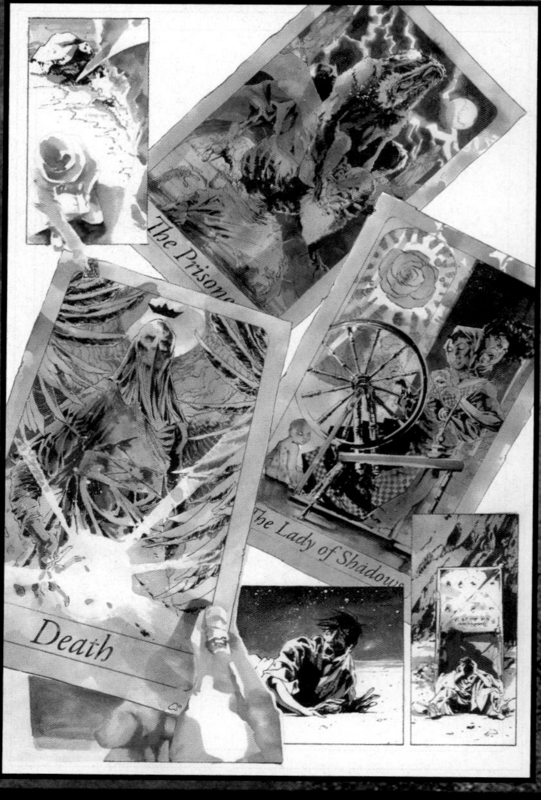
Death

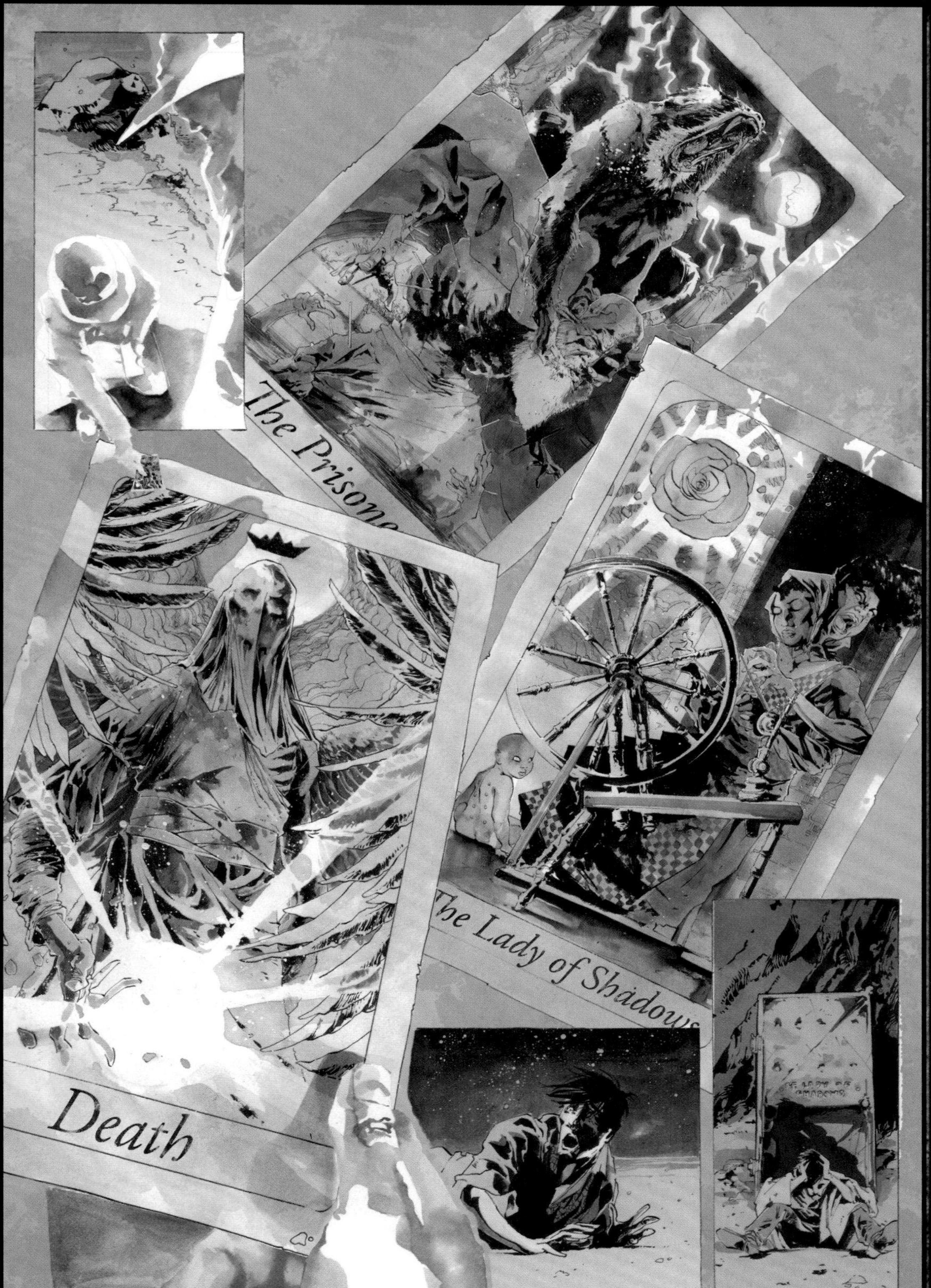
The Prisone
The Lady of Shadows
Death

Page 3

1. It is now morning. Roland and Eddie sit by the magic door and the remains of their fire. They have just eaten some lobstrosity meat for breakfast. Eddie asks Roland if he will enter the head of the woman on the other side of the door, just like Roland entered Eddie's head when he was on a plane to NYC. Roland says yes.

2. We come a little closer. Eddie asks if Roland is going to kidnap her. Roland says he is bringing her to Mid-World take part in a grand quest. Eddie gives a hoarse, cynical laugh. He says it's not a quest; it's a nightmare.

3. Roland now stands with his hand on the doorknob, but he has frozen. Eddie is pointing a gun at him. He wants Roland to bring him through too. All he wants is to smell the New York air and get a tub of fried chicken.

4. We close in on Roland's haggard face. His infection is returning and he looks terrible. Roland says that the door might not open onto New York City. It might not even open onto Eddie's universe. Besides, Eddie doesn't want fried chicken; he wants heroin.

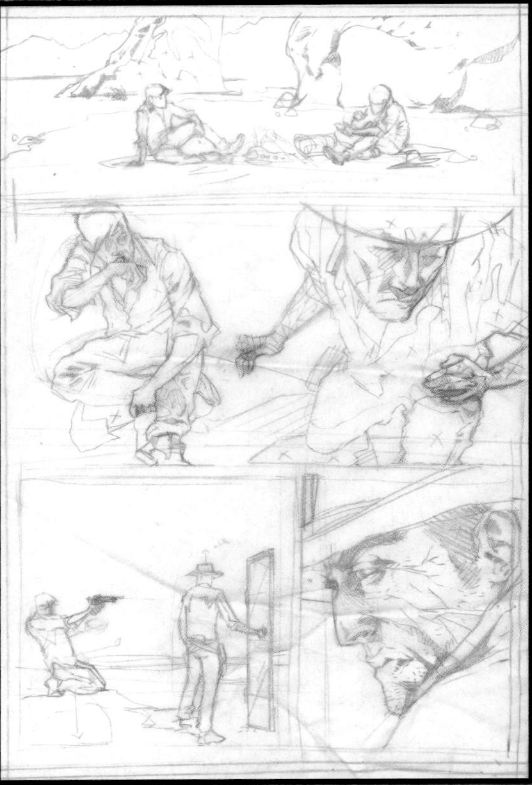

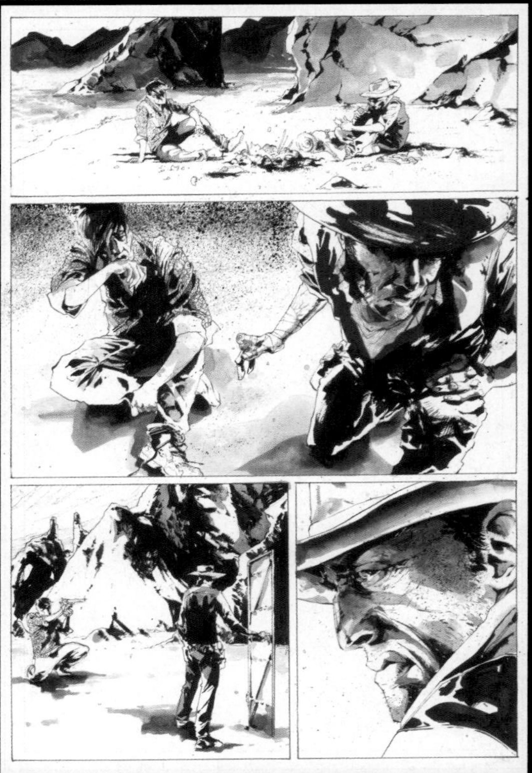

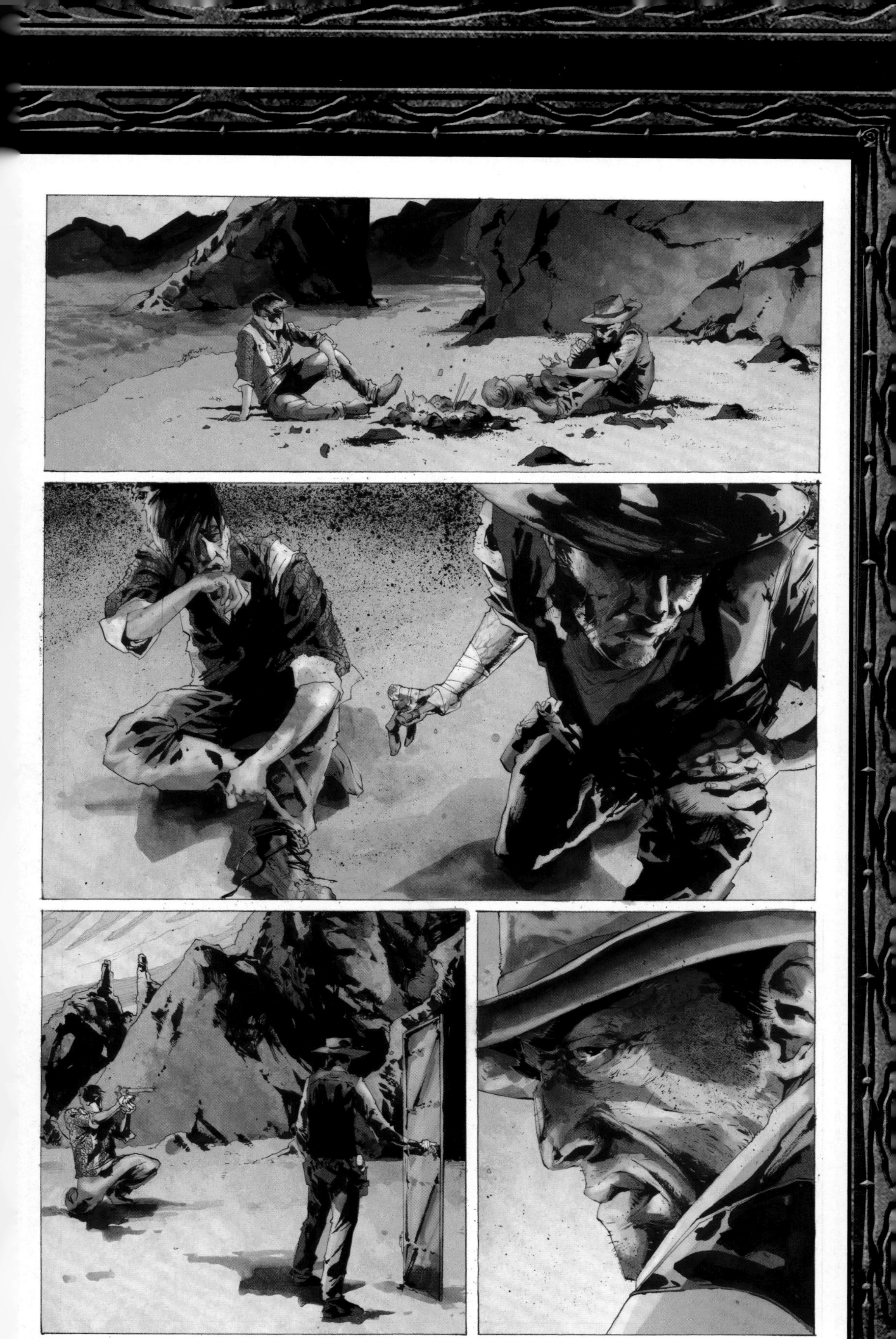

Page 4

1. Roland has opened the door. It appears to lead into the ladies department in a big US department store circa 1964. We see jewelry and makeup counters, artfully arranged pocketbooks and maybe some lingerie. Awestruck, Eddie has lowered the gun. Eddie asks if they are looking through the Lady of Shadows' eyes. Roland says yes, but Eddie replies that the movement looks more like a steady-cam from a movie than like the movement of someone walking. Roland understands, though he doesn't know what a steady-cam is. Roland asks Eddie if this door leads to a time before Eddie's when of 1987. Eddie says it must be sometime in the early 1960s. The clothes remind him of when he was a little kid.

2. Let's focus on what is happening inside the doorway. The Lady of Shadows has paused in front of a glass counter. She is handing a white scarf with bright blue edging to the snide white salesgirl standing behind the counter. We can tell that the salesgirl doesn't like the Lady of Shadows. Although we can't see the Lady's face, we see her hands. She is an African-American woman and her fingers are covered in gaudy rings. On her left pinky is a large fake diamond. On the third finger of her right hand is a large opal. (See The Drawing of the Three, 198-206, and 239)

3. The salesgirl grimaces as she folds up the scarf. As Eddie comments from off camera, the Lady of Shadows is one rude bitch. (See Drawing of the Three, 198-206 for dialogue.)

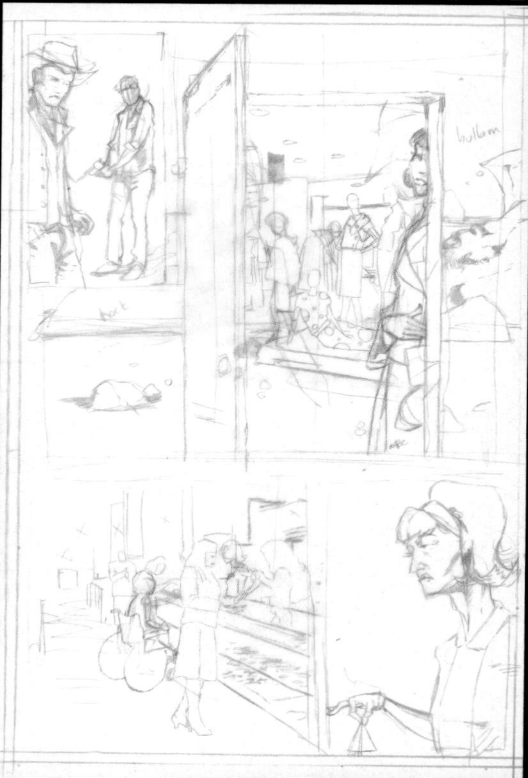

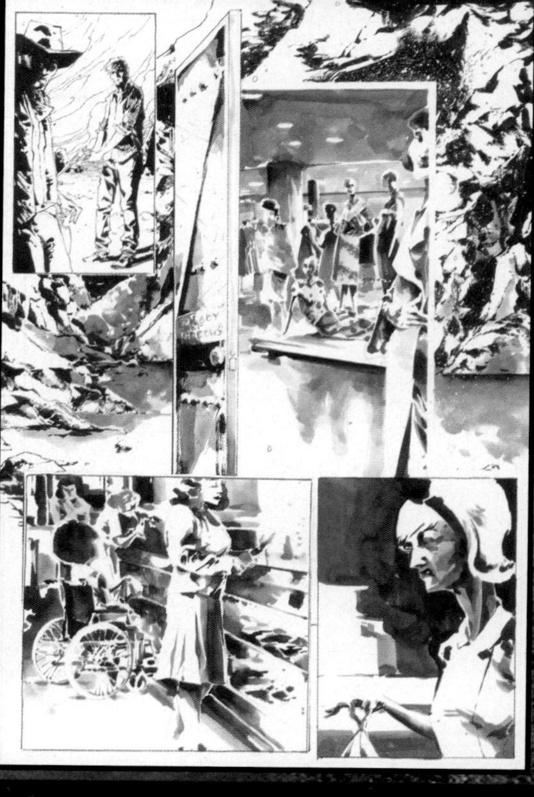

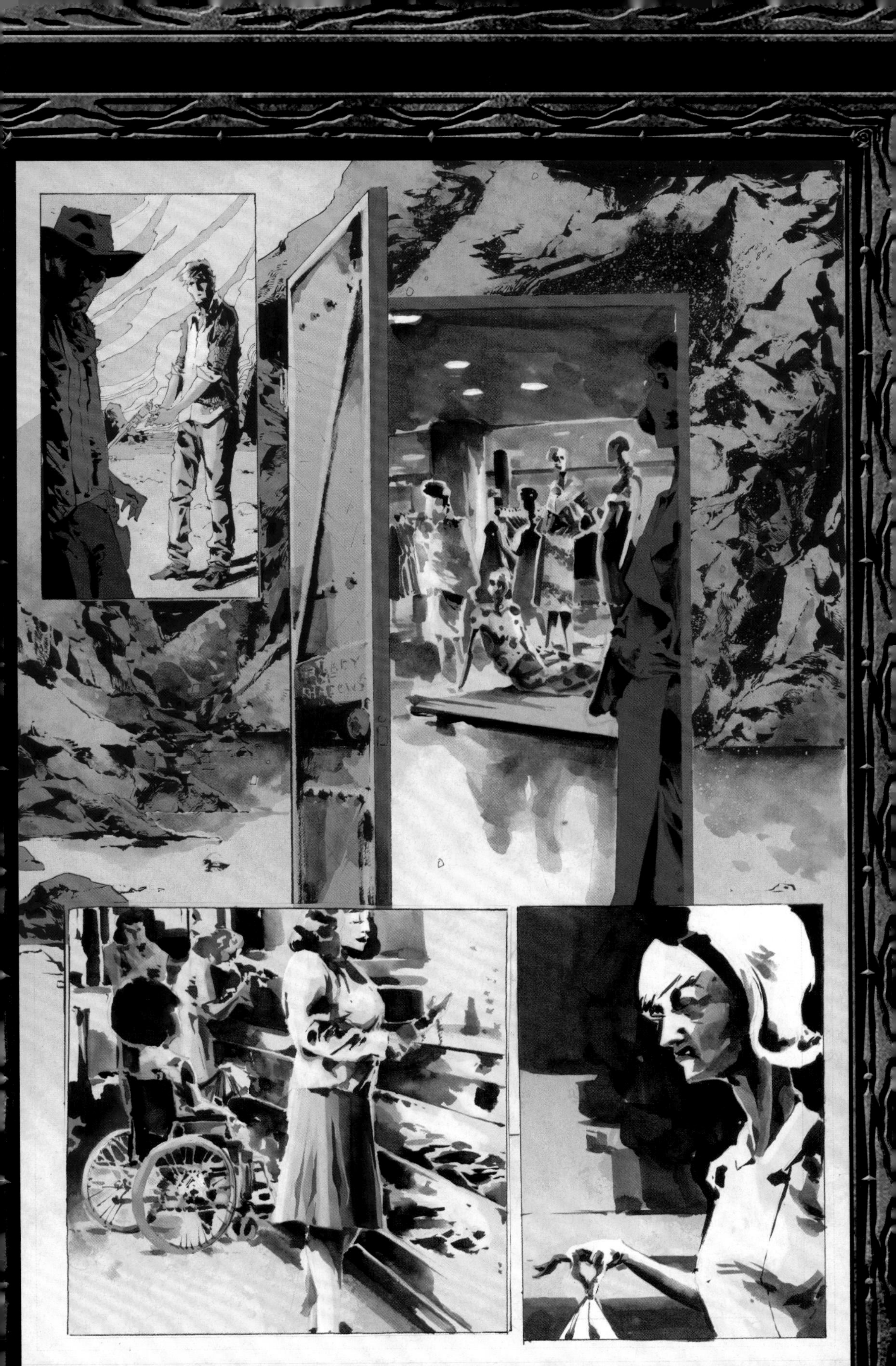